ST ANDREWS STUDIES
IN PHILOSOPHY AND PUBLIC AFFAIRS
Founding and General Editor:
John Haldane, University of St Andrews

Values, Education and the Human World
edited by John Haldane

Philosophy and its Public Role
edited by William Aiken and John Haldane

Relativism and the Foundations of Liberalism
by Graham Long

Human Life, Action and Ethics: Essays by G.E.M. Anscombe
edited by Mary Geach and Luke Gormally

The Institution of Intellectual Values: Realism and Idealism in Higher Education
by Gordon Graham

Life, Liberty and the Pursuit of Utility
by Anthony Kenny and Charles Kenny

Distributing Healthcare: Principles, Practices and Politics
edited by Niall Maclean

Liberalism, Education and Schooling: Essays by T.M. Mclaughlin
edited by David Carr, Mark Halstead and Richard Pring

The Landscape of Humanity: Art, Culture & Society
by Anthony O'Hear

Faith in a Hard Ground: Essays on Religion, Philosophy and Ethics by G.E.M. Anscombe
edited by Mary Geach and Luke Gormally

Subjectivity and Being Somebody
by Grant Gillett

Understanding Faith: Religious Belief and Its Place in Society
by Stephen R.L. Clark

Profit, Prudence and Virtue: Essays in Ethics, Business & Management
edited by Samuel Gregg and James Stoner

Practical Philosophy: Ethics, Society and Culture
by John Haldane

Sensibility and Sense: Aesthetic Transformation of the World
by Arnold Berleant

Understanding Teaching and Learning: Classic Texts on Education
edited by T. Brian Mooney and Mark Nowacki

Truth and Faith in Ethics
edited by Hayden Ramsay

From Plato to Wittgenstein: Essays by G.E.M. Anscombe
edited by Mary Geach and Luke Gormally

Natural Law, Economics, and the Common Good: Perspectives from Natural Law
edited by Samual Gregg and Harold James

The Philosophy of Punishment
by Anthony Ellis

Social Radicalism and Liberal Education
by Lindsay Paterson

Social Radicalism and Liberal Education

By Lindsay Paterson

St Andrews Studies in Philosophy and Public Affairs

imprint-academic.com

Published in the UK by Imprint Academic
PO Box 200, Exeter EX5 5YX, UK

Distributed in the USA by
Ingram Book Company,
One Ingram Blvd., La Vergne, TN 37086, USA

ISBN 9781845407520 paperback
ISBN 9781845407513 cloth

A CIP catalogue record for this book is available from the British Library and US Library of Congress

Cover Photograph:
St Salvator's Quadrangle, St Andrews by Peter Adamson from the University of St Andrews collection

Contents

Preface

Liberal education has long appealed to the left. Great works of literature have been consoling and encouraging, lessons from history have been inspiring, the ideas of moral philosophy have been invigorating, and the analytical precision of careful scholarship has been felt to deepen the understanding of where society has gone wrong and how it might be made better. Rather more than religion, liberal learning has for intellectuals provided a soul in a heartless world, and capitalism has stood indicted for excluding people from the best of the inherited culture.

During most of the period when modern concepts of liberal education have been influential in Britain there has been, furthermore, a radical strand of support for widening access to it. From the late-eighteenth century to the middle of the twentieth century, the main current of left-wing thought about education sought to extend an appreciation of what Matthew Arnold called the best that has been thought and said. These radical ideas may be traced from Arnold, J.S. Mill and T.H. Huxley, through liberals and socialists such as R.H. Tawney, A.D. Lindsay, Raymond Williams and Richard Hoggart, to the reforming politicians responsible for establishing the educational systems of the welfare state, and even, in the first half of the twentieth century, to quite revolutionary thinkers who sought to overturn the social order but who adhered nevertheless to a common understanding of liberal learning. British radicals of that sort often drew upon cognate thinkers in other countries, such as Antonio Gramsci and Hannah Arendt. This tradition of radical thought was always in creative and sometimes tense dialogue with exponents of liberal education who were of a more conservative disposition, most notably T.S. Eliot, F.R.

Leavis, Q.D. Leavis and G.H. Bantock. British socialist thinking about education has learnt a great deal from fruitful dialogue with moderate conservatism. The dialogue was aided by the conservatives' reciprocal openness to a range of thought, and indeed liberal education itself came to include the principle of democratic pluralism, often drawn in explicit contrast to the educational ideas of the mid-century totalitarian states.

Thus while secondary schooling for everyone was being established between the 1920s and the 1950s, it was taken for granted that the curriculum of that new system ought to be based on these core inherited ideas. When a new kind of adult education was being invented to provide education for the working class—most notably through the Workers' Educational Association, founded in 1903—it was supposed that the whole point was to give them access to culture that they had been denied. When good-quality book publishing was being revolutionised in the 1930s, led by Penguin, it was assumed by the editors who led that transformation that the market was for thinking people who leant to the left but who, being educated, wanted to make up their own minds about the great issues of the day. Liberal education in this sense was conservative as to content—the handing on of the cultural legacy—but, in the ideas of the radical thinkers, potentially revolutionary in its implications, because it would form the only secure basis for a proper democracy, in which the citizen would reach the same depth of understanding as the old ruling classes had acquired.

Yet in an abrupt and unprecedented reversal, the radical enthusiasm for that kind of curriculum then disappeared between the 1960s and the end of the century, leading to a retreat by most segments of liberal opinion from constructive discussion about the educational value of inherited ideas, and even from any serious debate about educational standards. Indeed, in many respects, there has been a withdrawal by the political left from truly educational debate altogether, replacing that with a direct concern only with such matters as social inequality and identity. Even more prominent than this in programmes of left-wing governments since the 1960s has been a vocational purpose—preparing people for employment—and a belief that education can lead to economic growth. Any kind of cultural aim has then just vanished.

The book tries to understand why radical thought in Britain originally interpreted education in broadly the same terms as did conservatives, and why the change has taken place more recently. It deals mainly with the twentieth century, but attention is given also to the origins of the ideas in earlier periods, mainly back to the middle of the nineteenth. While concentrating on Britain, it also pays attention to influential ideas from elsewhere, because radical debate and educational debate have never been wholly sealed in national boxes. The discussion is of ideas much more than events, concentrating on prominent left-wing thinkers about education, examining the debates in which they engaged, and reflecting upon the resulting educational policy and practice. The book is not an evaluation of effectiveness—of whether left-wing ideas about education are better than others, or whether the socialist interpretation of liberal education is truer to its spirit than a more conservative one. But insofar as events—such as policies and their effects—are necessary for the understanding of the ideas, there is inevitably some attention to how the debates impinged on practice.

The book may also be thought of as a case study of the role of ideas in the making of public policy. There are three ways in which ideas can enter into policy studies. One is very common, found in the investigation of the ideas of policy makers all the time: in education policy, these might be their beliefs about inequality, about intelligence, about the capacity of people to learn. But what is salient here is rather different from that, and may be succinctly summed up as being the study of ideas about ideas: I discuss in this book what was believed about inherited culture, how left-wing thinkers in theory and in practice understood the intellectual legacy of the past, and what they thought ought to happen to that inheritance in a new society. That is the second sense in which ideas might be studied in policy making, as a consideration of the philosophical systems which were adhered to by influential people. Yet even that way of describing the intention here is not enough, since it is impossible to escape some kind of evaluation of ideas when reflecting on what people thought. In that sense, the study of ideas in action, as it were, is a form of moral philosophy itself, broadly construed. It might be perverse to call this—the third way in which ideas might be studied in connection with policy—ideas about ideas about ideas, but casting judgement on what people thought about the systems of philosophy which they admired seems as inescapable as it would to these thinkers themselves, in their always normative relation to the past. They were interested in the traditions of European civilisation because they admired it and wanted, through socialism, to make it available to all. To put this differently, however important the aim may be of neutrally assessing the ways that people thought about culture, it seems impossible, when discussing this in connection with education, to avoid concluding that some of these ways were better than others, not in the sense of evaluating them in any instrumental sense, but better internally, as an expression of tradition. As we shall see in Chapter 4, moreover, that distinction between evaluating and understanding an inheritance was itself central to some of the later figures in the stories which are told here, notably in the ambiguous and complex writing of Richard Hoggart and Raymond Williams, who stood approximately at the end of a tradition in which the cultural past was held unquestioningly by the political left in high regard.

This way of looking at ideas in policy—of treating what people thought as an opportunity to reflect on whether what they thought was right—may be more apparently useful in the study of education than in some other fields, insofar as ideas might themselves be thought to be the stuff of education (though that claim, as shall be seen in later chapters, is now rather controversial). Nevertheless, it seems possible that considering what people in the past thought about the options in policy across a wide field, and considering also the systems of thought that were available to them, might be a way of stimulating new thinking about the political decisions that face us now. For all the multiculturalism that pervades Western thought today (the educational aspects of which are considered later in this book) the one culture that is generally not treated with respect is that of the past. Unless we are so hubristic as to believe that everything which came before us has been superseded, we might do well to return to the respect for what came before them which the socialist thinkers who are discussed here instinctively felt.

What is meant by liberal education is discussed throughout the book, but especially in Chapter 1, where the history of the ideas associated with that term is introduced. What is meant by 'social radicalism'—the left—is less precise, but because we are dealing here with highly self-conscious thinkers who wrote a lot, the definition is taken implicitly from them: people whose ideas are discussed here chose to define themselves as being on the left, usually as socialist or social democrat, in some cases as predominantly liberal (though they were all liberal in a very profound way, as we shall see), and in later periods as feminists or opponents of racism. Chapter 2 analyses ideas about liberal education by selected thinkers on the left in roughly the first half of the twentieth century, thus including periods when the Labour movement was rising to prominence, and eventually into government, when secondary education was expanding massively, when adult education was being invented afresh, and when—above all—universal suffrage from 1928 was creating a new democracy. Chapter 3 traces how these socialist ideas about a liberal education impinged on socialist policy and practice in that same period, both in schools and for adults. Chapter 4 examines the survival of some of these ideas in the first wave of mid-century revision of socialist thought, and Chapters 5 and 6 trace the profound change that then took place, as the great pioneering efforts of socialist reform ran into the sands of the growing affluence and access to opportunities which it itself had created, and as a generally growing scepticism of hierarchy and authority undermined the old respect for inherited culture. The impact of these changes on social democrats in government from the 1960s onwards is dealt with in Chapter 7. The final chapter considers whether the tradition of left-wing adherence to liberal education might finally have come to an end.

Acknowledgements

I am particularly grateful to Fiona O'Hanlon for kindly reading and commenting on a full draft of the text, picking up many errors and infelicities and discussing the ideas contained in it. I am also grateful for discussions of the general ideas, or of partial drafts of sections of the work, with David McCrone, Ian Martin and Colin Kirkwood, with students in post-graduate and Honours classes in the Schools of Social and Political Science and of Education at the University of Edinburgh, and with members of the audiences at colloquia at the University of Lyon (December 2006), the British Educational Research Association annual conference (September 2008), and the Institute for Advanced Studies in the Humanities, University of Edinburgh (May 2012). The series editor, John Haldane, made valuable suggestions for improvement to the manuscript, which have been incorporated here. The responsibility for interpreting the comments which people have generously made is entirely my own.

Chapter 1

Liberal Education

The concept of a liberal education is as old as thinking about education itself. It was first defined in ancient Greece, was adopted by the Romans to address the dilemmas of leadership, in Europe was imbued with strongly Christian themes when universities were founded from the eleventh century as places where young men would be equipped to rule, began to acquire something of its modern aura with the ideas of refinement and freedom that grew in the Renaissance, and then fully entered modernity in alliance with Enlightenment freedom and the beginnings of modern ideas of democracy. As well as the persistent strand of concern with how to govern wisely, this very old tradition also was pulled between two poles of selection and of moral quality, 'merit' and 'worth' in Rothblatt's terms (2007). Who it was to be for, and what kind of person it would shape—not just what facts or ideas they would learn—have been of perennial concern, and what happens when merit and worth come into conflict has recurrently posed a challenge. If rulers are to be ethical and wise, do they also have to have intellectual merit to earn their power? Might intellect even be the means to wisdom? Above all, as democracy slowly brought everyone into this debate, and raised in connection with every adult the question of their fitness to take decisions about the direction of their society, what was the core of necessary knowledge, understanding and moral worth that would prevent democracy from becoming demagoguery?

The socialist thinkers and makers of policy whom we are considering in this book were heirs to these debates. Until towards the end of the twentieth century, they themselves had mostly had a liberal education of a traditional kind, often, until the middle of the century, in academically selective grammar schools or other elite schools and in the ancient universities. Where they did not have these privileges, their education beyond the elementary was in the firmly liberal traditions of the Workers' Educational Association and some similar organisations, deliberately designed (as we shall see later) to provide liberal education for those who missed out on it when they were young. For a very large part of the century, liberal education seemed the obvious path to take for the newly democratic polity out of which they hoped that socialism would grow. Only a small minority of revolutionary Marxists and an even tinier group of anarchists had serious doubts on this score. The essence of the liberal aims of reformist socialists was summed up in the middle of the century—at the high point of the influence of such ideas on socialist thought—by G.D.H. Cole, one of the influential socialist intellectuals whose contribution to the debate we shall consider in the next chapter:

> They were claiming mainly that the benefits of the superior education open only to the well-to-do should be extended, at least by way of opportunity, to the children of the poor. (Cole, 1952: 50)

One of the reasons that moderate socialists did not doubt this aim was precisely that the inherited ideas about liberal education had included an awareness of the dilemma of merit and worth, of selection and ethics. The capitalism which they wanted to overthrow, or to severely modify, had liberated the individual as never before in history, and none of these kinds of socialist had any doubts that this was an important advance in civilisation that had to be defended: these people were liberal democrats before they were revolutionaries. Liberal education appealed to them because they had themselves learnt through it to understand what, in their view, was oppressive about capitalism, and they had come to the position that the essence of the problem was that capitalist democracy contradicted itself. It offered freedom but denied its reality to all but a few. Though there was a crucial economic aspect to this—though the most dire social problem of capitalism was widespread poverty—the main strand of socialist thought at least until the 1950s held that cultural inequality was, in a deeper sense, more alienating than material deprivation. To be shut out from the inherited civilisation was to be ill-equipped to be a citizen, to be deprived of the essence of humanity. To these thinkers, overcoming that exclusion was both an end and a means. Socialism would make a reality of the educational ideals of liberal culture by enabling everyone to enjoy the benefits of that civilisation, and by so doing the liberal democracy which capitalism had been forced finally to accept would become a reality because it would have the educated citizens that it required.

Rothblatt (2007: 301) captures this polarity succinctly. On the one hand, 'liberal democracy believes that worth can be the result of education, especially liberal education.' Democratic socialists generally eschewed the romantic view, favoured by some kinds of revolutionary thinkers, that the working class were intrinsically virtuous on account simply of being oppressed; so education was as necessary to their virtue as to anyone else's. If that had seemed obvious to thinkers about education since Plato, then such well-educated people as the socialist intellectuals we consider in the next chapter would have been far too aware of their own relative obscurity in a long line of distinguished thought to doubt it. On the other hand, as Rothblatt goes on to say, 'social democracy prefers to begin with worth, an idea once found in the elite culture before sorting by the test commenced.' That view was not common until well into the twentieth century. To the main strand of socialist thinking in Britain in the twentieth century, the idea that human beings were born virtuous was insufficient. Most of these thinkers, despite the Christianity which most of them also accepted, probably felt uneasy with the idea that people were born in sin. But not being wicked was not the same as being virtuous, which required deliberate inculcation, and the only means to that end was the wisdom of the ages. Liberal education offered that potential because, since its Greek days, it had been an education that was not servile, but for free citizens, those with the capacity to govern. In a democracy, that was everyone. Only a certain kind of Marxist held that this history of ideals could be dismissed as a ruling-class illusion, and only later (as shall see) did it occur to more than a small band of far-left people that two-and-a-half millennia of thought about education and culture could be set aside. That liberal education contained within it an acute awareness of its own dilemmas was what gave it such longevity—the dilemma of how to create human worth and how to define what was meritorious in people and in ideas. To those socialist thinkers, education in the great traditions of cultured thought was self-evidently the only means by which the potential worth of everyone could be made real. And this was held to be self-evident because it was old, because it had been so evident to so many intellectually acute predecessors.

Victorian sources of twentieth-century ideas

The more immediate background to socialist thought about liberal education in the twentieth century was, however, its most recent re-thinking by Victorian liberals, especially in the work of the most lastingly influential of these people, Matthew Arnold. The Victorian age was reacting, in turn, to the reinvention of liberal education in the Enlightenment. Rothblatt notes that liberal education came to be attached to the attainment and settlement of civilisation (Rothblatt, 1976: 17). It was a word with wider significance than mere 'civility', since it connoted a social system. Civility might refer to personal duty, civilisation to the whole social organisation in which it might be expressed. 'Civility is a word that reaches towards civilisation' in that 'the end of a liberal education was something less than civilisation and something more than civility' (*ibid.*: 21–2). The evidence that someone was liberally educated, Rothblatt notes, was in their behaviour, style, taste, fashion and manners. To later socialist thinkers, as we shall see in the next chapter, that Enlightenment idea was immensely attractive, since one of the great horrors of capitalism (and, as they saw it, its degeneration into fascism) was its barbaric threat to civilisation, and at the individual level its destruction of moral integrity. Democracy required something much better: G.D.H. Cole called it 'a mental and moral relation of man to man' (quoted by Carpenter, 1973: 247). If it was the task of socialist politics to create a new social order—to safeguard and renovate civilisation—liberal education could prepare individual citizens to be worthy of it, by giving them the capacity to express it in their daily lives through a refined civility.

Liberal education was more than that. Before a socialist renewal of civilisation could come about it was necessary to educate citizens in ways that would help a peaceful revolution to be accomplished. As Rothblatt notes of liberal education more generally, it was thought to be 'the pathway to civilisation' (Rothblatt, 1976: 23). The means to that end was, first of all, literature, notably the literature of ancient Greece and Rome. The place of the ancient world in liberal education was questioned much later, though in fact rarely by the socialists of the first half of the twentieth century, to whom the ideal of Athenian democracy and of Roman social organisation rather appealed, but its relevance was understood to be the models of human problems and ideals which it offered. It was a version of what would later be called (inelegantly) multiculturalism. The liberal argument for studying cultures as remote and yet pertinent as those of the ancient world was always that they forced modern students out of any insular complacency, as explained by R.W. Livingstone in the midst of the destructive nationalism of the First World War:

> There is no absolute protection against self-absorption and blindness to our own weaknesses. Still a knowledge of other civilisations, with which we can compare ourselves, is some help. (Livingstone, 1916: 164)

Greece and Rome 'resemble us sufficiently to admit of comparison, yet are sufficiently different to allow a contrast' (*ibid.*: 185). Livingstone was one of a group of Oxford scholars who sought to widen access to that tradition at the beginning of the twentieth century; others in the group included the socialists R.H. Tawney and William Temple, to whose ideas we shall return (Palmer, 2004). Ernest Barker, writing in 1923, went further: the Stoic philosophy which Rome learnt from Greece was relevant to modern democratic politics because it 'proclaimed the equality of citizen and alien, man and woman, bondman and free' (E. Barker, 1923: 67). Three decades later, after an even more destructive conflict, R.R. Bolgar similarly concluded that studying the ancient world would put our own in perspective: anthropology, he wrote in 1954, has the virtue of giving us 'insight ... into the complexities of our own world' because 'nothing illuminates so vividly as comparison', but at least equally instructive for 'the mass states of today' is the comparison with 'ancient culture' and its 'spiritual centre in the small independent city' (Bolgar, 1954: 386). The linguistic and mental challenges of studying these civilisations were thought to be valuable in their own right, but the main point was that nothing which modern societies confronted had not been debated carefully by the Greeks and Romans (Campbell, 1968). By considering their dilemmas, modern students could thus be freed from the parochialism of the present.

The emergence of civility as a criterion was both tied to specific social classes and also, through the idea of civilisation and Enlightened reason, in aspiration universal. Rothblatt notes that 'every age has its model of an educated man', and in eighteenth-century Britain this was linked to 'a country gentleman, a city merchant or financier, or a London professional man' (Rothblatt, 1976: 59). Such a demeanour involved 'liberality', such as 'good temper' and 'generosity', and also 'sociability', an openness to social connections that readily became a sense of social responsibility. These were all attributes of the rising middle class, and hence were products of capitalism, and they corresponded also to particular features of middle-class lifestyle, as Rothblatt further notes, places where conversation could readily take place—coffee houses, chocolate houses, salons, clubs, small tables for cards or for tea to encourage intimacy, comfortable broad seats (*ibid.*: 63).

Liberal education was more than just the culture of a specific new class, however, since it also pointed towards universal reason, and thus was ready for adaptation by diverse tendencies of political thought in the nineteenth century. On the one hand, and eventually leading directly to later socialist interest in liberal education in the twentieth century, the general connection between Enlightenment reason and one kind of radical critique of capitalism led a minority of radical thinkers to see knowledge and reason, spread through education, as the means to bringing about a better society. This minority current eventually became the socialist thought about education that we consider in the next chapter. G.D.H. Cole, for example, noted admiringly the debt of Robert Owen to William Godwin, in the ideal of a humane capitalism which Owen tried to construct at New Lanark. Godwin, Cole said,

> saw mankind becoming more and more rational with the growth of knowledge; for he thought that to know the good and to act upon that knowledge were but two inseparable aspects of a single process. Accordingly, his entire philosophy turned upon education as a means of making men more rational and therewith better. (Cole, 1952: 46)

Cole acknowledged his own debt to this line of thought through its Victorian phase in the work of the early pioneer of Christian socialism, F.D. Maurice, who was professor of English literature and history, and later of theology, at King's College, London, between 1840 and 1853: 'F.D. Maurice and his friends, no less than Owen, had a deep belief in the central importance of education as a moral and social force' (Cole, 1952: 46–7). Maurice's socialism has been described as 'approximat[ing] a mild Tory paternalism' (Reardon, 2006), and his educational beliefs led him to pioneer the provision of liberal education for working-class adult students: he helped to establish a 'working men's college' in London in 1854, and was its first principal, remaining active in it till a few years before his death in 1872. Also in this same line of religious or aesthetic objections to capitalism is the writing of the art critic John Ruskin, which influenced the cultural outlook of the first generation of twentieth-century socialists. His essay on 'The Nature of Gothic' (1853) was reprinted specially for the inauguration of the London working men's college, because of its denunciation of the dehumanising effects of industrial capitalism (Hewison, 2013). He wrote in 'Ad Valorem' (1860) that 'the rich not only refuse food to the poor; they refuse wisdom; they refuse virtue; they refuse salvation' (Ruskin, 1979 [1860]: 271).

John Henry Newman

Radical opposition to capitalism in the nineteenth century was not, however, the main way in which liberal education left a legacy for twentieth-century socialists. Whatever they might eventually recognise in the minority current through Maurice and others, they were more directly the heirs to the dominant strand of Victorian liberalism, which itself was the main heir to the Enlightenment. Two features of liberal education were strongly encouraged by Victorian liberalism. One was the idea of curricular breadth, the belief that the liberally educated ought to know about the full range of human affairs. Sociability and civility would depend on the empathy created by such broad understanding. This view was reinforced by the ideas of 'faculty psychology', the theory that the mind had distinct aspects, or faculties, and that the purpose of education was to stimulate them all (Albrecht, 1970; Hergenhahn, 1997: 167–8). The ultimate goal was overall mental strength, which could be achieved by paying attention to all the aspects of the mind, for example the philosophical, the literary, the scientific, the religious. Mental training, even drill, was the means to these ends of a broad intellectual capacity. Rothblatt (1976: 130) points out that, according to this theory, the teacher became centrally important, having the knowledge, judgement and intellectual rigour to direct the training that was required. Through these concerns, Rothblatt notes, intellectual aims—the training of mind—came to dominate educational goals, not displacing ethical goals but becoming the means to achieving them. Thus nobility, dignity or generosity were thought to be best attained, not by direct training, but through developing the intellect.

Mental training through breadth of mind, though an important aspect of the educational legacy of Victorian liberalism, was only a tributary to the strongest current, which might best be described as a sense of moral purpose. That readily became a severe critique of capitalism, and hence was attractive to socialists from Maurice onwards; it also ensured that the socialist thought about education had its origins in the mainstream of liberal thought. The most influential thinkers here were John Henry Newman and Matthew Arnold, whose legacies stretched right across the spectrum of liberal and even quite conservative beliefs in the twentieth century. In owing a debt to them, socialist thinking about education up until the middle of the twentieth century was part of a broad, liberal, humanistic culture, not at all external to dominant ways of thinking or alienated from the dominant culture of Western civilisation.

Newman's main influence on ideas about liberal education was through the lectures which he gave in Dublin in the

1850s that were later published under the title of 'The Idea of a University'. They were delivered in his capacity as the principal of a new Catholic university of Ireland that the church had invited him to help to establish. Newman's conversion to Catholicism from Anglicanism in 1845 had caused a great stir in mid-century debates, having resulted from a serious breach within the Church of England between high-church and low-church currents, the former—the Tactarians led by E.B. Pusey, professor of Hebrew at Christ's College, Oxford—close to Catholicism. Newman's theological and philosophical beliefs were hostile to utilitarian ideas, and formed the main themes of his lectures. Yet it would be quite inaccurate to suppose that Newman thought that education should only be for its own sake. In his view, it was always a preparation for life. The aim was moral and social—to create 'a habit of mind... which lasts through life, of which the attributes are, freedom, equitableness, calmness, moderation, and wisdom' (Newman, 2011 [1873]: 167). His point was only that 'knowledge is capable of being its own end' (*loc. cit.*), not that it had no effects beyond itself. 'That further advantages accrue to us and redound to others by its possession, over and above what it is in itself, I am very far from denying' (*ibid.*: 168). His point is simply that pursuing knowledge for its own sake is a natural instinct of human beings, and ought to be fostered.

Newman meant by liberal university education a programme of study that would give the student access to an intellectual tradition 'which is independent of particular teachers, which guides him in his choice of subjects, and duly interprets for him those which he chooses' (*ibid.*: 167). Tradition is thus the central force, shaping any education that would be judged to be worthwhile in the ways that Newman would favour:

> [The student] apprehends the great outlines of knowledge, the principles on which it rests, the scale of its parts, its lights and shades, its great points and its little. (*ibid.*: 167)

It is in these respects, he says, that such an education may be called 'liberal'. Thus liberal education need make no claims beyond its own self-justification:

> That alone is liberal knowledge, which stands on its own pretensions, which is independent of sequel, expects no complement, refuses to be *informed*... by any end, or absorbed into any art. (*ibid.*: 171; his emphasis)

He acknowledged two more specific social aspects of the ideas that made his thought appealing to later generations of social reformers. One was a precondition: he notes Cicero as pointing out that (in Newman's words, quoting Cicero)

> only after our physical and political needs are supplied, and when we are 'free from necessary duties and cares,' [are] we... in a condition for 'desiring to see, to hear, and to learn.' (*ibid.*: 169)

The current of thought about liberal education that defined its essence as being not for servility is thus associated with a view that it is not deliberately for anything specific at all. The freedom to learn for its own sake became, with Newman and the influence which he had, a fundamental liberal freedom, and thus demanded of later generations of political reformers that the social conditions be put in place to ensure that everyone could truly enjoy that freedom just as they might enjoy freedom of speech or freedom before the law.

The other social aspect is the consequences that Newman readily acknowledges to flow from liberal education (even though he is emphatic that consequences are not its justification). Yet even here he is careful to distinguish between intellect and ethics. 'Liberal education makes... the gentleman' (*ibid.*: 179). That is good in itself, though is not enough to make a good person:

> It is well to be a gentleman, it is well to have a cultivated intellect, a delicate taste, a candid, equitable, dispassionate mind, a noble and courteous bearing in the conduct of life — these are the connatural qualities of a large knowledge. (*ibid.*: 179)

But intellect is not the same as virtue. Despite his listing nobility here, we can recognise the same idea as Rothblatt noted from the eighteenth century, that the aim of liberal education was intellectual, not directly ethical. Such a view then bequeaths the idea that, though liberal education might be conducive of virtue, it is not itself virtuous, is 'no guarantee for sanctity or even for conscientiousness' (*ibid.*:

179). From this idea comes a principle of intellectual detachment that, as we shall see in the next chapter, strongly influenced the main current of moderate socialist thought about education in the first half of the twentieth century. Whatever well-educated people might do with their education was separate from that education. Education was not propaganda, however mildly and however much in favour of liberal principles of freedom. Indeed, education was liberal precisely because it prescribed nothing moral.

There was also a third, much more muted, social implication of Newman's thinking about education. Despite his major concern with university education, he was not opposed to 'the education of the people' (*ibid.*: 194). Indeed, 'the more education they have, the better.' Nor was he opposed to the widespread dissemination of some knowledge of the sciences, or of history, biography or political economy. But 'recreations are not education', which is difficult and requires persistent hard work:

> Education is a high word; it is the preparation for knowledge, and it is the imparting of knowledge in proportion to that preparation. We require intellectual eyes to know withal, as bodily eyes for sight. (*ibid.*: 195)

That intellectual challenge—of giving working-class people access to a truly university education—though remote from Newman's thoughts became a central concern of socialist thinkers in the twentieth century.

Matthew Arnold

Despite Newman's eschewing of direct social purposes, the idea of liberal education that emerged partly under his influence came to have a firmly social aspect. Newman contributed what Strike (2004: 321) has called 'an ideal of human flourishing' with a central role for the intellect, 'an ideal of cognitive liberation' in which 'the life of the mind liberates people from servility to unreflective tradition and prejudice'. But there also followed 'a political ideal, [in which] good citizens are people who are capable of critical reflection and rational dialogue'. The pre-eminent exponent of this version of liberal education, and the person who left the strongest legacy to the twentieth century in this connection, was Matthew Arnold.

As Stefan Collini points out, Arnold is inescapable, having had an enormous influence on how we think about culture (Collini, 1988: 3). Arnold's belief that—as Collini (*ibid.*: 87–8) puts it—culture could 'unify and heal' is 'one of [his] most potent legacies', and it certainly appealed to many on the political left in their thinking about what the educational response should be to the divided society that capitalism had created. Collini notes that his legacy in the 1920s and 1930s was strongest among those who proposed that English literature could lead to cultural renewal. A prominent official example was the Newbolt Report of 1921 on the teaching of English in schools in England. The wider cultural influence was through the social and political writing of T.S Eliot, F.R. Leavis and I.A. Richards, aided by the biography of Arnold which Lionel Trilling published in 1939, views to which we return below. These developments, as Collini puts it, established '"English" as the successor-subject to Classics, and even the successor-religion to Christianity' (Collini, 1988: 1123). Arnold's ideas about culture were ultimately the reason why literature came to be central to the idea of liberal education in Britain in the twentieth century, a view that appealed particularly to the political left.

Dover Wilson has suggested that there were four phases in Arnold's writing—successively as poet, as literary critic, as 'prophet of culture', and as theologian. It is the central two, and especially the third, that concern us here, but it is always as well to remember with Arnold that the poetry and the Christian belief are not far in the background. Arnold was born in 1822 in Middlesex. His father, Thomas, was a school teacher whose significance for later educational reform lay in his renovation of Rugby school as its head teacher from 1828, making it into the model for the high-status independent schools that, by the mid-century, saw their role as preparing young men for imperial leadership. As well as making school discipline stricter, Thomas also reformed the curriculum, placing the classical languages at its core and introducing also modern languages, history and mathematics. His aim was 'first, religious and moral principle; secondly, gentlemanly conduct; thirdly, intellectual ability' (quoted by

L. Strachey, 1918: 182). Matthew—who was a pupil at Rugby—acquired from the success of his father's changes an aim to make such a curriculum available much more widely: in Dover Wilson's words, Matthew 'dreamed for the rest of his life of an indefinite multiplication of Rugby day schools promoted by the State' (Wilson, 1930: 169). Matthew's own main paid occupation was as an inspector of schools, from 1851 until 1886, just two years before he died. This practical experience was as important to his views about education as were his being a poet and his Christianity. His understanding of what needed to change acquired a depth and a realism from the drudgery of travelling all over England to test pupils on the knowledge which the schools were supposed to impart. His ideas about how schools might shape citizens in a liberal fashion was influenced by the more interesting official visits he made to France in 1859 and 1865 to report on its school system for the Newcastle and Taunton official committees of enquiry into aspects of school education in England.

Arnold became professor of poetry at Oxford University in 1856, a very part-time commitment, but his first public impact was through his writing as a literary critic and as a critic of Victorian culture and politics. He took a comparative approach to both tasks, referring to other European literary traditions, and all the time aware of what Collini calls 'the towering presences of the classics' (Collini, 2008a). Collini sums up Arnold's approach to literary criticism:

> His work as a critic remained curiously backward-looking, always more alert to the ways in which the great heritage of European literature might animate and discipline contemporary sensibilities than it was to the innovations and expressive possibilities of the present. (*ibid.*: 7)

This approach established the importance of tradition in the analysis of English literature, and a perception of its significance for contemporary concerns.

He was then drawn into wider social criticism through his thinking about education, in numerous articles in periodicals and notably in his book *Culture and Anarchy* that was published in 1869. Its dominant concern was with how education might be used to make democracy work, a topical interest in the aftermath of the Reform Act of 1867 that significantly widened the franchise to include some of the male working class. He was apprehensive about democracy, recognising the threat of populism and demagoguery, but saw it as inevitable, and in any case was instinctively favourable to it and to the liberal republican tradition of revolutionary France. It was above all through this book that his ideas survived to influence later thinkers.

Rothblatt points out that, in his thinking about liberal education, Arnold was essentially returning to eighteenth-century ideas, in three respects (Rothblatt, 1976: 149–50). He sought what Rothblatt calls an 'holistic culture, where self and society are integrated and in accord, so that education is harmonious with the stated aims of society'. In Arnold's words:

> What interests me is English civilisation... —the humanising, the bringing into a harmonious and truly humane life, of the whole body of English society. (Arnold, 1891: 85)

Second, liberal education was 'a restraining force', the way to safeguard civilisation, but it had its effects not through imposition by the state but through making people civilised so that their free choices do not degenerate into anarchy. As Arnold put it:

> We are believers in freedom, and not in some dream of a right reason to which the assertion of our freedom is to be subordinated. (Arnold, 1960 [1869]: 78)

The personal qualities required to exercise freedom responsibly were pre-eminently those which education could create, much more than the ethical development that religion can bring about: what education can provide are 'the power of intellect and knowledge', 'the power of beauty', and 'the power of social life and manners' (Arnold, 1980 [1878]: 595), with the result, as Trilling (1939: 265) put it, that 'culture is reason involving the whole personality; it is the whole personality in search of the truth.' Education would further enable democracy to work effectively by enabling all social classes to contribute to public debate:

> It is well for any great class... to be able to say for itself what it wants, and not to have other classes, the so-called educated and intelligent classes, acting for it as its proctors. (Arnold, 1891: 106)

Social inequality baulked this ideal: 'the religion of inequality' has the effects 'of materialising our upper class, vulgarising our middle class, and brutalising our lower class' (Arnold, 1980 [1878]: 601).

The third feature which Rothblatt notes in Arnold's thinking about liberal education was that it rested on what Rothblatt calls 'a standard based on commonly-accepted canons of taste' (Rothblatt, 1976: 150), as expressed in the idea of 'the best that has been thought and said'. Arnold describes *Culture and Anarchy* thus:

> The whole scope of the essay is to recommend culture as the great help out of our present difficulties; culture being a pursuit of our total perfection by means of getting to know, on all the matters which most concern us, the best which has been thought and said in the world. (Arnold, 1960 [1869]: 6)

The purpose of doing so is explicitly to bring about change: 'through this knowledge, turning a stream of fresh and free thought upon our stock notions and habits.'

Matthew Arnold and the curriculum

Of these three principles, the third is most explicitly about the curriculum. Arnold expanded on this, both in relation to styles of teaching and learning and also in thinking about what was to be learnt. The method should be 'by reading, observing, or thinking' (Arnold, 1960 [1869]: 163), the aim being to realise each person's 'true aspirations and powers' (quoted by Walcott, 1970: 59). The means would be the development of what he saw as ideals of human character: 'conduct, science, beauty, manners' (*ibid.*: 112). This is recognisably the heir to the eighteenth-century ideas about liberal education. The reason why literary criticism would have a central role is that Arnold interpreted it very broadly: as Collini notes, it was the name which Arnold gave to the 'task of general judgement' (Collini, 1988: 55). Arnold emphasised detachment in this work (with one of his many variations on his leitmotiv):

> Criticism... obeys an instinct prompting it to try to know the best that is known and thought in the world, irrespectively of practice, politics, and everything of the kind; and to value knowledge and thought as they approach this best, without

> the intrusion of any other considerations whatever. (Arnold, 1980 [1864]: 247)

The aim of such critical practice is then 'to create a current of true and fresh ideas', and

> its business is to do this with inflexible honesty, with due ability; but its business is to do no more, and to leave alone all questions of practical consequences and applications. (*ibid.*: 249)

These consequences, he said, will always take care of themselves, because they 'will never fail to have due prominence given to them'. The detachment from 'practice' links Arnold to Newman, despite their different views about social purpose.

It is this affinity which Arnold seeks to establish between culture and education that has made his ideas so influential. The very indeterminacy of the word 'culture' helped it to gain currency, though also—as we shall see in Chapters 5 and 6—laid the educational ideas deriving from Arnold's influence open to criticism by those who did not share his belief that culture in his broad sense ought to be widely disseminated. Arnold's recurrent definition of 'culture' is as 'sweetness and light' (Arnold, 1960 [1869]: 54), a phrase that, though easily caricatured by writers in the more cynical twentieth century, conveys the twin aspects that appealed to his successors. He sometimes replaced 'light' with 'wisdom' or 'intelligence' (*ibid.*: 90 and 72); the word 'enlightenment' would capture the collection of ideas, and relates them to the intellectual tradition which Arnold inherited and which he passed on. 'Sweetness' is proper or right behaviour, but also has an aesthetic aspect: Arnold sometimes associated it with 'beauty', and he thus linked education to action, to 'the noble aspiration to leave the world better and happier than we found it' (*ibid.*: 44). Culture, he said, 'is, or ought to be, the study and pursuit of perfection', and the relevant components of perfection are 'beauty and intelligence, or, in other words, sweetness and light' (*ibid.*: 72).

Rothblatt sums up these ideas in terms that would fit better to twentieth-century modes of expression: 'culture' is 'values implied or expressed in behaviour', and points out also that the word can describe 'the many and subtle interpenetrations of history, society and education' (Rothblatt, 1976: 10). Trilling makes explicit the implication that appealed to liberals and socialists in the twentieth century: culture 'is a method of historical interpretation which leads to political action' (Trilling, 1939: 271). Though Arnold admired the ideas of Newman—who was, Dover Wilson explains, after his father the strongest influence on him—he was always more willing to link culture to worldly concerns as he pursued the aim of educational reform that his father had started. Arnold interpreted Newman politically, especially in opposition to what he saw as the 'hardness and vulgarity of middle-class Liberalism' with its motto of 'doing as one likes' (Arnold, 1960 [1869]: 63).

Arnold thus renewed the idea that liberal education prepared people to govern responsibly, which in a democracy would ultimately mean the whole adult population. Rothblatt explains this current of thought in the nineteenth century more generally (Rothblatt, 1976: 154). The leaders of the ever-restless industrial society, he points out, had to have an understanding of social change. Thus it was now not enough, he notes, to have style, conversation and manners: what was needed was 'universal knowledge... a magnificent effort of the rational mind'. So the prime focus of Arnold's political attention was on the state as it was changing under the pressure of middle-class politics. Dover Wilson describes Arnold's view of the state 'as a framework of the national community through which the best of the nation might find expression' (Wilson, 1930: 185), and Trilling (1939: 186) notes that Arnold agreed with Edmund Burke that the state is 'the nation in its collective and corporate character'. Arnold developed these ideas through his work in France, which persuaded him that the state could enlighten society by sponsoring a system of effective public schools which would prepare people to be democratic citizens. Arnold described the state as something which citizens create—the 'organ of our collective best self, of our national right reason' (Arnold, 1960 [1869]: 97).

Democracy would make the need for good general education all the greater but more difficult to meet. The question as Arnold saw it was essentially how to recover democratically the natural authority of the old ruling class:

'the difficulty for democracy is, how to find and keep high ideals' (Arnold, 1980 [1861]: 454). Trilling notes that, for Arnold, democracy requires intellect since it requires everyone to judge for themselves, and requires tolerance of diverse points of view, judging each according to reason. This required a detachment from factionalism, emulating the old aristocratic dispassion: the aristocratic 'grand style', Arnold said, 'may go along with a not very quick or open intelligence; but it cannot well go along with a conduct vulgar or ignoble' (Arnold, 1980 [1861]: 439). Arnold saw fanaticism as lacking sweetness and thus also as lacking light, and the dispassionate citizen had to be as rationally detached as the effective cultural critic. Collini describes Arnold's complex position here by referring to 'his emphasis on experience, judgement, and sensitivity rather than theory, doctrine, or literalism' (Collini, 1988: 95). Arnold thus insisted on absolute standards of judgement, and was opposed to any kind of relativism:

> A kind of philosophical theory is widely spread among us to the effect that there is no such thing at all as a best self and a right reason having claim to paramount authority,... and that there is nothing but an infinite number of ideas and works of our ordinary selves... pretty nearly equal in value, which are doomed either to an irreconcilable conflict, or else to a perpetual give and take. (Arnold, 1960 [1869]: 120)

Thus, despite what is sometimes claimed, Arnold firmly believed that science ought to be included in liberal education, and that understanding scientific ideas was important to being a citizen. He was a friend of T.H. Huxley, who was an eloquent pioneer of science education (and the most effective proselytiser of Darwin's ideas). He wrote to Huxley in 1880 that 'the dictum about knowing "the best that has been known and said in the world" was meant to include knowing what has been said in science and art as well as letters' (Armytage, 1953: 352). He told Huxley that he had thought about using the word 'uttered' but retained 'said' solely on the grounds 'that the formula runs so much easier off the tongue with the shorter word'. He indeed defined culture very broadly: 'in determining generally in what human perfection consists', culture must be taken to include '*all* the voices of human experience which have been heard upon it, of art, science, poetry, philosophy, history [and] religion' (Arnold, 1960 [1869]: 47; his emphasis).

Huxley himself was in no doubt that liberal education should include science, drawing no distinction in principle between social and natural sciences:

> Education is the instruction of the intellect in the laws of Nature, under which name I include not merely things and their forces, but men and their ways. (Huxley, 1971 [1868]: 79)

In the speech he gave at Aberdeen University in 1874 upon being elected rector there, he substituted 'science' for 'ancient languages' in a passage taken from John Stuart Mill's analogous address at St Andrews seven years earlier (Mill, 2011 [1867]):

> In cultivating... science as an essential ingredient in education, we are all the while laying an admirable foundation for ethical and philosophical culture. (Huxley, 1874: 212)

He also, as in the tradition of liberal education, believed that the effect of such an education would be to change the student's very identity: 'the fashioning of the affections and of the will into an earnest and loving desire to move in harmony with these laws' (Huxley, 1971 [1868]: 79).

It is in the context of the insistence by Arnold both on absolute standards and also on tolerance and reason that we should judge his comment that 'men of culture are the true apostles of equality' (Arnold, 1960 [1869]: 70). He would like to do away with social class altogether, because he understood class as an economic matter, and believed that the cultural standards which he espoused were equally relevant to all classes. Education was the means by which to create a common culture based on standards of morality and of reason, and the proper education of school teachers would be necessary to bring this about. He noted in one of his reports as a school inspector the need 'to elevate and humanise' teachers, bringing them 'intellectual sympathy with the educated of the upper classes' (Arnold, 1889 [1852]: 20).

In Newman and in Arnold, nineteenth-century developments in thinking about liberal education thus left a legacy that was ready for reinterpretation by socialist thinkers. There was consideration of the new challenges posed by democracy, and how a liberal education that had once been conceived to prepare the aristocracy for rule might be adapted when every citizen had a role in governing. There was the sense that capitalism had released a destructive anarchy that could be overcome only through the calm reflection that would be encouraged by liberal education. There was the resulting sense that detachment from factional strife ought to be the prime aim of liberal education's pedagogical methods. Moderate socialists, especially, found these appeals to democracy and to reason attractive—as we shall see in the next chapter—since it allowed them to dissociate themselves from those revolutionary currents of thought (by the twentieth century mainly Marxist) which rejected everything that the liberal tradition had bequeathed. Thus the sense of tradition in nineteenth-century ideas about liberal education also appealed to the mainstream of twentieth-century British socialism, the feeling, with Ruskin, that the collective riches of society which capitalism had denied to the working class included cultural as well as material wealth (Ruskin, 1979 [1871]: 375–6). The growing attachment to the Enlightenment principles of reason was also associated with the increasing status of science, which appealed directly to twentieth-century socialist ideas about the rational planning of society. Rothblatt notes that liberal education first started to include research as one of its foundational ideas in the late-nineteenth century, welcoming innovation, boldness, questioning and discovery (Rothblatt, 1976: 157): 'the new meaning of a liberal education that superseded all the others was the search for truth—not abiding truth, but contingent truth, based on facts and sources' (*ibid.*: 196).

The legacy for twentieth-century socialism required reinterpretation, however, as few of the nineteenth-century writers about liberal education would have been content to call themselves socialists. Wilson notes that Arnold distrusted socialism 'as too rigid, and inclined to level down', especially in a cultural and intellectual sense. In Arnold's words: 'socialistic and communistic schemes have generally ... a fatal defect; they are content with too low and material a standard of well-being' (Arnold, 1980 [1878]: 589). Arnold disliked any kind of strong, centralised state, such as was being constructed in his own time in Prussia. But it is perhaps precisely because the twentieth-century socialist thinkers about liberal education took their main inspiration from these non-socialist currents of liberal thought that they had to find ways of reconciling the great traditions with radical ideas about the state, democracy and equality, in which, as Wilson says in a paraphrase of Arnold's ideas, 'the service State... function[s] through a bureaucracy which attracted the best brains and spirits of the country' (Wilson, 1930: 186). To reject all that had gone before would have been rhetorically easy but intellectually unsatisfactory. In the end it would not have been realistic either, since, if the nineteenth-century thinkers had anything to teach, it was that the past lives on, whether in the ideas about wisdom and justice derived from ancient Greece and Rome, or in the respect for the old cultured class in medieval Europe that even Marx admired. 'The best that has been thought and said' was not confined to any one place or time.

The twentieth-century socialist heirs to this also had to develop their ideas in a context that included other, contemporaneous ways of taking forward Arnold and Newman, and so, before we turn to socialist thought about liberal education, we look finally in this chapter at the non-socialist thinking about education, culture and democracy which emerged powerfully in Britain in the period between the two world wars. Though socialists often cast their arguments as deriving from an older tradition, in actual practice the debates in which they were engaged were with liberal and even conservative exponents of a different kind of understanding of the significance of the past for the era of mass democracy.

Liberal education and mass democracy

Strauss comments on an ambiguity in the meaning of the word 'liberal' in the phrase 'liberal education', arising from the persistence of the older ideas which we have noted from Rothblatt. There is here, Strauss (1968: vii) says, 'a premodern sense' of 'liberal', in opposition to 'illiberal' rather than to 'conservative', and signifying 'much the same as "virtuous"'. In fact, generally this meaning of liberal 'goes together with a conservative posture', which we might note is not necessarily at all consistent with the dominant understanding of 'liberal' since the nineteenth century as being concerned above all with 'individual freedom' (Waldron, 1987: 129). Arnold's doubts about approving of people doing what they liked left as strong a legacy as his warmth towards the interventionist state.

Through the intense political debates from the late-nineteenth century to the middle of the twentieth, there was thus a broadly conservative current of thought that claimed the tradition of liberal education as its inspiration. A starting point for understanding this is the doubts about populist democracy that Arnold and others expressed. Arnold was rather appalled by reading de Tocqueville's *Democracy in America* when it appeared in 1835, showing, in Wilson's paraphrase of Arnold's response, 'a society without culture, without traditions, without anything that could rightly be called State institutions' (Wilson, 1930: 170). In a letter of 1848, Arnold wrote to his mother that 'I see a wave of more than American vulgarity, moral, intellectual, and social, preparing to break over us' (Arnold, 1895 [1848]: 5). In his later essay on 'Equality' (1878), after praising the high cultural standards of the pre-revolution French nobility which were being maintained for the whole population by republican France, he commented that 'in America, perhaps, we see the disadvantages of having social equality before there has been any such high standard of social life and manners formed' (Arnold, 1980 [1878]: 587).

Twentieth-century responses to liberalism also doubted whether the sacrifice of community in the name of freedom was consistent with that aim of liberal education which valued education's contribution to citizenship, since being a citizen presupposes a stable society in which the individual can act politically. Strike (1991: 434) has noted the conflict between freedom and community in liberal thought about education. On the one hand, there is the aim to 'provide the opportunity for children to explore and freely choose from among as wide a range of cultural goods and patterns of life as is practical'. Strike calls this 'neutral education'. On the other, there is the more activist aim 'to develop such characteristics as are required for citizenship in liberal society'. He further notes that what is in this formulation merely a tension becomes irreconcilable if the community is identified with the state, which is why liberals regard 'the identification of community with state [a]s the greatest danger to liberty' (Strike, 1991: 474).

Socialists were particularly ambivalent about this because, however much they placed freedom ahead of all other political goals (which democratic socialists in Britain tended to do), their objection to capitalist anarchy was, with Arnold, based on a valuing of community or solidarity. Thus one of the recurrent principles which they faced, as we shall see in the next chapter, was the need (again in Strike's words) for an education which 'subjects the values and moral traditions that form local community to criticism and rational appraisal' (Strike, 1991: 474). Only such an education, Brian Barry has argued, could truly be described as liberal (Barry, 2001: 194–249). Nevertheless, what almost all currents of political thought about education in Britain in the early twentieth century had inherited from the nineteenth century and from the Enlightenment was an attachment to universal values and the belief that they could be best transmitted by passing on high culture—'the best that has been thought and said'—to each succeeding generation. The ideal was summed up by Karl Mannheim, one of the founders of the academic sociological study of education, who was professor of that subject at the Institute of Education in London from 1946, having established a distinguished reputation as a sociologist in Weimar Germany before being forced into exile in 1933. In his influential *Ideology and Utopia,* he argued that 'participation in a common educational heritage progressively tends to suppress differences of birth, status, profession, and wealth, and to unite the individual educated people on the basis of the education they have received.' The reason for this is that education, under the influence of class-less intellectuals, now can be universal without obliterating class:

> One of the most impressive facts about modern life is that in it, unlike preceding cultures, intellectual activity is not carried on exclusively by a socially rigidly defined class, such as a priesthood, but rather by a social stratum which is to a large degree unattached to any social class and which is recruited from an increasingly inclusive area of social life. (Mannheim, 1936: 155–6)

In Britain, a common admiration for universal values was aided by the fact that intellectuals were, in Heyck's (1998) terms, highly integrated with the ruling elite, regardless of their own political ideology: there was never any of that alienation of radicals of the left or of the right from the state which was occasioned by revolution and war in most other European countries. Thus the right did not see universal liberal or democratic values as a threat to stability, and the left did not regard stability and continuity as being inconsistent with profound social reform. The place in which discussion about the proper interpretation of tradition happened in Britain was thus more often the university or the public debates deriving from it than the partisan arguments of politics. The resulting restrained intellectual style for the twentieth century is summed up by Judt (2012: 56) in terms that remind us how much this style itself owes to the ethical ideas of proper conduct contained in the eighteenth-century development of liberal education:

> It entails knowing how to 'be' an Oxford don; understanding intuitively how to conduct an English conversation that is never too aggressively political; knowing how to modulate moral seriousness, political engagement and ethical rigidity through the application of irony and wit, and a precisely-calibrated appearance of *insouciance*. It would be difficult to imagine the application of such talents in, say, postwar Paris.

Judt describes the whole generation (right or left) born around 1905 as 'without question the most influential intellectual cohort of the century' (*ibid.*: 36). A member of that generation, Cyril Connolly, described its effects: 'we grow up among theories and illusions common to our class, our race, our time. We absorb them unawares and their effect is incalculable' (Connolly, 1983 [1948]: 141–2). One of the most prominent features was a loss of that optimism which dominated the Victorian age, though not its intellectuals:

> In spite of the slow conversion of progressive ideas into the fact of history, the Dark Ages have a way of coming back. Civilisation—the world of affection and reason and freedom and justice—is a luxury which must be fought for, as dangerous to possess as an oil-field or an unlucky diamond. (*ibid.*: 261)

Trilling notes that the pessimism was itself part of the intellectual heritage: Arnold resembled both Wordsworth and T.S. Eliot in writing 'for a small group of saddened intellectuals for whom the dominant world was a wasteland' (Trilling, 1939: 79), like Eliot, Lawrence and Yeats conveying 'the loss of a certain culture' (*ibid.*: 421).

The importance of *Scrutiny*

The particular threat which alarmed many intellectuals in Britain at this time was mass culture accompanying mass democracy. The most influential group of writers expressing that concern was around the journal *Scrutiny*, founded in 1932 by the literary critics L.C. Knights and F.R. Leavis. They shaped the debate, and thus shaped also the left-wing response to the debate; indeed, writers for the journal included several on the left whose ideas we consider in the next chapter. The most prominent contributors other than these were literary critics: Q.D. Leavis (married to F.R. Leavis), I.A. Richards and, specifically on education and somewhat later, G.H. Bantock. The link between social critique and literary criticism was firmly in the tradition of Arnold.

The views about mass culture in this group were characteristically expressed in Q.D. Leavis's book *Fiction and the Reading Public* (1932), a pioneering study of audiences in the sense that it surveyed readers of popular fiction as well as analysing such writing in literary-critical terms. Though not in any sense a left-wing book, the critique of capitalism was as clear as in Arnold. '[P]robably the most terrifying feature of our civilisation' is the effect of 'Big Business' in 'destroy[ing] among the masses a desire to read anything which by the widest stretch could be included in the classification "literature"' (Q.D. Leavis, 2000 [1932]: 270 and 17). The book, she says in conclusion, has 'isolated and shown the workings of... tendencies which, having assumed the form of commercial and economic machinery, are now so firmly established that they run on their own and whither they choose' (*ibid.*: 270). Her argument is that there was a time in the past when there was not this debilitating divide between high and mass culture. In the eighteenth or even the nineteenth century, she says, everyone could read the same novels, and there was a real meaning to the concept of the 'common reader'. The common culture was even stronger in the Shakespearian age and in the century that followed, in contrast to the time at which Leavis was writing:

> Elizabethan popular writers were able to make use of a rich speech idiom; they wrote for a people whose social intercourse had developed the art of conversation... There was here no poverty of emotional life needing fantasy to nourish it, no relief in vicarious living. (*ibid.*: 88)

This culture was sustained through the religious revolutions of the seventeenth century, stimulated by the elegant and complex writing of such widely read works as the Authorised Version of the Bible, *Pilgrim's Progress* and *Paradise Lost*. The highbrow novel, addressed to a minority audience, Leavis says, did not make a significant appearance until the late-nineteenth century.

The problem now, she argues, is not only that popular taste has been vitiated, but also that most 'intelligent educated reader[s]' no longer have 'an explicitly literary training', many indeed having been 'alienated... from culture' by their pursuit of science (*ibid.*: 74–5 and 191). The popular tradition was in any case destroyed by the popular press, but also by other features of popular culture that are 'inimical to mental effort', such as cinemas and jazz music (*ibid.*: 224). The effect of the press was a combination of ownership by large conglomerates, yielding an artificial homogeneity of content and style, and pressure from advertisers, without whom a mass press would not have been financially viable (*ibid.*: 182–3) The result is that

> the traditional editorial style [of the Victorian age]—the rounded and majestic period, the elaborate argument, the moderate tone—had to go; it was replaced by the bright snappy style that picks out the 'human' features of a topic in three simple paragraphs. (*ibid.*: 183)

This was not just about style, however: it was a loss of that seriousness of purpose which had remained strong throughout society between the seventeenth and mid-nineteenth centuries. She notes that Arnold could write for readers who would share a meaning of key terms that could no longer be assumed:

> Arnold's critical idiom betrays the conviction that certain important terms essential to his argument—'culture,' 'right reason,' 'the will of God,' 'the best self,' 'perfection'—do not need defining; he addresses himself to the general reader... and yet can assume that his idiom will be intelligible them. (*ibid.*: 189)

In support of her claim about Arnold's audience, she notes that *Culture and Anarchy* was quickly made available in a sixpenny pocket edition, and later in an even cheaper paper form.

For the group around the *Scrutiny* journal, the response to such a crisis was to assert the value of 'community' (Mulhern, 1979: 309). Literature became what Mulhern calls, in his history of *Scrutiny*, 'the new repository of moral values'. F.R. Leavis aimed to create a new distinterested intelligentsia which could apply its literary-critical judgement to the problems of mass society. The main reason for the faith in literature was that, in Q.D. Leavis's words, 'the novel can deepen, extend, and refine experience by allowing the reader to live at the expense of an unusually intelligent and sensitive mind' (Q.D. Leavis, 2000 [1932]: 74). Unlike Arnold and most of his generation, the *Scrutiny* group paid far more attention to novels than to poems or plays, but the approach to literature was the same as his, seeing literary criticism as a criticism and potential reformation of life: in Arnold's words, by considering 'the best that is known and thought in the world, and by in its turn making this known, [criticism] create[s] a current of true and fresh ideas' (Arnold, 1980 [1864]: 248–9).

The *Scrutiny* writers avoided outright pessimism by placing some faith in education as the means of counteracting the tendencies which they described. Though the details of that response varied between left and right, the common premise was, as Mulhern points out, that education, though 'complicit with the "economic process"' that was destroying community and culture, could be 'a centre of opposition' to that, especially through literature (Mulhern, 1979: 101). Educational concerns were, indeed, at the heart of the whole *Scrutiny* project, following the introduction of compulsory elementary education in England and Wales in 1870 and Scotland in 1872. There was then what Sutherland has called 'alarmed pessimism' occasioned by 'the fear inspired in the cultured classes of late Victorian and Edwardian England by the Foster Education Act of 1870. If Demos could read, what reading-matter would the monster demand?' (Sutherland, 2000: xviii). Half a century later the apprehension was all the greater since that mass of people now also could vote and was even being offered (by the left) access to secondary education. F.R. Leavis turned his attention increasingly to education, writing in 1943, and echoing Arnold's distrust of American individualism and populism, that

> we are told that the century to come is to be the century of the common man, and we read in papers, books, and pamphlets of the changes that are to be made in education in the interests of democracy. Remembering what the claims of democracy have done for education in America, we cannot, some of us, help asking, as we note how the stress falls when these changes are discussed over even the most honoured signatures: 'But what about the interests of education?' (F.R. Leavis, 1943: 163)

He justified this concern in terms of what would be most effective in establishing a true democracy:

> If... the essential standards and essential ends [of education] are lost sight of or sacrificed as of merely subordinate importance, democracy will have been ill served and the common-ness of the century of the common man will be of an order that it is not exhilarating to contemplate.

Scrutiny solicited comments on the Spens report of 1938, which (as shall be discussed more fully in Chapter 3) proposed the restructuring of secondary education in England and Wales into three tiers; academic, technical and 'modern'. The report recommended that 'the first aim of all English teaching should be to enable a child to express clearly, in speech or writing, his own thoughts, and to understand the clearly expressed thoughts of others' (Board of Education, 1938: 219). Then there is an aim that was close to thinking in the *Scrutiny* circle:

> The second objective, which can only be attempted after the first is more or less successfully attained, is the development of the power thus acquired to benefit the child as a social

> being, and to help him to take his place as a thinking individual and a wise citizen.

F.R. Leavis summarised the invited comments in an editorial article. He agreed with those which argued that, when liberal education was for only for a small number of people, the majority received 'what might be called a tradition of liberal training', in family, home, or church. The tradition was broken by the industrial revolution; even worse, the dehumanising spirit of the factory and of the elementary school 'has spilled over into the secondary school' (F.R. Leavis, 1939: 256). Leavis argued also that:

> Schools and colleges are, or should be, society trying to preserve and develop a continuity of consciousness and a directing sense of value—a sense of value informed by a traditional wisdom. (*ibid.*: 242)

One critic of Spens in the *Scrutiny* collation had argued that it was too concerned with the vocational uses of education. What should have been proposed, this critic said (in an argument reminiscent of Newman's), was 'a period of general preparation, of contemplation,... necessary before even preparing for any particular activity' in life (*ibid.*: 250). L.C. Knights applied a similar argument to the training of teachers, writing about the results of a survey which he had conducted of training colleges in England and Scotland. The problem, he said, was that teaching at the colleges was mechanical, and not aimed to stimulate deep knowledge. Students were not encouraged to discuss what they were learning, and were regimented even in their 'private study'. But this could not be solved without attacking 'the general state of English culture at the present time', in which 'behind the educational system stand the cinema, newspapers, book societies, and Big Business—the whole machinery of "Democracy" and standardisation' (Knights, 1932: 259).

The most obvious response to all such concerns was perhaps conservative. Mulhern commented that the *Scrutiny* group was 'profoundly at odds' with Marxist and social-democratic ideas, and were closely tied to the tradition of Burke, Cobbett, Shelley, Carlyle and Lawrence, 'propounding the idea of a disinterested clerisy centred on literature and capable of guiding the moral life of an aberrant society'

(Mulhern, 1979: 306). The leading educational voice in the group was Bantock, though mostly after the Second World War. Writing in *Scrutiny* in 1951 (Bantock, 1951: 32), he gave two reasons why Arnold still mattered in the middle of the twentieth century. One was that the 'cultural situation' had grown worse 'along the lines which Arnold indicated', in the sense of 'degeneration of standards'. The other, and more important, was the need for a formal curriculum taught by well-educated teachers, embedded in a tradition of culture. Bantock calls this Arnold's 'protest against the romantic idea that the source of enlightenment lay within the self', in favour of 'the reassertion of a classical ideal [that] involved a submission to an external discipline'. Bantock accordingly was highly critical of child-centred ideas, such as those of John Dewey, professor of education at the University of Chicago (1894–1904) and at Columbia University (1904–30) the extensive influence of whose thought we consider more fully in Chapter 6. Bantock commented:

> Children nowadays are encouraged to be 'creative' in a vacuum, as it were, without the mental stimulus that only subject-matter of value, and the direct intervention of the teacher can provide. (*ibid.*: 39)

T.S. Eliot's even more conservative writing on education and tradition had influenced Bantock (and most writers for *Scrutiny*). He doubted the effects on standards of 'educat[ing] everybody' (Eliot, 1948: 108), even if the intention was to adjust the teaching to the capacities of the child, since, he said, the necessary testing would 'substitut[e] for classes, elites of brains, or perhaps only of sharp wits'. The attempt to adjust education to the needs of society would destroy education by restricting it 'to what will lead to success in the world', and would 'restrict success in the world to those persons who have been good pupils of the system' (*ibid.*: 101). Eliot's main reason for distrusting liberalism was that it destroyed tradition without which social order would collapse, an argument which is in essence the same as Arnold's, but without Arnold's faith in education as a means of renewing tradition. Eliot thought that 'a "mass culture" will always be a substitute-culture' (*ibid.*: 107), but he did not accept the false choice that would restrict culture to an elite. Bantock points out that it is inaccurate to say that Eliot was interested only in high culture (Arnold's sense of culture), because he used two senses of the word. High culture was the refinement of culture in the anthropological meaning of 'all the characteristic activities and interests of a people' (*ibid.*: 31). He wanted to believe that culture was a unity, in which the elite would provide standards for the mass. The question was how to form the elite, since Eliot believed that the disparity of cultural background in the elites to which meritocratic recruitment would lead would undermine that unity of cultural outlook that is necessary for leadership. His solution was that the elite had to be attached to an existing class, though how that class was to be perpetuated remained therefore problematic, and would have to depend at least in part on heredity. There is a sense, nevertheless, in which what Eliot was describing was the elite of intellectuals who debated these ideas across the political spectrum between the wars, the last time at which that was possible before the massive social mobility and educational expansion of the second half of the twentieth century destroyed the cultural unity permanently (Mulhern, 1979: 312).

John Carey (1992) has pointed out that a contempt for mass culture was the common view of intellectuals in the first half of the twentieth century, and certainly Eliot's position seems a cardinal instance. Yet even Eliot's position is not straightforward, and offers a strangely democratic form of ultra-conservatism, even if we are sceptical, seventy years on, of his return to a past of monastic elites leading the rest in a kind of secular version of holy sacrament. We may judge Q.D. Leavis's similar admiration for the common culture that she discerned in Shakespeare's or Milton's England to be romantic wishful thinking, but it does not in principle exclude even the poorest and most culturally marginalised in society from participation in the highest culture, given the right kind of education and other cultural opportunities. These conservatives were far away from a belief that schools are inevitably an expression of the existing social order.

It is not surprising then to find that *Scrutiny* had a significant influence on the political left (Hilliard, 2012). In anticipation of themes that are explored in greater detail in the next chapter, this view of the debate around *Scrutiny* helps to set the context, and partly explains why the best approach to understanding left-wing thought on education at this time is as part of a dialogue with the rest of what we might call humanistic ideas. Mulhern (1979: 175) judges that *Scrutiny* had 'a clear general bias towards the Left', in the sense that it was 'anti-fascist, anti-war, anti-capitalist' (*ibid.*: 95). But it was not socialist. There were three important respects in which *Scrutiny* provided a bridge across which ideas could travel between left and right. One was class. There was a rather paradoxical sense in which the sociological interests of the Leavises, and other writers for *Scrutiny*, inclined them to favour an almost Marxist view that class was entirely an economic matter, not a cultural one. It was economics that had created the mass culture that they deplored, and it was economics that was forcing education in a utilitarian direction. The very commonality of mass culture thus ensured that there were no longer separate class cultures as there were in the more hierarchical society of Arnold's time. If that meant a shared mediocrity, at least it pointed to a way out, through education and through the wider dissemination of those critical standards that would refine literature until it could, once again, create a common culture worth admiring. Imaginative literature provided the common bond, as recalled for example, at the end of the century, by the Marxist historian Eric Hobsbawm, who arrived as a young refugee in London with his aunt and uncle in 1933. He said of Leavis:

> No don in his century had a greater impact on the teaching of literature. He had an awesome capacity to inspire generations of future schoolteachers who, in turn, inspired their bright pupils. (Hobsbawm, 2002: 94–5)

He attributes the growth of left-wing history-writing in Britain to the fact that in the final years of secondary school 'literature took the space left vacant by the absence of philosophy' (*ibid.*: 97). As was pointed out by Raymond Williams, one of the socialist writers who (as we shall discuss in Chapter 4) followed directly from the *Scrutiny* group, F.R. Leavis's view of literature was that it distilled (or ought to) the essence of culture, and in that sense it was potentially the property of everyone (Williams, 1961: 247 and 249). Only the later cultural definitions of social class on the left could break this link, as shall be seen in Chapter 5.

The second opening to the left was through the idea of community, which itself was the social elaboration of the idea of culture. Mulhern (1979: 330) calls *Scrutiny* a 'radical romantic counterpoint to the conventional wisdom of liberal-Fabian educational policy, a latter-day variation on the romantic/utilitarian antinomy that constitutes one of the abiding structures of industrial-capitalist culture'. That may be true, but it does not explain the close affinity between even Eliot's critique of a philistine, mechanical society and the very similar indictments from intellectuals on the left. This idea of a community of culture set against the anarchy of capitalism is discussed further in the next chapter. Once again, it was a link of humanistic understanding across the political spectrum that was lost later in the twentieth century when the arguments for a common culture were no longer so unproblematically shared, and when the utilitarian conceptions—what Mulhern calls the Fabian ideas—came to dominate actual left-wing policy on education.

And it was education that provided the third and strongest link from *Scrutiny* to the left, a sharing of the tradition from Arnold. There was an optimism about very many of these writers, a sense that with education everything was possible. At the time, that view inspired most strongly a commitment to adult education. Later, as secondary education expanded, the same view came for a while to influence left-wing thought about a common curriculum for school pupils, building upon the Leavisite practices which inspired Hobsbawm. There might have been disagreement about the extent to which the best that has been thought and said could be appreciated by everyone, but there was no sense at all that the effort was not worth it.

Chapter 2

Socialist Intellectuals: Reason and Enlightenment

Ideas about liberal education on the political left in Britain in the first half of the twentieth century are examined here particularly through the views of three of its most prominent intellectuals – R.H. Tawney, Harold Laski and G.D.H. Cole. These three matter because they were so famous at the time and so influential. As one biography of Laski has commented: 'it is difficult to recapture the hold over the mind of the left between the wars exercised by the socialist trinity of Cole, Laski and Tawney' (Kramnick and Sheerman, 1993: 251). We look also at other thinkers too, and in the next chapter trace the development of the ideas discussed in this chapter in the context of left-wing policy and practice, but it is not unreasonable to suggest that the way in which culture and education were thought about on the left can be captured in the words of these three men.

Who were they, then, and why do they matter? Tawney was the most extensively involved in education, being one of the pioneers in adult education from the beginning of the century. He was born in 1880 in Calcutta, where his father was prominent in the Indian education service. He epitomised the close intellectual connection at this time between academic learning of a quite traditional kind and radical political activism. He was educated at Rugby School, acquiring a sense of socially responsible leadership from the ethos laid down by the reforms of Matthew Arnold's father. Subsequently as a student at Balliol College, Oxford, he was, as Terrill (1973: 24) put it, attracted by 'the social idealism of Edward Caird and the socially oriented religious liberalism of Charles Gore [later Bishop of Oxford]'. That moved him to 'the social moralism out of which his socialism later grew' and he became a member of the executive committee of the Workers' Educational Association in 1905 shortly after it had been established by Albert Mansbridge. He taught classes under its auspices while holding academic posts in Glasgow and Oxford Universities and—for most of his career (1920 until his retirement in 1949)—at the London School of Economics, becoming professor of economic history there in 1931. In his academic work he was distinguished as an historian of seventeenth-century England, and was elected a Fellow of the British Academy in 1934 for his work in that respect. Alongside this, he was also firmly on the political left throughout his adult life, 'a democratic socialist with philosophic roots in Christian humanism' (Terrill, 1973: 269). This was evident not only in his most influential books—notably *The Acquisitive Society* (1921) and *Equality* (1931)—but also in his direct service to the Labour Party, standing unsuccessfully for election on several occasions and, much more influentially, writing many important policy papers for them. The title of his detailed *Secondary Education for All* (1922) coined a slogan that shaped Labour's thinking in this connection for four decades, and he later judged that the 1944 Education Act (a product of the wartime coalition but implemented by Labour after 1945) embodied principles inspired by his 1922 work (Tawney, 1964 [1949a]: 152). His biographer Lawrence Goldman assessed *Equality* as 'an important milestone in the development of socialist thinking in Britain and a prescient guide to the intentions and achievements of the Labour government after 1945' (Goldman, 2004). His political ends were also served by his long period, from 1928 to 1944, writing for the *Manchester Guardian* newspaper, his contribution amounting to around 90 articles on education, often as unsigned editorials (Terrill, 1973: 84).

Tawney's aim in serving the Workers' Educational Association was to extend to the working class the benefits of that kind of education he had enjoyed, and the sorts of scholarship that he engaged in. As Stefan Collini has put it: Tawney's work was 'associated... with the obligation of the educated and the privileged to put their talents at the service of the working class' (Collini, 1999: 177). He was a pioneer of the W.E.A.'s university-style tutorial classes, the aim of which was to bring the same standards of rigour and evidence to adult education as were found in classes at universities. A collective tribute to him published on the occasion of his 80th birthday in 1960 showed how highly regarded his work in adult education had been:

> His first glory was that of a teacher when he met those gardeners and plumbers and potter's throwers on level terms, respecting their shrewdness of judgment whilst winning their confidence with his scholarship, obtaining their liking by his natural equalitarianism of manner, whilst offering them such treasures of history as Oxford had taught him to discover for himself... The thousands of [W.E.A.] University Tutorial Classes which have flourished in Britain have been, quite literally, offshoots from these first two of Tawney's. (Creech Jones, 1960: 6)

His legacy has indeed stood the test of time (Wright, 1987: 130–54). Goldman notes that whereas 'the influence of other socialist thinkers of this era [first half of the twentieth century] like Harold Laski, G.D.H. Cole, and Sidney and Beatrice Webb has faded since their deaths,... Tawney remains a living presence' (Goldman, 2004). Tawney remained respected by both the right and the left of the Labour movement even in the bitterly divided 1980s (Wright, 1987).

Nevertheless, for all his prominence and the untypical longevity of his legacy, at the time we are considering here he was only one of several public intellectuals in Britain who shaped the way in which the left thought about education. Indeed, so far as the general public was concerned, Harold Laski was probably even more prominent, 'at bottom a mass preacher and public teacher, one of the most widely read and listened-to public intellectuals' of the twentieth century (Kramnick and Sheerman, 1993: 590). Although written about his reception in America, a further comment by Kramnick and Sheerman (1993: 453) sums up something of

Laski's public persona: he was perceived there as 'the foreign, Jewish, intellectual radical that Americans could immediately call up in their minds when they envisioned a "socialist"'.

Laski was born in 1893 in Manchester, son of a very successful cotton exporter; both his parents were prominent members of the Manchester Liberal Party. He attended Manchester Grammar School, and then had an adventurous undergraduate career, switching from history to science at New College, Oxford, and, in that connection, working on eugenics as a student volunteer with Karl Pearson at Imperial College, London; Laski's first published article was on this topic, appearing when he was only 17. At Oxford, Laski then changed back to history, gained a first-class degree, and worked for a while writing 'vigorous left-wing editorials' for the *Daily Herald*, the fledgling left-of-centre newspaper founded in 1912 (Newman, 2011). In 1911, he married Frida Kerry, also at this time an enthusiast for eugenics. The marriage was against his parents' wishes, a rift which took a long time to heal. From Frida he acquired a strong attachment to the case for women's rights. His academic career started in Montreal in 1914 (at McGill University), after which he moved to Harvard, from where he met and became friends with many leading American intellectuals, notably Felix Frankfurter (later an adviser to President Roosevelt) and the leading American academic lawyer, Oliver Wendell Holmes (like Frankfurter a member of the Supreme Court). Laski and Holmes remained very close friends, despite the difference of age (Holmes having been born in 1841) and despite sharp differences of politics, Holmes being a conservative.

While lecturing at Harvard, Laski also was active in American socialist politics and trade union affairs, attracting much controversy as a result. When he returned to Britain in 1920 to a post as a lecturer at the London School of Economics he become involved with the Labour Party and with the Fabian Society, the organisation that had been established in 1884 to press for socialist transformation by gradual means, and that had become the leading intellectual institution on the reformist left in Britain, helping to set up the Labour Party and guiding its ideas. Laski became professor of political science at the L.S.E. in 1926 where he remained until his death in 1950. During the 1930s, he was prominent in the Socialist League, the main left-wing pressure group in the Labour Party, which campaigned for a Popular Front that would combine all political forces on the left, analogously to the movement that came to power in France with the election of Leon Blum in 1936 as the Socialist prime minister of a coalition also involving the Communist Party and the centrist Radicals. The particular concern of Popular Front campaigning in Britain was the reluctance of the National Government in the 1930s to confront the rise of fascism on the continent of Europe. The Communists were too insignificant in Britain to make a Popular Front a serious political choice (and in any case were wholly unreliable as allies, as Laski and others discovered when they repeatedly changed their position on cooperation with socialists and liberals). Nevertheless, the Socialist League was important because it shaped general political views in the 1930s and because it included many people who were to become prominent in and around the Labour government of 1945, notably not just Laski—who was an elected member of the party's National Executive Committee from 1937 to 1949—but also Stafford Cripps (Chancellor of the Exchequer, 1947-50), Aneurin Bevan (Minister of Health, 1945-51) and Ellen Wilkinson (Minister of Education, 1945-47); we return to Wilkinson's ideas and policies in the next chapter. Tawney, too, joined the League, but less enthusiastically (Terrill, 1973: 78).

Newman (2011) describes Laski as 'the best-known socialist intellectual of his era', because his main political influence was probably through his public writing rather than directly in the Labour Party, where he tended to attract the ire of the leadership for his dissenting views; indeed, on several occasions he tried to displace Clement Attlee from the leadership on the grounds that he was uninspiring and too cautious in his commitment to social reform. Laski was most famous for his books and articles, becoming, as Collini has put it, 'emblematic' of the public intellectual between the wars, even—despite his radical views—embodying 'the tastes of the average educated Englishman of the period' (Collini, 2006: 133). He was also as committed as Tawney to adult education, where, as shall be discussed later, 'he stood by the traditional mission of teaching "humanly enriching" high culture' (*loc. cit.*). Like Tawney, but with a less insistently religious flavour, he 'tapped into th[e] vast stream of ethical socialism, usually via William Morris' (Kramnick and Sheerman, 1993: 249).

Though he admired Tawney (13 years his senior), Tawney thought him rather meretricious and distrusted his move to the almost Marxist left in the 1930s, but Laski's public prominence depended in large part on his intellectual dissent, on his challenge to the cautious conservatism that had seemed to engulf Britain when its global power declined and, particularly, when it seemed incapable of doing anything to resist the collapse of European democracy. For all his Marxism, Laski remained—as we shall see—an absolutely firm proponent of liberal democracy, and his academic writing and teaching were particularly concerned with the distribution of power, with pluralism, and with the problems raised for democracy by the growth of the state. In this respect, he shared concerns though certainly not a political position with his quite different colleague at the L.S.E., Friedrich von Hayek, later highly influential on the development of the anti-state ideology of the New Right in the 1970s and 1980s.

G.D.H. Cole, too, was an adult educator, and he also was thus very active in the W.E.A. He, too, benefited from the elite liberal education that the Victorian era had bequeathed: born in 1889, he attended St Paul's School in London and Balliol College, studying classical history and philosophy. He, like Tawney (and many others), was influenced by William Morris: 'I became a Socialist, as many others did in those days, on grounds of morals and decency and aesthetic sensibility' (quoted by Carpenter, 1973: 5). He was involved in the Fabian Society and the Labour Party as a student. He developed from these early intellectual and political interests the ideas of Guild Socialism which first established him as a public figure, an almost anarchist set of ideas in which the state would become irrelevant because workers and communities would take control of their own local society and economy. Much of his writing on this topic was in the radical weekly *New Age* which had become, by the eve of the First

World War, one of the most prominent in Britain, with a vaguely Christian socialist philosophy. Cole, like Tawney and Laski, was shaped by the thinking of Oxford idealist philosophers whom we examine further below, notably by T.H. Green through the work of John Neville Figgis, who argued that only small communities could truly embody the spirit of mutual support and the ethical principles that Green and his associates had advocated (Boucher and Vincent, 2000).

The Guild Socialist movement collapsed, although it was influential on the early Labour Party, helping to prevent its becoming as centralist in its philosophy as many socialist parties were becoming at that time. Cole then converted himself into an economist and political scientist, becoming an academic at Oxford University, first (1925) as a reader in economics and later (1944) as professor of political and social theory. Cole continued to be influential on the Labour Party's economic policy, for example being a member of the Economic Advisory Council for the second Labour government in 1930 (Howson and Winch, 1977: 24). After the fall of that government and the formation of the National Government in 1931, Cole 'worked hard once again to produce a radically socialist alternative to mainstream labourism' (Stears, 2004); he, like Laski and Tawney, joined the Socialist League. He wrote very widely, both in periodicals such as the *New Statesman* and in books, so much rivalling Laski as the leading socialist intellectual that the two 'actively disliked each other' (Kramnick and Sheerman, 1993: 250). In particular, Cole wrote a highly influential series of popular books aiming to introduce general audiences to such topics as the state of Europe in the 1930s, the condition of the world economy, and what socialism might mean. His biographer notes that academic critics sneered at him for writing too much, but these 'were among the most significant things he did', filling 'an important gap in mass education' (Carpenter, 1973: 182). One reason the books mattered is that they 'demonstrated the existence of a literate population eager for the latest political information at a reasonable price', and thus taking advantage of the growth of popular publishing that we shall consider in the next chapter. Cole's aim,

Carpenter says, was to do 'everything well, rather than one thing superbly' (Carpenter, 1973: 183 and 222).

Later, in 1941—combining his academic and political activities—Cole led the development, at Nuffield College, Oxford, of the Social Reconstruction Survey, a pioneering sociological investigation of Britain with the aim of informing the development of social policy for the post-war world. But his main contribution as a socialist intellectual was, again like Tawney and Laski, as an educator. He was a tutor for the W.E.A., and worked also to improve its administration. As we shall examine in detail shortly, and also like Tawney and Laski, he was, as Stears (2004) notes, 'unstintingly committed to offering a broad-based, non-vocational, liberal education to those who had missed out on formal educational opportunities'. He died in 1959.

There were many other prominent and influential socialist intellectuals, whose ideas we shall also look at more briefly. The most influential was the philosopher A.D. Lindsay, born in Glasgow in 1879, educated at Glasgow Academy, Glasgow University and Oxford University, lecturer and later professor of philosophy at these two universities, master of Balliol College, Oxford, and founder of the new university of Keele in the 1950s. He, too, was influenced by the idealist philosophy ultimately deriving from T.H. Green that was the dominant tone at Glasgow and Oxford when he was a student, and, even earlier, he acquired from his parents and from his upbringing the commitment to social reform that was a feature of the United Free Church of Scotland to which they belonged (like several early Labour MPs from Scotland, such as the Reverend James Barr). Lindsay met Tawney as an undergraduate, and became involved in the W.E.A. and in other efforts to widen access to Oxford teaching. He was active in the Labour Party, and in the 1930s in various attempts to create a Popular Front. Thus Lindsay in several respects epitomised how permeable the boundary was between being a member of the social and educational establishment and being a radical critic of it.

Other such intellectuals were the philosopher C.M. Joad, a great part of whose writing and speaking was devoted to widening access to philosophy; he wrote—in a passage that could provide a manifesto for any such radical intellectual—that the working class, too,

> want to explore the higher reaches of the human spirit in literature and art, in religion and philosophy; to understand man's craving for beauty and holiness, and to be introduced to some of the concrete manifestations of that craving in paint and sound and stone. (Joad, 1945: 156–7)

But Tawney, Laski and Cole provide particular insights to understanding left-wing views of education in Britain in the first half of the twentieth century because they wrote a great deal of a sustained kind about the education that, in their view, a socialist programme should favour. And because they were so prominent, these views mattered.

The origins of socialist ideas about education

The starting point for understanding such views is that the most influential socialist thinking on education and cultural matters generally—the kind of thought we are considering here—believed itself to be in the mainstream of European civilisation, indeed to be the only way of saving that tradition from barbarous destruction. It was the direct heir to the Victorian liberalism of Matthew Arnold and his contemporaries. Socialist ideas about education were part of the core European culture in the 1920s and 1930s, an instance of what Collini (2006: 189) calls the 'irreducibly plural' character of any social order: 'general ideas', as he says, 'are not necessarily to be found "outside" it', and indeed those socialist ideas on education that did position themselves outside that dominant tradition of European culture were, at the time, quite uninfluential and unimportant. This is perhaps the most important feature of the whole body of belief that is being examined in this chapter: unlike much later writing about education from a point of view that is critical of capitalism and other aspects of the established social order, the most important left-wing educational thought in this period considered itself to be recovering all that was most valuable in that cultural inheritance, and thus in effect placed itself in the humanistic mainstream. Capitalism was repugnant, indeed, partly because it deprecated the importance of intellectuals (Ulam, 1951: 102), an echo of Arnold's castigating the bourgeoisie as philistines (Kramnick and Sheerman, 1993:

119). These thinkers never believed that there was anything intrinsically alienating about the dominant culture: the problem lay not in the culture but in blocked access to it.

The first source of socialist principles was in the idealist philosophy of late-Victorian Oxford, extending its influence to the whole emerging British welfare state by the middle of the twentieth century (Bogdanor, 2006; Boucher and Vincent, 2000). Harris (1992: 123) defines this school of thought as including

> anyone who thought that knowledge rested on certain a priori categories, who viewed society and/or the state as having a real corporate identity, and who saw the prime concerns of social science as being the interpretation of 'meaning' and 'purpose' rather than the discovery of causal laws.

He notes that these ideas permeated the nascent welfare state in the first half of the twentieth century, providing an 'emphasis on corporate identity, individual altruism, ethical imperatives and active citizen-participation' (*op. cit.*: 137).

These ideas stemmed ultimately from German conceptions of the state, especially Kantian and Hegelian, and were spread initially by university teachers such as T.H. Green (1836–1882), student of Benjamin Jowett at Balliol College, and later professor of moral philosophy at Oxford; Sir Henry Jones (1852–1922), student at Glasgow under Edward Caird (who had himself associated closely with Green when at Oxford in the 1860s), and then lecturer or professor in moral philosophy at Aberystwyth, Bangor, St Andrews and Glasgow; and Thomas Jones (1870–1955), student of Henry Jones, lecturer in political economy at Glasgow University and as professor at Queen's University, Belfast, member of the Cabinet Secretariat, 1916–30, and president of the University of Wales at Aberystwyth, 1944–50. A.D. Lindsay commented later that Green and his associates and pupils were influenced by the critique of competitive society, and of inequality, by Carlyle and Ruskin, but unlike them were democrats (Lindsay, 1930: 152): 'they had got from Kant, and Kant got from Rousseau, a profound belief in the worth and dignity of the ordinary man.' The role of the state was to enable each individual to realise that potential fully; in Bogdanor's words (2006: 149):

> From Rousseau and Hegel, Green derived the notion that state action to remove 'obstacles' to self-realisation, ignorance for example, would enhance rather than restrict freedom... Thus education, and in particular humanistic education, played a vital role in creating the good society.

The sense of duty could be shared by democrats and by proponents of autocracy such as Carlyle because of a shared understanding that, in Dower's words (1930: 46): 'a man's job is not merely making a living or a fortune, but his main channel of service to others.' Green believed that education could form a common culture, and, as Ulam (1951: 66–7) notes, saw the inclusion of the working class in politics as an essentially educational task.

Ulam (1951: 17) explains that students in this late-nineteenth-century tradition were encouraged to admire 'the Graeco-Roman world of ideas and literature' for its discipline, to celebrate knowledge for its own sake, and to see education as a means to order and beauty. Moral absolutes, they learnt from Plato, transcended time and place, and therefore also the ephemeral divisions made by the social-class structure of capitalism. Harris (1992: 127) points out that Plato's thought appealed, through the idealists, to those who believed in a strong, ethically informed state because of his 'emphasis on society as an organic spiritual community', his 'focus on justice rather than force as the basis of the state' and his 'vision of the ethical nature of citizenship', in which 'individual citizens found happiness and fulfilment not in transient sensory satisfactions, but in the development of "mind" and "character" and in service to a larger whole.'

As important as was the ancient world to this unity of thought between established educational institutions and radical critics was Christianity, even among those who, unlike Tawney, eventually lost any explicitly Christian faith: in Ulam's words again, Christian ethics were based on an 'aesthetic combination of intellect and emotion which represent[ed] the quintessence of Western civilisation' (Ulam, 1951: 18). Lindsay notes that the tradition from T.H. Green (and Oxford generally) went back to the seventeenth-century Puritans for ideas about democracy (Lindsay, 1930: 152). Hopes for Christian salvation (and their secular residue) then also explain a third point about this shared tradition—its individualism. Ulam (1951: 21) pointed out that, unlike in Hegel's own thought, for these British intellectuals at the beginning of the new century (whether socialist or liberal) the State was a means to the end of liberating individual citizens. As with Matthew Arnold, it was an expression of citizens' best selves, what Ulam (1951: 21) calls their 'higher instincts'.

Thus the socialist intellectuals must first of all be understood to be liberals. Collini (1999: 187) points out that there was no clear distinction in Britain before 1914—the intellectually formative period for the leading thinkers we are considering—between moderate socialists and progressive liberals, all those who believed that the state had to be used to remove the impediments to the individual liberty of classical liberalism. Socialism was merely the latest development of British liberalism (Hynes, 1976: 261). Even the most left-wing of the three, Laski, who moved closest to being a Marxist, was a liberal, and—perhaps most importantly for our purposes—had an essentially liberal impact on public debate: 'a socialist by allegiance and a liberal by temperament', as George Orwell described him in 1943 (quoted by Kramnick and Sheerman, 1993: 470). Kenneth Morgan (1987: 93) says of Laski that

> more than any of his contemporaries, he sought to provide intellectual links between liberalism and socialism. His life was a prolonged intellectual engagement with the twin concepts of liberty and of equality.

G.D.H. Cole was an 'heir of... Edwardian Liberalism' (Carpenter, 1973: 11), and his 'socialism was humanistic, emphasising major liberal values such as democracy and freedom' (*ibid.*: 3). For him, 'democracy... was more than a political principle; it was a moral relationship' (*ibid.*: 50). He described himself as 'a radical individualist as well as a socialist', and said that if the Labour Party forgot its radicalism it would in effect have abandoned its socialism (Cole, 1949: 210). Looking back later he thus concluded that 'I was never under any temptation to become a Communist, because my attitude was basically pluralistic and libertarian' (Cole, 1958: 7).

Tawney was 'steeped in the presocialist radical and utopian tradition', modified by the influence of T.H. Green's ideas (Terrill, 1973: 175). Thus he admired early radicals such as William Lovett, a leader of the Chartist movement of the 1840s, from whom he concluded that 'the condition of any genuine democracy is education' (Tawney, 1964 [1920]: 27), and Robert Owen, pioneer at New Lanark of a humane capitalism and of an education system that transferred 'emphasis from discipline to kindness' (Tawney, 1964 [1953a]: 35). The tribute paid to Tawney when he was 80 described the moralism of his book on *Equality* as being in the tradition of 'Carlyle, Ruskin and Morris' (Creech Jones, 1960: 9). Collini (1999: 178) notes that Tawney was recognised as Victorian even during his lifetime—'part Victorian moralist, part Old Testament prophet.' Continuity of a tradition of liberal freedom, leading to democracy and the social reforms that it might bring about, was supreme. In Tawney's words (quoted by Terrill, 1973: 151–2):

> It is not certain, though it is probable, that Socialism can in England be achieved by the methods proper to democracy. It is certain that it cannot be achieved by any other; nor, even if it could, should the supreme goods of civil and political liberty, in whose absence no Socialism worthy of the name can breathe, be part of the price.

Though initially acquired in the intellectual milieu of late-Victorian and Edwardian universities, the belief in democracy, liberalism and the value of Western civilisation then was intensified by the experience of the First World War and of its aftermath leading to the near collapse of these values in the 1930s and 1940s. Socialist intellectuals shared in that general sense of foreboding which, we saw in the last chapter, pervaded intellectual culture in the 1920s and 1930s: 'all of them agree', notes Samuel Hynes in his account of this mood in the 1930s, 'that war is a serious and immediate threat, and that the future of western culture is at stake' (Hynes, 1976: 196). The continuity of tradition was felt to have been broken by the slaughter of young men in the First World War, so that those who were writing in the 1920s 'were like the survivors of some primal disaster, cut off from the traditional supports of the past' (*ibid.*: 20). John Strachey, who became a Labour MP and a member of the Cabinet in the 1945 Labour government, described the consequences for left-wing thinkers thus in 1934:

> My generation of Englishmen became conscious of the break-up of our old world, not by realising that its economic foundations were shattered, but by a sudden and bewildering loss of faith in the whole moral, religious, and social ideology which we had inherited. (Strachey, 1934: 66)

Virginia Woolf (1940) described the feeling as like standing on the tower that was culture as it gradually tilted over towards collapse.

Imaginative writers such as Woolf provided one of the strong links that bound together all points in the ideological spectrum in an awareness of disintegration. The most prominent and influential, on left and right alike, was T.S. Eliot. Hynes notes that he 'managed to be both a model and a patron to the radical young', despite himself being a 'classicist, royalist, and Anglo-Catholic', providing the abiding metaphor of a waste land. Judt (2012: 73) draws a parallel between Eliot and Matthew Arnold, each 'the voice of a certain moral nervousness in the face of modernity, passed through a literary and increasingly religious sensibility'. All the left-wing poets between the wars saw Eliot as their model, along with other great English exponents of the sense that an epoch was ending. Stephen Spender, for example, characterised the legacy in this way in 1937, referring to the young John Cornford who was killed when fighting as a volunteer in the International Brigades that went to Spain to support the democratic republic against the fascist rebellion:

> When I say that modern poetry is political, I am not thinking of John Cornford giving up poetry in order to fight the fascists in Spain, but of the fact that the best poetry of our time, the outstanding poems of Thomas Hardy, the war poems of Wilfred Owen, Eliot's *Waste Land*, much of Auden's poetry, is concerned with the individual faced by an unprecedented crisis in the history of civilisation, and with far-reaching public calamities such as the Great War, the prospect of a greater war, and the crisis of the capitalist system. (Spender, 1937: 19)

Good poetry—however political—had to be universal, which is 'that which is true in the widest possible context... Universality in poetry cannot be attained by a "correct" attitude of mind' (*ibid.*: 29–30).

Auden was the leader in the 1930s in this linking of left-wing views with a sense of cultural collapse, and—as we shall examine further below—had well-developed ideas about the place which education might have in bringing about a new civilisation:

> We live in an age in which the collapse of all previous standards coincides with the perfection in technique for the centralised distribution of ideas; some kind of revolution is inevitable, and will as inevitably be imposed from above by a minority; in consequence, if the result is not to depend on the loudest voice, if the majority is to have the slightest say in its future, it must be more critical than it is necessary for it to be in an epoch of straightforward development. (Auden, 1977 [1933]: 317)

Laski made the point in a more explicitly political way, linking it to the challenge of persuading democracy to be aware of the importance of what it had inherited:

> Fear of a complete breakdown is never long absent from the thought of any observer in the West who is honest enough to admit that what was generally accepted, say from Hume and Adam Smith to the Peace of Versailles in 1919, as the permanent aims of our civilisation, are now under microscopic examination by the very peoples whom we hoped to persuade to its acceptance. (Laski, 1952: 152)

The sense that civilisation was breaking down accompanied and reinforced a moral conservatism among socialists at that time. Henry Jones distinguished two kinds of socialist thought—instrumental and ethical (Boucher and Vincent, 2000: 165–6). On the whole, British socialists—as distinct from communists—were of the latter kind, believing that not only was capitalism itself morally unacceptable, preventing (as they learnt from the idealist philosophers such as Green and Jones) the full realisation of each person's best self, but also that it had morally deplorable effects: greed, selfishness, destructive competition, irresponsibility, alcoholism, violence. Rose sums up the ethical principles of this view as essentially religious:

> The Labour Party preached a kind of twentieth-century Wesleyanism. Socialism would be brought about by an ethical revolution based on broadly Christian principles, just as nineteenth-century evangelicalism had transformed a

> brawling, hard-drinking proletariat into respectable chapel-going Victorians. (Rose, 2002: 307)

Socialists of the first half of the twentieth century were morally conventional, admiring what Bogdanor (2006: 161) calls 'social obligation and mutual respect'. Kramnick and Sheerman (1993: 158) describe this as the 'ascetic, anti-materialistic, self-denying' aspect of British socialist belief. There was almost no hint whatsoever of the challenge to social norms which came later in the century, the 'hedonistic individualism' (Bogdanor, 2006: 161) which eventually destroyed this old sense of socialist respectability.

Out of this general sense of malaise, of traditions undermined, of impending catastrophe, then came, for many thinkers on the left, a belief in education as the only way in which civilisation could be saved. The inherited culture was not the problem, indeed was precisely what was best in the world that was going. Capitalism had separated all but a privileged minority from these traditions, from the power of the developed intellect to understand these very social changes, and from the aesthetic imagination that could enable people to bring about a better society. Cole summed up the premise of equality of opportunity: 'Socialism... involves the initial assumption that talents and capacities for service ought to be sought out and discovered wherever they exist... A Socialist school system has therefore to be so designed as to give every child its chance' (Cole, 1952: 63). Tawney agreed on the need to identify talent wherever it could be found, and suggested (in 1924) that 'rebuilding a tolerable civilisation' would depend 'at least in part on the deliberate cultivation of human faculties of which the proper name is education'. Education, in short, was necessary for democracy to work (Tawney, 1924: 2–4).

Civilisation and academic detachment

Thus socialist thinking about education until about the middle of the twentieth century was much more about recovering things of great value that were believed to be under threat from capitalism and war than about creating anything new, except insofar as a newly educated people would be a source of new imagination. The problem was widening access to the greatness of Western civilisation, not destroying it. An abiding principle was that of detachment, a belief that only socialists could be trusted not to distort education towards narrow class ends as the dominant social order was perceived to have done, and that only socialists could thus claim to be the true custodians of the tradition, respecting it as a tradition rather than selecting those parts of it which might suit any purpose of ideology or of power.

Detachment to these socialist thinkers meant academic detachment of a kind that would have been recognised by anyone who upheld the value of disinterestedness. The aim was, first of all—before any political purpose—imparting truth and an appreciation of the importance of truth. Laski, for example, argued that

> the business of a university... is... teaching students how facts are converted into truth. What it is seeking is the method whereby experience in any branch of knowledge can be connected with the structure of the universe. The pathway to that end is, above all, a training in scepticism.

Accordingly, 'a mind receptive to novelty, capable of wisdom, inclined to moderation—these are the excellences at which it aims' (Laski, 1930: 91–2).

Cole's own education taught him the importance of research, in which respect he was active in the Fabian Research Department, the New Fabian Research Bureau in the 1930s and in the Nuffield College Social Reconstruction Survey. Laski reached a similar position of academic detachment through experience, a common trajectory for socialists of his generation, moving from being an activist first to being primarily an intellectual and an educator. Kramnick and Sheerman (1993: 80) comment on the effect on him in 1914 of going to teach in Montreal: 'he arrived a political activist of a scholarly bent, given to spontaneous militancy. He left two years later a professional academic with little interest in "madly brave" deeds.' His mature philosophy was then summed up later (1935): 'the only duties the teacher owes to the university are the duties to think hard, to think freely and to think independently.' Students must, he said, have 'their minds turned upside down... by continuous questioning... —this is the real path of intellectual discipline' (quoted by Kramnick and Sheerman, 1993: 331). The business of the university 'is to do what practical men have never the time nor the knowledge to attempt—the cutting of fundamental principle from the raw material' (Laski, 1930: 147). Rational enquiry may well lead the honest thinker to principles of equality: 'what can the practical man grasp in that eternal challenge to English complacency which Matthew Arnold—a typical academic mind—flung at it in his famous "choose equality and flee greed"?' (*ibid.*: 141). But even this insight might be vouchsafed only to the very best minds: 'let it be freely admitted that the great academic mind is rare; there are thousands of bad violinists for one Paganini' (*ibid.*: 143). Access to education did not mean common outcomes of the learning thus acquired.

Laski thus saw himself as defending a tradition of detached academic work against the pressure from capitalism to reduce it to utility or mere decoration: 'the university, at the best, becomes a semi-technical school; and, at its worst, a graceful academy where the sons of practical men learn that modicum of cultivation which social success demands' (*ibid.*: 148). He was influenced in this connection by one of his American friends, the educational thinker Abraham Flexner, who argued that it was important for the humanist scholar to have the same detachment in assessing current society as in dealing with times far in the past (Flexner, 1928: 19–20): 'universities have no responsibility for action or policy, but complete responsibility for ascertaining, telling, and interpreting the truth—the truth in respect not only to stardust and atoms, but to pictures and poems and politicians and economic theories, present as well as past.' By 'humanists' he meant anyone 'who, divesting himself of his prejudices or prepossession, surveys his work and that of others from the standpoint of its value to civilisation'.

Since capitalism was believed to be the enemy of true scholarly values, asserting disinterestedness could be held to be a specifically socialist or at least democratic principle. John Strachey saw capitalism as hostile to 'the eternal cause of human culture, of science and of civilisation itself' (Strachey, 1934: 69). Laski agreed with the radical Archbishop William Temple that education was a means to ending the workers' 'spiritual and mental slavery' (Kramnick and Sheerman, 1993: 182): in Temple's words, 'education is the means of entrance into the fullness of life, individual and social' (Temple, 1922: 337). The liberal politician and philosopher R.B. Haldane believed that improved education beyond the elementary stage 'brings with it a new social ideal. To those who have reached it there comes the virtue of courtesy and urbanity'. Social reform is a consequence of such spiritual reform (Haldane, 1923: 16). Percy Nunn, professor of education at the Institute of Education in London, who was both admired and influenced by Tawney, said that the industrial revolution and urbanisation had cut off most of the population from 'sweetness and light' (Nunn, 1923: 11–12).

The resulting principle that the working class, having been deprived of access to the great human traditions, had to be educated if democracy could be made real was expressed repeatedly by socialist writers on education. In this they were drawing on a main current of liberalism (Strauss, 1968: 5). Without education, Laski held, the working class would not appreciate the value of what had to be defended: ignorance of tradition 'is paid for by the inability of the ignorant to realise the fragility of civilisation' (Laski, 1930: 221). Nunn argued that the aim of educational reform ought to be 'to place the true dignity and grace of life within reach of all who are qualified to achieve them. That can be done only by a system of education which brings the things of enduring and universal worth to the doors of the common people.' Laski thought that this would be impossible so long as capitalism persisted, because of

> the incompatibility of a capitalist society, even if its political form were democratic, with a life that was gracious and dignified not for some fragment of mankind especially favoured by birth or wealth or the chance possession of acquisitive skill, but for all men and women prepared to earn their bread by the sweat of their brows. (Laski, 1952: 245)

For Laski, the true citizen had to be educated to think freely and critically: 'the citizen must be able to… form judgements upon issues so complex that their very statement is incompatible with simplicity' (Laski, 1923: 49). Society had not equipped the citizen to exercise the responsibilities of democracy: 'we have made the electorate commensurate with the majority of the adult population, but we have failed, in any creative sense, to fit that electorate to grasp either its responsibilities or its powers' (*ibid.*: 48). Democracy would fail unless that widespread understanding was achieved. Though this was a political goal, the only way to achieve it was by detached study: 'only where mind meets mind in the free exploration of such values is there born that sense of the state which makes possible the conscious improvement of the social fabric' (*ibid.*: 53). Laski's purpose was clearly heir to the aims of Matthew Arnold:

> The state must seek to make each citizen realise himself to the full. So far as our efforts can make it so, he must be his best self. And he cannot achieve that self without an education which ends only with life. (*ibid.*: 54)

'There can be no training of the intellect', he said, 'which is not also a training of the character' (Laski, 1930: 94).

Laski suggested that the social relevance of education—its urgency in the face of social collapse—dictated nothing of its content or manner: 'every period of vigorous social effort has always been accompanied by a renewed faith in the possibilities of education. At times, indeed, as with the Reformation, the purpose has been subordinated to some special end, but it has at least been perceived that the cultivation of intelligence is essential to the success of any movement' (Laski, 1923: 47). Laski turned down requests to become a Labour candidate because, in the words of Kramnick and Sheerman (1993: 177), 'it was more important to be a teacher and thinker, more important to write than live a life of active politics.'

Even in the intensely political 1930s, socialist thought in this connection valued disinterestedness, indeed came increasingly to do so. Hynes sums up Stephen Spender's view as against those of 'hard-line communist[s]'. What a 'bourgeois' writer writes 'need not be propaganda for his own class':

> If he is truly an artist, his work will perform art's historic role of revealing... the reality of the present and the past. So art will serve the revolution by telling revolutionaries the truth. (Hynes, 1976: 105)

'A great deal is said about saving culture,' Spender wrote in 1939, 'but the really important thing is to have a culture to save.' In the end, the revolutionary cause matters less to the democratic socialist than integrity: 'all Marxist criticism which judges writers by their declared political opinions or insists on their having declared opinions is hasty and approximate at best, and, at worst, destructive' (Spender, 1939: 23–4). The best-known such statement from the 1930s is by E.M. Forster in 1939: 'I hate the idea of causes, and if I had to choose between betraying my country and betraying my friend, I hope I should have the guts to betray my country' (Forster, 1965 [1939]: 76).

In such desperate political and military circumstances as faced the world in the 1930s, and even as many previously quite moderate socialists moved to the left, the overriding principle of saving civilisation from fascist barbarism remained strong. Fascism was, first of all, simply stupid. 'It is important', wrote Laski, 'that the makers of the Fascist movements were fundamentally uneducated men' (Laski, 1940: 60). It was only by destroying proper education that the Nazis could have triumphed, could have broken 'the hold of the old German traditions of decency and respectability upon the younger generation'. The fascist 'attitude to reason, indeed, could not have been more permanently or effectively symbolised than by the burning of books. The literature they thus committed to the flames was, in large part, the creator of the values they had come to deny' (*ibid.*: 66).

Generally it was also believed by socialist thinkers, whatever their detailed ideological position, that moderate socialism was better able to promote civilised values than communism. This growing scepticism about communism did not reach its sharpest point till the late 1930s, as a decade of partisan conflict between socialist and communist parties seemed firmly to place communists against liberal democracy. In the words of Wood (1959: 120): 'instead of the oasis of escape from the wasteland which the British intellectuals believed they had discovered in communism, they found only a mirage concealing a desert of hatred, intolerance, deceit, and conformity.' The importance of proper education underlined the preference for gradualism, since education—as opposed to propaganda, indoctrination and moral exhortation—could not be hurried. Only through adult education, Laski argued, can 'social change... proceed in a peaceful fashion', and only in that way can there be any safeguard for the continuity of tradition that the communists as much as the fascists were felt to threaten:

> For where men understand the delicate complexity of civilisation they will be careful of its mechanisms and its traditions. It is where they are ignorant of, and careless about, the long effort that has gone into building that they are prepared in blind anger to destroy. (Laski, 1923: 58)

Education for its own sake

One purpose of detachment was to defy vocational usefulness. Laski deplored the tendency for universities in the USA to be 'less a thinking-shop which it ought only to be than a place for the manufacture of degrees which are really tickets to enable you to learn on what subject the holder has been given enough facts to enable him to pass an examination… I miss in American life the tonic quality of Oxford where men sit down to examine great things greatly' (Holmes and Laski, 1953: 53). One important aspect of this was a distrust of specialism. Laski proclaimed a 'need for breadth of learning against the limited horizons of both specialism' and also 'the practical man', specialism being 'learning without wisdom', and practicality 'habit without philosophy' (Laski, 1930: 92–3). He wanted his students to have a broad, humanistic education of the characteristic liberal kind:

> I have encountered a student in his third year who had not read *Pride and Prejudice*, because his subject was, he explained, history and not literature. I am inclined to believe that there is no more final test of university adequacy than its effectiveness in creating a widespread curiosity in books… When I find the student who has made great literature his own personal province, I know that I have found the man whom it is invariably a privilege to teach. (Laski, 1930: 109)

It was not that left-wing thought deplored the practical application of knowledge, but merely that breadth and detachment were believed to prepare people better for life, and better therefore for the practical application of the intellect than any more explicit attempt to inculcate useful knowledge might achieve. This was a tradition of useful liberal education that could take authority from Newman, as Laski noted when explaining 'the elementary conditions which will enable a student to enter a professional school, on the one hand, or his life's career, on the other, with a mind trained to distinguish substance from shadow'. Such conditions, Laski said, 'depend, as Newman said of his own university ideal, "on the slow, silent, penetrating, overpowering effects of patience, steadiness, routine, and perseverance"' (Laski, 1930: 119–20). This view—that liberal education was in the end the best kind of useful education—was common in socially committed liberalism in the early twentieth century, exemplified by the Liberal cabinet minister R.B. Haldane, who, with Tawney, was a founder of the British Institute of Adult Education in 1921. Haldane wrote widely of the need for university reform if Britain was to be able to compete successfully with German economic advance. Arguing in 1923 that 'the new conception of education must be that of education as an end in itself, a power liberating from the fetters of ignorance', he nevertheless, like Laski later, followed Newman in proposing that 'if the practical man or the artist has wide knowledge he is pretty certain to be the more capable because of it' (Haldane, 1923: 15 and 8). The view persisted right through to the mid-century. Thus Cole, when contesting the Oxford University constituency in the 1945 election as a Labour candidate, accepted the need for technical education, 'but I believe that this can be done, not merely without sacrificing the culture that we have inherited from the past, but in such a way as to deepen and enlarge it and to penetrate culture with the spirit of science and science with the best achievements of that older culture' (quoted by Carpenter, 1973: 204).

The importance of both detachment and liberal education for its own sake was most evident in debate about teaching in the W.E.A. G.D.H. Cole was vice-president for a decade, to 1938. He celebrated its commitment to free enquiry that was liberal and non-vocational (Carpenter, 1973: 117). The method that was most appropriate for teaching adults was freedom of debate:

> Absolutely open discussion, absolute freedom of teaching—these are the bedrock principles on which our movement is securely based. We stand for education, not as a form of propaganda, open or disguised, but as a way in which we can help one another to increase our knowledge, to

> strengthen our minds, and to arrive at a fuller understanding of the world around us. (Cole, 1925: 101)

The pedagogical aim was to remove people from the immediate pressure of events and their own lives, even if only for the couple of hours of a tutorial class, although more readily achieved in residential adult education such as at Ruskin College in Oxford (Buxton, 1908: 195). Cole gave us a vignette of his own teaching style:

> What I have done... is usually to select a quite short period —perhaps the last thirty years, or any similar period during the past two to three centuries—and to take as the subject of the class the study of this period from a number of different points of view, trying to relate, for example, its economic and its political history, the history of one country to that of another, and its economic and political record to its achievements in literature, philosophy and science. (Cole, 1932: 146)

Laski summed up the mood: 'a good [W.E.A.] tutorial class is the one place in modern England where you may catch again that sense of spacious exhilaration which came to men like Erasmus in the dawn of the Renaissance' (Laski, 1923: 56). L.T. Hobhouse, the academic economist who shaped the 'New Liberalism' that led the Liberal Government of 1905–16 to found the modern welfare state, searched even further back for the analogy that would describe the aims of adult education: 'where a body of keen students is gathered together, there, in the good medieval sense, is a University' (Hobhouse, 1909: 711).

If there was a political aim, said Laski, it was by an indirect route, to ensure that, as the *Manchester Guardian* put it in a comment about him in 1936, 'Labour must become a literate movement' (Kramnick and Sheerman, 1993: 319). Cole was of the view that 'those of us [among W.E.A. teachers] who are Marxians or Socialists hold this faith—that we serve Marxism and Socialism better by this method than by turning education into propaganda. We may all be propagandists, too, out of class; but we do not mix the two' (Cole, 1925: 101). Archbishop Temple was also closely involved in W.E.A. activities, and urged that the liberal education which it would provide should distinguish what is transitional from what is permanent (Sadler, 1985b). Tawney believed that education was necessary to enable people to make up their own minds. Education demands 'faith and courage', said Cole, 'for it means trusting our fellow men with the opportunity to decide for themselves' (Cole, 1925: 101).

The W.E.A. was often in direct competition with its rivals on the left in the field of adult education, notably the National Council of Labour Colleges and the Plebs League, Marxist organisations with the explicit purpose of furthering socialism (a conflict of ideas to which we return in Chapter 3). Cole had no sympathy for the Labour Colleges (Carpenter, 1973: 117). His biographer notes that, for Cole, 'propaganda had a place, but it should come after the development of the individual's mind so that he could tell good arguments from bad ones, and judge for himself on the basis of reliable information' (*ibid.*: 117; Cole, 1925). In Cole's words:

> For the most part, then, British Socialists in modern times have felt able to work without qualms for the democratic development of the existing educational structure, and have not felt impelled to denounce it as, in its very nature, an instrument of indoctrination in capitalist and anti-socialist beliefs. (Cole, 1952: 48)

Though Laski occasionally taught at Plebs League events, 'his heart and his efforts were focused on the more enrichment-oriented ideals of the W.E.A.' (Kramnick and Sheerman, 1993: 182). He protested that 'if working-class education ever becomes the servant of a theory its merits as a movement will be destroyed' (quoted by Kramnick and Sheerman, 1993: 182–3). As Kramnick and Sheerman (1993: 183) note, 'he was a professor and could not totally abandon the academic ideal of objectivity which the trade-unionist Pleb[s] League dismissed out of hand.' Laski, like Cole, would leave his partisan affiliation at the door: 'I certainly can no more allow the [Labour] party to control my political affiliations... than I can allow the university to control my ideas' (Kramnick and Sheerman, 1993: 373). William Temple believed that the far-left view of education would destroy it. Tawney, too, insisted that propaganda had no place in W.E.A. teaching, as harmful to its true purposes as the kind of adult education that was merely about leisure (Terrill, 1973: 86). For such a mild-mannered person, his contempt for the kind of ideology that took its lead from the Soviet Union shows how deep the divisions were, and reminds us how close he was in this respect to George Orwell:

> The chicanery, discreetly termed relativism, which dismisses ordinary human virtues, from honesty to mercy, as bourgeois morality; falsifies ethical standards; and applauds as triumphs of proletarian heroism on one side of a frontier episodes denounced by it as Fascist atrocities on the other, appears to me nauseous... a long-familiar poison. (Tawney, 1964 [1952]: 178)

Liberal education and tradition

If non-utilitarian detachment was the goal, tradition was the means, not only as something valuable in itself but also as the best way of rising above the moment. Tradition detached from the everyday was a compensation for tawdry commercialism: 'it is deep comfort,' Laski wrote, 'in a grimly acquisitive society, to know that the priests move at their tasks... [A]s we contemplate the press and hurry about us, it is in general... pleasant to know of a place where men are remote from, and careless of, the commonplace immediacies of the marketplace' (Laski, 1930: 122). Cole, like most moderate socialists, was deeply attached to British traditions. His socialism 'emphasised what had to be done to liberate the tendencies he loved in English society' (Carpenter, 1973: 6), and he sought a way to 'recognise nationality, yet keep class loyalty alive' (Carpenter, 1973: 38). He also took from this tradition a concern with academic standards: 'socialists cannot, however, by any means afford to accept a lowering of the quality of higher education in the interests of social equality' (Cole, 1952: 61). Tawney's biographer describes a dominant concern in the 1930s of socialists who were not revolutionaries as being 'how to change England without wrecking it' (Terrill, 1973: 80). Tawney, Terrill notes, 'did not feel... cultural alienation from his own society, or from the West', his work being full of 'biblical and classical allusions, snippets from Shakespeare, Milton, Burns, and Tennyson' (Terrill, 1973: 237 and 234). A.D. Lindsay saw the problem as being that articulated by Kant, of finding standards that are 'corrigible and progressive, creative and authoritative' (Lindsay, 1957 [1950]: 145). As in the line of Scottish dissenting ministers of religion, he had (his daughter commented in her biography of him) 'a great love for tradition and continuity, and a readiness to challenge the forms of tradition whenever they failed to grow with the spirit' (Scott, 1971: xiii). He could thus describe himself as simultaneously conservative, liberal and socialist.

> He was a conservative in his love of the traditions in which societies have their life; a liberal in his dislike of both the exclusiveness to which tradition is liable and the doctrinaire planning which disregards its living structure; a socialist in his passionate concern that all men should be included. (*ibid.*: xiv)

Respect for tradition, then, very commonly took the form of valuing a canon of great works as a means of bringing all citizens into a common culture while stretching their intellect and their imagination. Tawney argued that 'no one can be fully at home in the world' without acquaintance with the cultural traditions of society, in which he included 'literature and art, the history of society and the revelations of science'. There was no sense that any of these accomplishments were beyond the experience of any social class: they were the imaginative means by which great minds had given insights into 'the heights to which human nature can rise and the depths to which it can sink' (Tawney, 1964 [1953b]: 88). Learning through such a canon is important in itself: Tawney believed that 'the enjoyment of great literature is an end, not a means.' We ought never to subordinate the intrinsic worth of literary works to the study of the social context of their production. The purpose of understanding the social context was to clarify references in the texts, but above all to gain insight into genius, as for example in the source of Walter Scott's greatness as the founder of the historical novel through his own experience of the contrast between the civilised enlightenment of eighteenth-century Edinburgh and the still wild lands of the region between that city and the border of England and Scotland:

> Such knowledge [of the social context of literary production] not only is a tribute owed to genius by posterity, but can become... the foot of the ladder leading into the world of imagination which genius has created. (Tawney, 1964 [1949b]: 196)

Even while respecting the studying of social context, it was always important that it be 'kept in due subordination in the background of our minds' (*loc. cit.*) while we respond imaginatively to the works themselves.

Laski, likewise, believed that any educated citizen should know the most important elements of the inherited culture first hand, giving as examples Shakespeare, Plato, Aristotle, Locke, Hobbes, Rousseau, Adam Smith and Ricardo. Without encountering difficulty, the student learns nothing worthwhile:

> It is essential for the student to encounter... the great mind which has formed the civilised tradition. He will rarely find it easy to wrestle with; but he will gain infinitely more from surmounting the difficulties of the supreme book than by digesting a second-hand summary of what the supreme book contains. (Laski, 1930: 97)

Laski would not stop at the works of the past, and would extend the canon to the great writers of the present, including those with whom he disagreed fundamentally on political matters: one of the recurrent features of the socialist intellectuals of this period is their own imaginative understanding of ideas that transcend political positions. Thus he could give a detailed exposition of T.S. Eliot's *Notes Towards the Definition of Culture* that is even-handed and sympathetic even while disagreeing with Eliot's 'profound disbelief in the quality of the ordinary man'. Rather as with Tawney's comment on Scott, that political disagreement did not prevent Laski from summing up Eliot's book with unqualified admiration while also explaining, respectfully and tentatively, why he disagrees with the political implications:

> I have summarised at some length and, I hope, fairly, Mr Eliot's attitude because it is at once one of the most clear and far-reaching attacks upon the emerging tendencies of our age. If we call this, as I think we are entitled to call it, a revolutionary period, Mr Eliot is seeking to enunciate what is hardly less than the outline of a counter-revolutionary philosophy. He argues that our present values are in a condition of disintegration. But his desire is not to discover how to move forward from this condition to a new integration, but how to restore values which were already in advanced decay at least half a century ago. (Laski, 1952: 120–1)

Laski thus does not disagree with the main premise of Eliot's analysis, that the tradition of high culture is important. There is nothing incompatible between a socialist principle of widening access to that culture—through public libraries and museums, for example—and defence of its main sources, the universities (*ibid.*: 119–20, 121). He invokes from within the high cultural tradition the many writers who have protested against social exclusion from it, writers such as George Sand, Carlyle, Mill, Herzen and Whitman. He disagrees with Eliot's educational proposal that most people should be content with vocational training: only 'insight into the heritage' of high culture can make people human, and there need be no contradiction between preparing someone for even a quite menial economic role and equipping them to appreciate 'what is most dignified in human nature':

> To train a man to be a 'skilled agricultural labourer' does not mean that we waste our energies and our substance if we teach him also to appreciate the beauties of Shakespeare or Dickens, to recognise why Goya was a greater artist than W.P. Frith, to realise that the music of Bach and Beethoven can bring things into his life more precious than he will find in the music of Sousa or George Gershwin, to explain to him at least in outline what science is, and how it has developed, and to give him some sense of the movement of world-history, not least of the place of his own country in that movement. (*ibid.*: 129)

As Kramnick and Sheerman (1993: 198) comment on such ideas, and Laski's doubts about the cultural value of Joyce, Proust and Dos Passos, 'politically radical, Laski was socially and culturally conventional', but Laski's judgements were from within a tradition, not a rejection of it. What Laski would then change is not what is judged valuable in such a curriculum, but who that would be for: 'none of these things ought to be the private possession of an elite.' There is a common humanity that ought not to be divided by class, and the resolution is to be found in making available to everyone the best that has been thought and said, because all these cultural accomplishments are 'part of the process of making man at home in the universe, of giving him perspective, of helping him to grasp how these forces work which determine his own destiny' (Laski, 1952: 129). 'Most men and women go through life', he wrote, 'completely ignorant of the intellectual heritage of civilisation.' But that is to deprive them of the most important social aspect of their humanity, what 'gave life its grace, dignity and fullness' (quoted by Kramnick and Sheerman, 1993: 182).

> Personal relations apart, no one who has been vouchsafed companionship in the investigation of that heritage but knows it as the source of the main joy life can offer. To deprive men of access to it does not destroy the impulse of curiosity; it merely deflects it into channels from which no social good can emerge. Education is the great civiliser, and it is, above all, absence of education which provokes the brute in man. (Laski, 1930: 220)

Such views of the inherited tradition were dominant on the left. In a lecture admired and quoted by Tawney (1924: 32), Percy Nunn linked the ideas to the compulsory school curriculum:

> The proper function of the elementary schools is something much more than to protect the State against the obvious danger of a grossly ignorant populace or to 'educate our masters' in the rudiments of citizenship. And unless it is done, unless the natural hunger of the people for knowledge and beauty is wisely stimulated and widely satisfied, no material prosperity can in the end save the social body from irretrievable degradation and disaster. (Nunn, 1923: 12)

A.D. Lindsay insisted on the importance of reading great literature (Scott, 1971: 182–3). C.M. Joad (1945: 167) argued that great literature enlarges our vision, giving 'more scope for our sympathy and insight in life... Literature makes life more interesting'. Virginia Woolf (1940: 33) believed that no writer should try to escape the tradition of great writing if they wanted to be any good. Even John Strachey's version of communism in his most left-wing period in the 1930s meant culture, science and civilisation (Thomas, 1973: 110–11).

The conclusion was also widely drawn, with Tawney, that engaging with the great minds of the past, as well as being valuable in its own right, was also the most effective means of combatting fascism and of bringing about radical political change. Auden was particularly effective—as Hynes (1976: 55) puts it—at translating 'modern movements and systems of belief' into parables, thus stimulating an interplay between social movement and the imagination. Tawney argued that 'cooperative study and discussion with our fellows' is not only necessary for effective social action but is also the means to understanding truth (quoted by Terrill, 1973: 181). This connection between 'tolerance and the appeal to reason' (Tawney, 1964 [1953b]: 94) and bringing about social change is one reason why 'all serious educational movements have in England been also social movements' (*ibid.*: 88). Education, he believed, is the means by which we transcend our personalities and relate to others, both living and dead. Social movements require education and require the 'training of mind and character'. Action requires reflection if control of political change is not to be surrendered to experts (Tawney, 1924: 3–7).

Laski believed that immersing students in a tradition was an effective way of stimulating their sense of social responsibility:

> It does not mean their training to a narrow political end, or their indoctrination with some system of social dogmas. It means the conscious fostering, in whatever avenue may offer, of that sense of responsibility to the social heritage which all men should possess. (Laski, 1923: 53)

'Love of knowledge for its own sake' was what had created the civilisation that is thus passed on (Laski, 1930: 120). One reason why the democratic parties in Germany had been discredited by the fascists was that they had 'repudiat[ed] national traditions' (Laski, 1940: 62).

The fullest academic development of such ideas at this time was by Percy Nunn, and it was from him that Tawney took the belief that, without educational renewal, democracy, and even the whole future of civilisation, would be at stake. More systematically than any other writer on education in the 1920s and 1930s, Nunn sought to analyse the balance required between tradition and change in order that education could bring about true social improvement in a democratic way. He had written that 'the same élan vital which brought the society to that point [of development] urges it so to train its young that they may maintain its traditions and ways of life' (Nunn, 1923: 2). He had argued also that

> a sane and courageous pursuit of the principle of individuality in education is above all things necessary, if our civilisation is to strengthen its now precarious foothold between the tyranny of the few and the tyranny of the many. (Nunn, 1920: v)

This could be achieved by means of education provided that traditions are maintained and renovated:

> A school fails to fulfil its purpose unless it is a place where the young are taught to accept and to maintain the best-tested traditions of thought and action handed down from the old time before them. Again it fails unless it serves as a 'jumping-off place' for a generation trained to be eager for new adventures in life. (*ibid.*: 58)

It was not enough to do what 'conservative reformers' had done for generations, merely 'to seek improvements in the practice based on this ancient faith'. Nor was it acceptable to follow the destructively revolutionary route, those who 'would have us reject it altogether, and build education anew on some form of the dogma of natural goodness' (*ibid.*: 102). A child had to be shaped by tradition and also learn from it how to think about society as it is changing:

> A school is a place where a child, with his endowment of sensibilities and powers, comes to be moulded by the traditions that have played the chief part in the evolution of the human spirit and have the greatest significance in the life of today. (Nunn, 1923: 7)

So in deciding whether any particular subject should appear in the curriculum the main consideration was whether it was 'one of the great movements of the human spirit, one of the major forms into which the creative impulses of man have been shaped and disciplined'. The main means by which children should be brought into contact with these great ideas was through the books in which they are expressed, because in that way education can take them beyond the limits of their own experience (Nunn, 1920: 122).

Since tradition was important, there also arose for Nunn —as for the socialist thinkers whom we have been considering in this chapter—the question of the balance that was to be struck between universal principles and national ideas. On the one hand, 'the whole burden of my argument is that the things which have universal human value are the things of most importance in education' (Nunn, 1923: 6). But, like the dominant strand of moderate socialism in Britain, there was also an attachment to national traditions: 'the universal can be apprehended only where it lives in concrete embodiments.' He was impressed (in 1920) by the importance of 'social heredity' in keeping alive the very existence of formerly submerged nations, such as Serbia and the Ukraine (Nunn, 1920: 61). Although there is a 'common European tradition based mainly upon the Graeco-Roman and Christianity, and it is vastly important for the happiness of the world to deepen and vivify men's consciousness of it, even this lacks the concreteness needed to form the basis of popular education... In short, a nation is the largest social unit whose ethos has the necessary individuality' (Nunn, 1923: 6).

This embedding of the universal in the particular culture was the way to reconcile the need for cultural traditions with the importance of fostering individuality. Nunn argued that the recent liberalising tendencies in education—the greater attention to the individual pupil—was

> inspired by the Christian principle of the immense value of the individual life, or, if you prefer to put it so, by the Kantian principle that no man ought to be treated merely as a means but always also as an end in himself. (Nunn, 1923: 3)

It was then up to the teacher to introduce the pupil to the tradition while always being aware of the individual needs of each learner:

> It will be [the teacher's] task to create and maintain an environment in which his pupil's impulses towards the arts and sciences will be awakened, and to shepherd them unobtrusively in the right directions. Himself steeped in the best traditions of his subject, he must see that, by inspiration, suggestion and criticism, those traditions are revealed to the young inquirer, and are allowed to make their appeal to him. (Nunn, 1920: 98)

In short, as Jonathan Rée has argued (Rée, 1987: 214) 'socialist hopes' in this period (and earlier) included the belief 'that educational opportunity should be extended not as an indirect means of social levelling, but for knowledge's own dear sake; and that capitalism is to be hated not only for its economic injustice, but for the injuries it inflicts on working people's intellectual culture too'. The yearning to escape capitalism was for 'a better existence, envisaged mostly in aesthetic terms as the life of painters, poets, philosophers and musicians'.

Liberal education and reason

There was one specific feature of the tradition of liberal education which particularly appealed to socialist intellectuals: the belief that reason was not only paramount but was also itself intrinsically socialist in the sense that, as Rée (1987: 214–5) puts it, socialism was, 'at bottom, the only reasonable arrangement of humanity'. It was believed that 'the inadequacy of all non-socialist social fabrics [would] be evident to any truly educated mind.' As Terrill (1973: 207) points out in his biography of Tawney, 'there existed that faith in reason which true socialism shares with liberalism', quoting Laski in his *A Grammar of Politics* approvingly paraphrasing Jeremy Bentham: 'social good is the product of coordinated intelligence' (Laski, 1925: 24). Kramnick and Sheerman (1993: 159) note Laski's abiding faith in reason, no matter how far to the left he drifted in the 1930s: they record his lecturing to cooperative societies in Manchester in 1936, in the face of the crisis of capitalism and of the collapse of democracy across much of Europe, on the political relevance of founding 'a great periodical' and new 'learned treatises' on 'the spirit of cooperation'. Such faith in reason was common across the left-wing spectrum. John Strachey, on the left, was a socialist because he believed in reason (Thomas, 1973: 37). His daughter described him as 'a complete intellectual', and noted his lack of any mode of conversation other than the rationally organised: 'riding, sawing wood, doing anything that didn't occupy his mind. I don't remember comfortable easy silences with him' (quoted by Thomas, 1973: 299). Sidney and Beatrice Webb, likewise, venerated detached reason: Sidney argued that a socialist policy for education should 'train up the most efficient and most civilised body of citizens, making the most of the brains of all', developing everyone to 'the margins of cultivation'.

C.M. Joad argued that education has three aims, the most important of which is the last: earning a living, becoming a democratic citizen, and 'develop[ing] all the latent powers and faculties of [the pupil's] nature and so to enjoy a good life' (Joad, 1945: 23). Reason is what made people free, and thus was the essential feature of liberal education:

> A 'liberal' education, both Aristotle and Plato would have agreed, is one which, as the name suggests, makes a man free, free both of the cravings of the unsatisfied body, which demand that the sense be titillated, and of the solicitations of the empty mind which demand that it should be kept occupied. (*ibid.*: 47)

The work needed to reach that state of intellectual understanding was a challenge, often requiring the mastery of 'what is difficult or dull', because without that sort of understanding the mind 'cannot engage in... disinterested inquiry, in speculation, in contemplation, in the satisfaction of curiosity and the joy of mental adventure' (*ibid.*: 48). The senses and the emotions, as much as the intellect, had to be educated in reason—the senses to appreciate beauty, the emotions to train character (*ibid.*: 50).

Socialist thinkers believed that capitalism was the enemy of reason and of the intellect, a specific version of their general belief that capitalism was destructive of high culture. Knowledge and virtue, Terrill (1973: 242) notes, were thought to be closely linked, and in that sense socialists thought of themselves as recovering a core feature of Enlightenment reason, restoring faith in education and in the 'rationalistic foundations of the dynamics of... social democracy'. William Temple valued liberal education because it enabled students to distinguish sense from nonsense (Sadler, 1985a). Education, said Tawney, brings people together because it is about ideas that they can share: it is 'the process by which we surmount the limitations of our isolated personalities and become partners in a universe of interests which we share with humanity' (Tawney, 1964 [1949b]: 191). The Workers' Educational Association firmly held to the principle of reason as any university:

> The disinterested desire of knowledge for its own sake, the belief in the free exercise of reason without regard to material results and [on the grounds that] reason is divine, a

> faith not yet characteristic of English life, but which it is the highest spiritual end of universities to develop, finds in the Tutorial Classes of the Workers' Educational Association as complete an expression as it does within the walls of some university cities. (Tawney, 1964 [1914]: 85)

Cole, also describing the Tutorial Classes of the W.E.A., said that their aim, like a university and unlike 'the general run of work in a technical college or evening school', is aimed 'rather at making people think and reason for themselves than at imparting a definite body of knowledge' (Cole, 1932: 131).

One important aspect of socialist adherence to reason was an appreciation of the importance of science, both as an admirable principle in itself—a means of understanding the world—and as a means to improving society. They carried forward into the twentieth century the nineteenth-century liberal admiration for Darwin in particular as having provided a rational basis to explain human origins and development. They thus inherited T.H. Huxley's insistence that liberal education ought to include science. Often that became agnosticism or atheism. Laski, as Kramnick and Sheerman (1993: 363) note, 'regarded science as both the death-knell for religion and the source of progress and all that was good'. Science was respected too by left-wing thinkers who retained a religious faith, such as William Temple, who argued that the former 'neglect of science' by education was 'a great evil', although he also feared, writing in 1930, the 'greater evil' that education was now becoming imbalanced in the opposite way, through neglecting the humanities—'the great movements of mankind, their achievements and failures...; their loftiest aspirations and deepest feelings':

> The citizen, when trained, will be chiefly scientific in dealing with inanimate things, chiefly sympathetic in dealing with living things, and, all his faculties alert, will be open to receive the vision of God. (Temple, 1958 [1932]: 167–9)

Proclaiming socialism's adherence to reason was a common theme in the left-wing response to fascism, an evidently irrational system of belief. Cole derided fascism as nonsense, to be combatted by reason (Carpenter, 1973: 187). Laski thought the 1930s were not an age of great literature because rationalism seemed cold beside all the 'ardent emotion which demands belief in terms of a blind faith insisting on the surrender of the right to think freely' (Laski, 1952: 34). This 'cult of unreason' was opposed to 'the diversity which civilised living requires' (*ibid.*: 35). It was a serious indictment of fascism that it had broken up 'the great international community of organised knowledge' (*ibid.*: 36). Although Laski retained some faith that the Soviet Union might help to save the world from this great wave of irrationalism (*ibid.*: 60–1), he was as hostile to totalitarian communism as to any system of thought that required uncritical acceptance of anything: 'the rationalism of the Communist, like that of St Thomas Aquinas or of Cardinal Newman, begins only at the point where the creed has been accepted' (*ibid.*: 206). 'A great culture', he believed, 'cannot be the outcome of minds not free to roam where the spirit takes them' (*ibid.*: 189). Great writers make absolute rulers uneasy: 'no one ever expects that a Shelley or a Byron or a Walt Whitman will arouse the enthusiasm of courtiers whether at Windsor or at the Kremlin', which was why poets such as Anna Akhmatova were persecuted by the Soviet regime (*ibid.*: 239). 'Decadent art is... obsequious art', to power, money, popularity or unintelligibility (*ibid.*: 240).

Concern with the importance of education in rational principles was closely linked to concern with the quality of democratic leadership, and the capacity of democracy to bring about worthwhile social change. This grew partly in response to the massive loss of young potential leaders in the First World War: in 1915, Laski wrote to the future Labour leader George Lansbury that he was worried about the death of so many of his Oxford acquaintances, asking 'where we shall get the intellect for the next generation' (quoted by Kramnick and Sheerman, 1993: 85). Thus, asserting the importance of intellectual education as a preparation for leadership became part of the left-wing response to the perceived collapse of the old social order, their rational response to Eliot's pessimism. Cole believed that, though not all irrational elements in human beings are evil, 'reason [i]s the human quality which, as civilisation advances, ought more and more to exercise a paramount and coordinating control.' The means was not only to be 'book learning', but also judgement—common sense, 'the intelligent choice of means' and moral vision which could be objective because shared by society. It was a pragmatic 'reasonableness' rather than an abstract rationality:

> This does not mean that civilisation involves a belief in the entire rationality of man, even potentially, but only that it does imply a belief that the rational elements in men ought to be encouraged, and their reasoning faculties developed to the fullest possible extent. (Cole, 1950: 76)

A.D. Lindsay drew from the teaching of T.H. Green and other philosophical idealists of the Oxford school that the necessary intellectual leadership could come only from the education of everyone. Green and his successors 'knew well how much democracy asks of the ordinary man, and therefore how entirely inadequate Hedonism is as a foundation of democratic theory' (Lindsay, 1930: 156). It was not up to the liberal state to substitute for these educated and popular decisions, though it should specify 'what could and what could not be expected of individuals' (Lindsay, 1930: 155).

Laski thought that capitalism had so impoverished the education of ordinary people that 'the necessary tools of intellectual analysis are incapable of being used. Knowledge and the power to make experience articulate become the monopoly of the few' (Laski, 1930: 220). The only way to develop that intellectual power was through formal, even abstract, learning: experience is not enough. Thus he believed that however useful trade union activity might be, or however much a sense of the dramatic may come from cinema, football or the music hall,

> citizenship is the power to contribute one's instructed judgement to the public good. It is a thing of the mind, and it demands, for its development, a training that is vigorous and unrelenting. It above all seeks a discipline of thought which comes only from the ability to handle the world about us, to relate the causes and effects of phenomena. (Laski, 1923: 50)

Consequently, Tawney believed, teachers ought to be 'men and women of culture' who need a liberal education. C.M. Joad, likewise, believed that all teachers—whether technical or not—require a good general education (Joad, 1945: 24).

Such concerns with the rational intellect made most left-wing thought in the period between the world wars sceptical of child-centred education, sometimes explicitly in doubts about John Dewey. Laski wrote to Holmes in 1932, paraphrasing Abraham Flexner, about 'the harm done to education by Dewey and his followers in telling teachers that the child ought to study the thing it finds pleasant' (Holmes and Laski, 1953: 1385). The result of this is, Laski said (as Joad did later), that 'effort seem[s] an evil on the ground that it is unpleasant. In the result the student fails to learn the need of that organised concentration of mind which gives understanding.' Cole, sceptical of 'free' or 'progressive' educational methods, though noting that there were some socialists among the pioneers of 'progressive' schools, nevertheless judged that they had not had 'any wide influence on the main body of Socialist thought' (Cole, 1952: 49).

Even some left-wing thinkers who were sceptical of the general admiration for intellectual and academic knowledge were doubtful about child-centred ideas. An example is Auden. Unlike most of the people whose thought we have been considering, his main teaching experience was not of adults but of children, in a school in Helensburgh (near Glasgow). Perhaps as a result, he was ambivalent about designing the curriculum around academic study, 'with its bias towards abstract knowledge divorced from action', and its preference for 'interpretation rather than creation' (Auden and Worsley, 1939: 31). He believed that liberal education with an academic bias was all very well to train administrators for the Empire, as Thomas Arnold's reforms at Rugby were intended to do (*ibid.*: 35). But most pupils, he thought, needed no more than a quite basic education, and so compulsory schooling ought not to be dominated by the 'academic tradition'. From that compulsion, it would then be necessary to 'select… candidates for mind-training very carefully' (*ibid.*: 38–9). Yet, despite these doubts that liberal education of the academic kind could be provided for everyone, Auden was equally sceptical of the child-centred philosophy, which he attributed to the belief from 'Rousseau and romantic anarchism' that 'the individual is born good and made evil by society' (*ibid.*: 34). He accepted that such beliefs had had the beneficial effects of encouraging people to study children and to try to understand what their needs are, and he also accepted that education is bound to be more effective if children are treated kindly and with common sense (*ibid.*: 37). But the premise that 'the most wonderful thing in the world is love' was naïve or worse. Teaching on that basis becomes 'management by flattery, persuading people that your suggestions are really their own'. As a result, 'the freedom they boast of is bogus', and the liberal teacher of this kind 'becomes the secret service of the ruling class, its most powerful weapon against social revolution' (Auden, 1977 [1932]: 313). However appealing to left-wing thought child-centred education later came to be—as we shall see in Chapter 5—it was regarded as eccentric at this time.

Intellectual tensions with democracy

Auden's doubts about the academic tradition of liberal education did also perhaps indicate a further tension within left-wing thought: there was often a sense that liberal education might be not be straightforwardly consistent with democracy insofar as democracy always has a tendency to anti-intellectual populism. In Joad's words:

> The activities and adventures of the mind, the sensitiveness to and interest in ideas which are a condition of civilisation and upon which its continuance depends—these things are anathema to the popular press and almost unknown to its readers. (Joad, 1945: 32)

On the whole, when faced with such doubts, left-wing intellectuals did not abandon their faith in intellect, and, when not actually doubtful about democracy, merely asserted a faith that a better-educated democracy would no longer be in danger of philistine degeneration.

There was a recurrent admiration on the left for what were thought to be the virtues of an old kind of aristocracy—of high moral standards, detached from the strife of party competition (as the liberal left thought education should be), and liberally educated for leadership (which was why the democratic response was thought to be to liberally educate everyone). Joad invoked the spirit in a description of the garden at the socially elite Winchester School, one of those 'peculiarly English' 'blends of the works of nature and man which seem in our own country to be more readily achieved, and more happily and easily graced by beauty than in any other'. It is the result of 'a long tradition of secure men living dignified and leisured lives', and it embodies

> faith in the ability of the human reason to discern the steps that are necessary to the making of a better world, in the disinterestedness of the desire to take the steps which reason discerned and in the determination of the human will to overcome whatever obstacles withstood the realization of the desire. (Joad, 1945: 90–2)

Appreciation of aristocratic disinterestedness and responsibility was a recurrent theme from socialist intellectuals. A.D. Lindsay praised the aristocratic values of Balliol College, by which he meant 'an intense care for distinction and values, a life of the kind of leisure and free conversation among equals which helps to cultivate the things of the spirit, and a wide and generous toleration' (quoted by Scott, 1971: 110). Democracy without academic values, he believed, risked demagoguery (*ibid.*: 306). Lindsay drew here upon the Scottish academic tradition in which philosophy was at the core of the curriculum, unifying its disparate subjects by linking them to a criticism of life (Emmet, 1971: 401–2).

Laski admired the leisured culture of the aristocracy, writing to Wendell Holmes in 1923 that 'the English aristocracy at its best' was 'cultured, generous and spacious-minded' (Holmes and Laski, 1953: 479). In their biography of Laski, Kramnick and Sheerman (1993: 43) link the development of these opinions to the influence of eugenic ideas—and especially Laski's early mentor, Karl Pearson—on a wide range of political thought in Britain at the beginning of the twentieth century, both left and right: 'one should [not] underestimate the common elitism that characterised both the Liberal-Fabianism interventionist eugenicists and the far more *laissez-faire* Spencerian attitude of Pearson in 1911.' West (1975: 162–3) traces such views further back, to what he calls the 'Victorian intellectual paternalism' of John Stuart Mill and others of his generation of early liberals, the belief that only having 'knowledge, rationality or culture' makes people truly free.

There was also a less straightforwardly ideological source of the admiration for ruling elites—a preference of personal style, the ascetic aloofness of an intellectual class confident of its own capacity to define the new world that its members thought they could discern arriving. Kramnick and Sheerman (1993: 193) sum this up in the case of Laski and his wife Frida: 'in their combination of intellectuality, plainness and puritanism the Laskis resembled many middle-class socialist intellectuals.' They note two moral strands among such thinkers. One was the ethical socialism deriving from William Morris that we have already noted, but the other was a vision of 'a socialist Britain managed and planned by technocratic, scientifically trained experts' (Kramnick and Sheerman, 1993: 156). As a result of his friendship with Wendell Holmes, Laski 'would balance a lingering faith in the leadership role of learned and cultivated gentleman like Holmes with a democratic commitment to the "upwards and onward-ers" that Holmes disliked'. Virginia Woolf (1940: 18) believed that a small educated elite had produced all that is good, although she also thought that their ideas had to be tempered by experience. A.D. Lindsay, influenced again by Scottish philosophical and theological concerns, perceived the dilemma as being how to reconcile democracy with the necessity of an educated elite that would lead and govern (Scott, 1971: 233). Ulam (1951: 117) comments that it was only the theological constraint that held Lindsay back from a more extreme preference for elites. Cole, Carpenter (1973: 247) notes, believed that people of his education, class and ideological understanding were able to judge other people's best interests: 'by the democracy I stand for I mean making the people really free and self-governing, not the votes they record when they are neither', a state of enlightenment that required not only a sound education but also better health, housing and other material conditions.

Even Tawney, the most instinctively egalitarian of the intellectuals we are considering here, believed that understanding came only as a result of thorough study which, in a capitalist society, most people had not had the chance to have: 'being exploited', he said, 'is no guarantee of virtue' (quoted by Terrill, 1973: 50). Terrill (1973: 228) notes that 'if in Arnold it was an appeal to cultural distinction that diluted his democratic proclivities, in Tawney it was the moralist's appeal to right relationships', a form of moral elitism. Tawney was sometimes as apprehensive as Arnold of the dangers of populist democracy, fearing that it 'may be tempted... to pander to popular tastes, instead of instructing them' (Tawney, 1964 [1949a]: 163). The studying needed to understand social change is not easy compared to 'cinema, dogs, arts or the austerities of the daily press' (Tawney, 1964 [1953b]: 11). If democracy were

> merely a more widely disseminated cult of betting-coupons, comforts and careers, there might be some gain; but it would hardly be worth the century of sweat which, together with some tears, has been needed to produce it. (Tawney, 1953: 191)

An important educational consequence of the common socialist respect for educated elites was a thorough commitment to selection on the basis of merit—what later came to be called meritocracy. Terrill (1973: 183) points out that Tawney's Christian pessimism prevented his holding to a 'rationalist optimism' in which nurture would always be able to overcome the defects of nature. He was in favour of 'multilateral' schools—places where all the children of a neighbourhood would be educated together: an 'educational system... worthy of a civilised society' requires that 'the children of all classes in the nation attend the same schools' (Tawney, 1964 [1931]: 144). But there would be differentiation according to aptitude:

> The time has come when all full-time post-primary schools should be placed on the same administrative and financial basis, and while providing varying curricula for different types of capacity should be equal in staffing, equipment and amenities. (Tawney, 1938)

Differentiation is needed because 'equality is not identity' (Tawney, 1924: 5): 'there are diversities of gifts, which require for their development diversities of treatment' (Tawney, 1964 [1931]: 146). It was the mapping of opportunity onto wealth that was 'a barbarity' (*ibid.*: 145). Tawney was not opposed to independent schools, provided they were opened on meritocratic grounds to able children of all social classes (Tawney, 1964 [1943]). The reason for 'prolong[ing] [the] education of all' was to allow 'intelligent selection' (Tawney, 1924: 4).

Similar views were widely held by socialist intellectuals, reflecting academic opinion such as that from Nunn (1920:

207) that variation in the curriculum ought to relate to 'differences in the ability, *ingenium* and needs of the nation's youth', not 'social distinction'. Laski believed, like Tawney, that it was important not to 'mistake equality for identity' (Laski, 1930: 232):

> Equality does not mean that the differences of men are to be neglected; it means only that those differences are to be selected for emphasis which are deliberately relevant to the common good.

Working-class educational potential

John Carey's strictures on the condescension towards mass culture by intellectuals in early-twentieth-century Britain certainly did not exclude those who regarded themselves as socialist or liberals. H.G. Wells, George Bernard Shaw, Virginia Woolf, Aldous Huxley, E.M. Forster, even (ambiguously) George Orwell: these and many others on the left can be found expressing pessimism about whether democracy could ever acquire the cultural and intellectual distinction that would be needed to enable it to operate as intended. When even such a mild and generous spirit as Tawney could express apprehension about popular culture, the faith of the left in democracy could not be said to have been unshakeable. In that sense, there was a strong current in left-wing thought between the wars that was heir to Carlyle rather than Arnold. Nevertheless, there is an important distinction, relating to the potential of education. The left intellectuals to whom we have been giving greatest attention here—certainly including Tawney—believed not only that democratising access to high culture was necessary, and not only that high culture need not be vitiated in the process, but also that, through education, such universal enlightenment was, without doubt, feasible. The problem was capitalism, not mass culture as such. Capitalism had distorted people's understanding of the culture that matters. Thus these thinkers were on the side of the autodidacts whom Carey praises and who, as he also explains, very many other intellectuals at the time ridiculed. As Goldman (2000: 298) notes, in a rejoinder to Carey, 'many of the intellectuals [active in adult education, among whom he lists Tawney, Cole and Lindsay] came to inquire and assist rather than lead. They admired the stoicism, endeavour and aspirations of the working-class élite with whom they mixed, and were careful not to assume a natural precedence.'

The characteristic position was summed up by Laski in 1930 (Laski, 1930: 216–7). One reason why democracy faces problems was inequality: 'Our inequality', Laski adapted from Matthew Arnold, 'materialises our upper class, vulgarises our middle class, brutalises our lower.' The solution, Laski believed, was education: 'the growth of education is increasingly destructive of the habit of deference.' Education would lead people to challenge inequality: 'the first result of education among the masses is the perception that whatever inequalities may be justified by social needs, the present inequalities are incapable of justification.' Thus wider education would bring into question that hierarchical system of values which Carey finds most intellectuals at the time to have endorsed, a challenge to the established moral order which Laski would welcome: 'the more we educate, in short, the more we reveal to the multitude the inadequacy of the moral principle upon which our civilisation is based.'

Such views do allow us to distinguish between the general tendencies noted by Carey and the position of some of the most influential of the socialist intellectuals. Terrill (1973: 23) concludes about Tawney, for example, that he saw 'education as a path to emancipation for every man, not as the preparation of an elite for the task of ruling lesser breeds'. Even some of the more hierarchically inclined of socialist thinkers in the 1930s and 1940s did have the honesty and percipience to see that deference was coming to an end, a process hastened (as in many areas of British life) by the shared privations of wartime. Hynes notes of Virginia Woolf's essay 'The Leaning Tower'—which started life as a lecture to the W.E.A. in Brighton in 1940—that it was 'a diagnosis and an obituary of the 'thirties generation, the last generation to be elevated above "the rest of us" by their class and their education' (Hynes, 1976: 392). That the generation as a whole should reach contradictory conclusions—some confirming Carey's analysis, some very definitely not—was not surprising, since they were caught in the maelstrom of cultural collapse: they were, says Hynes, 'the only generation compelled to write while their superior position was crumbling'.

An important source of faith in working-class potential was direct contact with the students of W.E.A. classes and other such organisations. Laski's first work in that respect was in the USA, where he was influential in the development of Boston Trade Union College (Kramnick and Sheerman, 1993: 120). Amongst its aims were that 'organised labour must develop its intellectual resources if it is to realise its hopes in the coming social and industrial order.' Although Laski was never elected to political office in Britain, he was coopted in 1934 to the library committee of Fulham council (in London), to which his wife Frida had been elected as a Labour councillor, seeing this as an aspect of education for the workers (Kramnick and Sheerman, 1993: 339). Laski gave as his reason for rejecting the eugenic ideas that he had absorbed in his youthful work in Karl Pearson's laboratory that experience had led him to a more accurate understanding of why educational accomplishment differed among social classes: 'close, unremitting physical toil does not make for the occasion to show great mental powers' (quoted by Kramnick and Sheerman, 1993: 78). That came from a review of Pearson's *Life of Francis Galton* (the founder of the modern eugenics movement). Laski then traced his new view to his experience as teacher of adult students: 'many of us cannot have failed to have met trade unionists whose intellectual powers have been stunted by the hardships of the lives they have led.'

G.D.H. Cole, too, joined the W.E.A. when it was still small and growing (in 1913), and he and his wife Margaret were consistently active in it. Margaret Cole later describe the W.E.A. succinctly as

> the organisation founded by Albert Mansbridge and A.L. Smith of Balliol, with R.H. Tawney as one of its earliest tutors, for the idealistic purpose of bringing cultural education of high standard to those who had never had a chance of it in their youth. (M. Cole, 1949: 114)

Tawney's early educational career was dominated by the W.E.A., he was connected with it for a total of 42 years from 1905, and he was its president from 1928 to 1945. Tawney often said that his own education as a teacher was mainly through his work as a tutor for the W.E.A., noting in a lecture to mark the fiftieth anniversary of its founding that

> if I were asked where I received the best part of my own education, I should reply, not at school or college, but in the days when, as a young, inexperienced and conceited teacher of Tutorial Classes, I underwent, week by week, a series of friendly, but effective, deflations at the hands of the students composing them. (Tawney, 1964 [1953b]: 86)

That humility is not at all the intellectual condescension described of others by Carey.

Working-class educational potential was not imagined to lie in a possible future in which their material conditions would have been improved: it was now. The purpose of education was not individual social mobility and it was only indirectly about social revolution, if at all. Tawney called the concept of the ladder of opportunity the 'tadpole philosophy':

> It is possible that intelligent tadpoles reconcile themselves to the inconveniences of their position, by reflecting that, though most of them will live and die as tadpoles and nothing more, the more fortunate of the species will one day shed their tails, distend their mouths and stomachs, hop nimbly onto dry land, and croak addresses to their former friends on the virtues by means of which tadpoles of character and capacity can rise to be frogs. (Tawney, 1964 [1931]: 105)

He was not actually opposed to social mobility, arguing elsewhere that one of the purposes of education was to place 'the resources of character and capacity at the disposal of the nation', but '*La carrier ouverte aux talents*—promotion by merit—is neither the sole object of education policy, nor, in the view of this writer, the most important one' (Tawney, 1964 [1943]: 66). Laski, too, was critical of the career open to the talented, because it 'meant, in the immense majority of cases, that freedom was open to the man who had the gifts necessary to win his way to success in a fiercely competitive struggle' (Laski, 1952: 81). The Liberal politician C.S. Buxton wrote in 1908 that the concept of the career open to talents enticed people to desert their class of origin: Ruskin College, he said, 'is neither part of a ladder system by which a man can climb out of his class, nor an attempt to educate the rank and file. It endeavours to train and to develop the intellect of those who are, or will be, leaders of working-class opinion'. The W.E.A. aimed to bring '"humane" education within reach of all' (Buxton, 1908: 193).

Tawney thus argued that education liberates people primarily for the effect it has on their minds, enabling them to 'become partners in a world of interests which they can share with their fellows' (quoted by Terrill, 1973: 182). He argued for improvement of school education for all, and believed that, in the meantime, the main purpose of adult education was to compensate those who had missed out on a proper education in their childhood, those 'who need a humane education both for their personal happiness and to help them to mould the society in which they live' (Tawney, 1964 [1953b]: 96).

Tawney was probably the main author of the influential *Oxford and Working-Class Education* (1908; see Terrill, 1973: 38, and Harrop, 1987), and its themes reflect his abiding philosophy. It was in effect a joint report of the W.E.A. and the university, and advocated a large extension of Oxford University education to students beyond its doors. It argued that a general, liberal education is needed by people of all classes, even if they remain in the same class regardless of whatever educational benefits they might gain: 'technical and general education ought not to be distinguished on the ground that they are fit for different classes, but because they stimulate different sides of the same individual' (Oxford University, 1908: 51). This is as true of the professional as of the manual worker:

> In our opinion a man who will throughout life work with his hands needs a general education for precisely the same reason that it is needed by a specialist like a lawyer, or a doctor.

The purpose for all classes was personal refinement as part of becoming a responsible member of the community—in order that the student 'may be a good citizen, and play a reasonable part in the affairs of the world'. The manual labourer 'as a member of a self-governing nation... must acquire the civic qualities which enable him to cooperate with his fellows, and to judge wisely on matters which concern not only himself, but the whole country to which he belongs' (*loc. cit.*). The report is explicit that this entails a liberal education, and that it is not about personal economic advancement: thus such an education is envisaged as valuable in its own right even if it has no direct implications for the structure of social and economic inequality (as opposed to the indirect reforms that a well-educated democracy might gradually bring about). It quotes and agrees with one of the witnesses from whom the committee that issued the report had received a submission ('a workman, a student and a Trade Unionist'): 'the time has come for the working man to demand a share in the education which is called "liberal"', a label which implies that 'it concerns life, not livelihood', and in the sense that 'it is to be desired for its own sake, and not because it has any direct bearing' upon the worker's 'wage-earning capacity' (*ibid.*: 52). The report offers through this quotation a brief definition of liberal education that transcends class, and indeed which would, with minor modifications, have been acceptable to Matthew Arnold or John Henry Newman, and which draws upon the whole tradition since the Renaissance of thinking about liberal education, civilised style and moral character:

> By the avenue of Art, Literature, and History, it gives access to the thoughts and ideals of the ages; its outward mark is a broad reasoned view of things and a sane measure of social values; in a word it stands for culture in its highest and truest sense. This 'liberal' education should be a common heritage.

The curriculum which the committee proposed for an adult education of this kind was, in detail, also directly heir to the liberal-education tradition, based on reading lists consisting of the most up-to-date academic work on economics, sociology and social reform, on political thought, on imaginative literature in English since the late-eighteenth century, and on English and world history since the Middle Ages. Such a curriculum could not be described as sacrificing any degree of rigour, reach or intellectual challenge when it included, in a very lengthy reading of several hundred books, works by Arnold Toynbee, Alfred Marshall and Sidney Webb, by Keats, Wordsworth, Byron and Shelley, by Jane Austen and George Eliot, by Walter Scott and Charles Dickens, by Hazlitt, Matthew Arnold, Carlyle, Ruskin and

Emerson, by Bagehot, T.H. Green, J.S. Mill and T.H. Huxley (though no experimental science), and by Plato, More, Rousseau and Burke. As Jonathan Rée (1987: 216) comments on such proposals (referring to the nineteenth-century advocate of working-class education Joseph Dietzgen, whose influence was felt throughout these movements), 'over-optimistic' though it may have been, it was not 'crassly self-contradictory': it was not in principle any more unreasonable to expect the working-class people to rise to this challenge, if given the chance and suitable conditions, than to suppose that the most able members of the dominant classes could do so when selected for the degree programmes of the existing universities.

The problem with the present state of affairs was in the assumption that such an education was not suited to the working class, and 'the national Universities, which are the natural fountain-heads of national culture, have been regarded as the legitimate preserve of the leisured class.' This has not only 'wronged the working class'; it has also 'to a great degree sterilised the Universities themselves' (*loc. cit.*). If there is a social purpose, the report emphasises, it is for citizenship, not for any gain of social status or economic worth: the aim is 'not so much for facilities to enable [working-class] children to compete successfully with members of other classes for positions of social dignity and emolument, as to enable workmen to fulfil with greater efficiency the duties which they owe to their own class, and, as members of their class, to the whole nation' (Oxford University, 1908: 82).

Tawney developed these ideas in his own writing and educational practice over the following half-century, and never wavered from them to any significant extent. Adult education was not a tool for social engineering: it was about liberating the minds of working-class people where capitalism had fettered them. He meant by equality not the same economic conditions for all, but a common culture: 'differences of remuneration between different individuals might remain; contrasts between the civilisation of different classes would vanish' (Tawney, 1964 [1931]: 150). The aim of policy for schools should thus be, Tawney argued, 'to create the common culture which at present we lack' (Tawney, 1964

[1943]: 73). The person who becomes educated and yet remains in their own community enjoys 'the dignity, the social contacts, and, if they please, the intellectual interests and culture, which human nature demands' (Tawney, 1964 [1952]: 186). Percy Nunn put the point forcefully:

> If someone asks what good is poetry to the farm labourer, the reply is that a man's education, whatever his economic destiny, should bring him into fruitful contact with the finer elements of the human tradition, those that have been and remain essential to the value and true dignity of civilisation. (Nunn, 1923: 8)

After the election of the Labour government in 1945, Tawney argued (in a lecture in New York in 1949) that 'the essentials of civilisation, once the privilege of a minority, have increasingly become a common possession' (Tawney, 1964 [1949a]: 162), and 'the most important aspects of human beings is not the external differences of income and circumstance that divide them, but the common humanity that unites them' (*ibid.*: 175). Material improvement from the Labour government was a means, not an end: 'civilisation is a matter, not of quantity of possessions, but of quality of life' (*ibid.*: 174).

Tawney was the most visible and eloquent exponent of this view that an important goal of socialism should be enabling working-class people to enter into the social heritage, interpreting that to mean the same as would have been meant by Matthew Arnold by 'the best that has been thought and said'. But such beliefs were common among the socialist and liberal thinkers about education whom we have been considering. In Laski's view, no class should be permanently shut out from 'those qualities which, in their intricate combination, we call civilised living' (Laski, 1952: 20), and he subscribed to Tawney's view on the importance of secondary education: 'secondary education for all is fundamental to national welfare' (Laski, 1923: 53). Reflecting on the writers in France who foreshadowed the revolution of 1789, he argued that 'education was the only path to national unity' (*ibid.*: 47). The same was true, he noted approvingly, of Adam Smith, who, despite not being 'a protagonist of government interference', urged that 'the education of the people is a matter of urgent national concern.' He cited also diverse ideological support of the same point by Jeremy Bentham, James Mill, John Stuart Mill, Thomas Jefferson and John Adams. 'The citizen', he said, 'must be able to find his way about the great world, or else he ceases, in any real sense, to be a citizen. But that ideal would be attained only if a proper education is available to all:

> At present... [the citizen] has barely caught sight of the intellectual heritage he might share. He can read, though his taste has not been formed. He can write, though he has been given no real powers of effective self-expression. The knowledge he mainly acquires when the years of school are over is practical knowledge; and that means, for the most part, the ability to follow a routine the implications of which remain unexplored. (*ibid.*: 49)

A.D. Lindsay argued in the same vein, and saw himself as inheriting the tradition of extending university teaching to the working class that was pioneered by Edward Caird, Arnold Toynbee, A.L. Smith, Tawney and William Temple. His daughter quotes him saying that 'these W.E.A. members came to university partly for what might be called weapons —for that kind of knowledge which would give them the power and capacity to handle men and things.' That was not all, however, since they also wanted to learn how to think about 'the meaning and purpose of life', not merely how to do what they wanted, but also 'what they *ought* to want to do' (Scott, 1971: 70; her emphasis).

The terms in which the mainstream of the Labour movement rejected the Marxist education of the Labour Colleges then revealed further also what was distinctive and optimistic about a liberal education for working-class people. Laski was concerned about the 'cult of the extreme', views which 'treat the critic as an enemy' (Laski, 1952: 19–20). Cole welcomed the fact that the founder of the W.E.A. 'was no Marxist', because 'he did not set out to destroy "bourgeois culture" and to replace it by a new culture emanating from the proletariat as a class.' Mansbridge, in Cole's sympathetic view, believed that the working class could participate fully in the cultural heritage if given the chance:

> He thought... in terms of a great cultural heritage from which the workers were for the most part excluded, and wished to find a means of opening this heritage to them and,

> in doing so, of broadening it out to find room for their aspirations. (Cole, 1952: 45)

Cole firmly believed that the dominant current of thinking in British socialism about the educational needs of the working class was of this kind. He noted two views of these needs – either 'educational philosophy and practice to suit the needs of the class struggle' or that 'education rests in fundamental values which transcend class differences.' He concluded that 'in Great Britain,... the Socialist tradition is mainly on the side of the second view' (Cole, 1952: 46). Haldane, likewise, argued that 'there seems to be no reason why among the working classes generally higher education [meaning post-elementary education] should not in the end have a moulding influence, such as it has had on our middle and upper social strata' (Haldane, 1923: 13). L.T. Hobhouse, referring approvingly to *Oxford and Working-Class Education*, likewise said that 'the democratic educational movement of to-day... desires... to dignify and enrich the life of the working class itself, and to teach it to play its rightful part, with responsibility and honour, in the complex work of the modern State' (Hobhouse, 1909: 710).

Further than the belief that the working class had the capacity to benefit more from liberal education than from instrumental aims, there was even a sense that they were the best defenders of the great cultural traditions, a view consonant with the wider idea, which we have noted, that socialism was needed to save culture from capitalist philistinism. The working class were engaged in a heroic fight: 'the persistent search for knowledge has in it an epic quality' (Laski, 1923: 55). Like Matthew Arnold, Laski thought that they might ally themselves with the best of the aristocracy against the philistine bourgeoisie (Kramnick and Sheerman, 1993: 184). The problem with the upper classes (again as distinct from utilitarian business people) was not their ideas but their not being open to any influences other than their own: if Laski enjoyed the refinement of conversations with aristocrats, he also was frustrated by the superciliousness, writing to Wendell Holmes in 1922 that 'the upper reaches of the Civil Service' are

> very impressive, cold, precise, extraordinarily well-informed and with a knowledge that is most illuminating of the source

> of government ideas. Yet they all clearly had a certain curious class-bias—I mean the belief that the young brain of England is concentrated in Oxford and Cambridge. (Holmes and Laski, 1953: 428)

The working class were perfectly capable of sharing the role of cultural leadership that used to be the monopoly of the aristocracy because

> the working class has realised more urgently than others the significance of education. To them it has signified the mastery of their environment; to others, in too great part, it has been merely the symbol of an income-bearing career. (Laski, 1923: 54)

The purpose of all such widening of access to liberal education was to make a reality of mass democracy. In this sense, these socialist intellectuals were more directly the heirs of the Victorian liberals—notably of Matthew Arnold—than was any more conservative segment of opinion, because they saw, as Arnold did, that something radically new was required in order to preserve what was best and in order to place the understanding that comes from the great cultural traditions in the service of society. In Tawney's words:

> A common culture is thus a new creation, not a levelling down to the existing working class mentality nor a levelling up to the existing middle class or upper class mentality.

'The ability to resist delusion', he said, depends in part 'on the habit of intellectual initiative which it is one of the ends of education to develop'. That is why intellectually stimulating education had to be more widely diffused: it was 'the condition of the harmonious working of any society which does not frankly resort to coercion' (Tawney, 1924: 4).

Conclusions

The views of education and democracy that we have considered here were part of a common culture that stretched from the conservative right to those on the left such as Laski who, in the 1930s, adopted a form of Marxism. Highly critical of capitalism though these thinkers were, they were not outsiders and were not even, in any profound sense, alienated from the mainstream of European civilisation. Their dominant educational concern, in fact, was to enable wide access to the riches of that culture. Their being part of a spectrum is the main reason why a tight political definition of the group of thinkers we have been considering is not feasible. Most were close to the Labour Party and some were sympathetic to the communists, but none lost touch with liberals or conservatives, and all were in some ways influenced by the contemporary developments in thinking about liberal education that we considered in the previous chapter, such as in the journal *Scrutiny*, and thus were heirs to a tradition of thought about education that stretched back to the Enlightenment and even to the Renaissance.

They believed, first, that education had to reconcile merit and worth, to use the terminology of Sheldon Rothblatt that we have discussed. On the one hand, they included within the idea of the moral purposes of education an ethical critique of capitalism, and thus they reinvented the concept of worth to include how to be a democratic citizen. That way of conceiving of a liberal education had been contained within it for two millennia, in that it had always been thought of as freeing people from servility. On the other, they remained concerned with academic standards, and with the selection of people—for educational courses and for careers—and of material for the curriculum. That was a consequence of these thinkers' liberalism. They sought to remove barriers, to encourage talent to flourish, to make sure that people had more than one chance in life to gain the benefits of the cultural traditions that they valued. But they never imagined in any detail how everyone could benefit in these ways, and they always assumed, in fact, that only the most able could ever engage with the inherited culture in the depth in which they themselves had done. That their own direct contact with education as teachers was mostly confined to the kinds of students who turned up voluntarily in adult-education classes or at university may explain why their writing could mostly ignore the details of how a liberal education might be brought to everyone through the school curriculum. That gap then left a vacuum of thinking for the next generation of reformers, as we shall see in the later chapters.

They believed also, second, that liberal education should in some sense also be useless education in that it should at most be preparatory to citizenship or to a career, not imbued with practical purposes. In this sense they were direct heirs to John Henry Newman and to that strand of thinking about liberal education that stemmed ultimately from religious contemplation. There was always something monastic about these socialist thinkers' educational ideals, even if the seclusion amounted to no more than the peace of a two-hour evening class to which the adult students would come at the end of a hard day. Joad's image of the garden at Winchester reminds us that Matthew Arnold's ideal was to make available to the whole of society the kind of education that his father had inaugurated through his reforms at Rugby (Joad, 1945: 90–2). The same vision pervaded the grammar schools and senior-secondary schools of the post-1945 period, and then became one of the points of conflict when the curriculum for comprehensive education was being defined in the 1960s and 1970s. We return to these debates in later chapters, but the main point here is that the education which these socialists imagined may in some respects be thought of as a temporary refuge from society, preparing people to re-enter everday life.

The socialist thinkers were mainly, third, the direct heirs to Matthew Arnold and, through him, to the Enlightenment. Despite some rhetoric to the contrary, they were not really romantics. They thought of education as being about taste and manners, about universally valid principles, about civilisation. A contemporaneous comment from Dover Wilson in an essay on Arnold is directly revealing here (Wilson, 1930: 192). He notes that Tawney takes Arnold's essays on 'Equality' (which we considered in the previous chapter) as the text for his own book *Equality* (from which we have quoted at several places in this chapter), and then comments that Arnold's heirs are not conservatives (despite what had been alleged by Leonard Woolf, 1937: 225–30), but people like Tawney, 'who combine a passion for education ... with that profound belief in the possibilities of human nature and the value of human personality which is the heart of the democratic creed'. That optimism was an Enlightenment ideal which Victorian liberalism adopted wholesale, and which twentieth-century socialists then adapted by invoking the power of the democratic State as its main instrument. They were encouraged in that direction by the idealist conception of the State as the community's 'best self' that was brought to Britain in the late-nineteenth century from German thought by T.H. Green and his successors, the teachers in turn of the socialist thinkers we have been looking at. To men such as Tawney, Wilson (1930: 192) continued, 'education and the public service, both growing more liberal with each generation, and embracing a larger and larger proportion of the best and brightest spirits of the time within their ranks, are the two chariot-wheels of civilisation, the meaning of which is not power or wealth, or even the conquest of nature, but simply "the adorning and ennobling" of the spirit of man.'

Thus it was, fourthly, that intellect and morality could be placed at the service of democracy. Socialism for these thinkers was no more than the fullest flowering of democracy, the truest kind of democracy that could only be attained when no one faced any obstacles to becoming a full citizen. That required the capacity to judge as well as a developed sense of what is right, and so liberal education was essential. If liberal education had always been thought of as teaching people how to govern, then universal liberal education was the only kind of education proper to a democracy.

That then, finally here, is the main divide between socialist thought about education in the first half of the twentieth century and the conservative strands with which it was intimately entwined. Though the thinkers we have been analysing shared the critique of capitalism that was offered by the Leavises, by *Scrutiny* and even by the highly conservative Eliot, and though they shared with them a direct line back to the warnings about an uneducated democracy that started its modern journey with Thomas Carlyle, they did not share that tradition's pessimism. They did firmly believe that education was the key, that most people had the capacity to acquire the intellectual powers and the wisdom that would allow democracy to operate as was intended. In the words of Laski, summing up both the challenge and the optimism (Laski, 1923: 50):

> The safety, indeed the reality, of a democracy depends in no small part upon this, that the average man can be trained to

feel a moral responsibility for the results of the political process.

Chapter 3

Socialist Policy and Practice to the 1950s

Educational policy and practice on the left in roughly the first half of the twentieth century followed the principles which were expressed by the socialist intellectuals whom we have been discussing, and indeed they all, as activists, contributed to these developments. We look at three aspects of this: organised adult education, more informal encouragement of self-education mainly through publishing, and the approach to education which the Labour Party took when it was in power, for two short periods as a minority government in the 1920s and then much more influentially when it held a majority in parliament from 1945 to 1951. One reason to give attention to formal and informal adult education is that many of the ideas about how socialists should relate to the tradition of liberal education were shaped in the context of thinking about the education of adults, not directly at this time in connection with what children should study in school.

Workers' Educational Association

The dominant organisation on the left in adult education was the Workers' Educational Association, founded in 1903. Woodhams (2003: 74) has described it as 'the fourth plank in th[e] edifice' of the Labour movement—along with the party itself, the cooperative movement and the trade unions. 'Neither the Labour Party nor the Trade Unions were concerned with education in the liberal sense', and so the W.E.A. had a free hand to develop its own ideas and character. It had its origins, indeed, outside the Labour movement altogether, in various attempts early in the twentieth century to extend Oxford University teaching to people who were not full-time students, such as in the report *Oxford and Working-Class Education* whose ideas we discussed in Chapter 2. Fieldhouse notes that this 'Oxford reform movement... was very influential in the formulation of... radical-liberal ideology', led by Tawney, Lindsay, Cole and Temple. Reforming Oxford was one practical expression of what he calls their faith in 'the rationalist and reformist parliamentary road to socialism and to the bourgeois notion of representative democracy'. But the significance went far beyond the new socialist politics: the Oxford reformers 'encompassed the broad centre of the British political spectrum, accommodating notions of individual fulfilment, social purpose, public service, social justice and class emancipation' (Fieldhouse, 1985: 121). Blyth traces the origins further back still, in the Oxford of Newman (Blyth, 1983: 2–3). From that milieu had emerged the notion that liberal education had to be more than just a certain kind of content: to fulfil its hope of educating people out of servility 'there developed an interest in the actual process of liberating individuals from their depressed, economic condition' (Blyth, 1983: 5).

The specific organisational influence was Albert Mansbridge, son of a carpenter who was born in 1876 in Gloucester and who achieved most of his own education through attending university extension classes at King's College in London. He met Charles Gore (Tawney's friend), who was then a canon at Westminster, and was mentored by him for many years (Jennings, 2002: 57). Through Gore, Mansbridge came into contact with the Oxford reformers. Pursuing what became his life's work of widening access to this kind of education, he formed the Association to Promote the Higher Education of Working Men in 1903, and in 1905 this became the W.E.A. Harrison notes that Mansbridge was not a socialist: what enabled his project to succeed was his 'unique personal qualities' rather than any contacts in the Labour movement. Harrison comments that 'it seems odd that a movement for workers' education should have been based on a collection of Anglican bishops, Oxford dons, and self-educated working men rather than on the trade unions', but the key to the kind of liberal education that the W.E.A. came to espouse was that it 'was the fruit of Edwardian liberalism, and especially, because of Mansbridge's university friendships, of Oxford liberalism' (Harrison, 1961: 263–4):

> From Edwardian liberal Oxford and the radical nonconformist provinces the W.E.A. imbibed its peculiar strength—the strength of working-class self-improvement, of nonconformist moral earnestness, of a radical concern for social justice. (*ibid.*: 349)

The W.E.A.'s role was not only educational, but also to smooth the transition to mass democracy. Thus, at a meeting of the W.E.A. in Reading in 1911, Gore said that 'all this passion for justice will accomplish nothing, believe me, unless you get Knowledge' (quoted by Harrison, 1961: 266). Jennings notes that Mansbridge was also astute enough to obtain the support of the advocates of national efficiency, for whom better working-class education would be one response to the economic challenge from Germany and to the British army's alarmingly poor performance in the Boer War—people such as Haldane, Rosebery, Milner and the Webbs (Jennings, 2002: 96).

The W.E.A. established its educational respectability by summer schools run at Oxford in the years following its founding. The atmosphere was not socialist, but rather 'a mixture of confrontation and good humour, sharp dissent and mutual respect' (Rose, 2002: 270), in other words rather the same as in any undergraduate tutorial class. This (along with the national-efficiency case) won the admiration of Robert Morant, permanent secretary of the Board of Education, who agreed to Mansbridge's enthusiastic pressing for public funding for three-year 'tutorial classes', the aim being to create for part-time W.E.A. students the same stimulus, assessed by the same standards, as undergraduate university education. The classes became the linchpin of the W.E.A. in England and Wales, though not in Scotland where—for reasons that shall be explained later—the universities were already somewhat more open to working-class access.

With such aid, but also above all with the enthusiasm for a liberal education of many working-class people, the W.E.A. grew rapidly over the first half of the century and shaped the

Labour movement profoundly. By the 1930s, it had around 60,000 students, one fifth of whom were in the three-year tutorial classes (at a time when there were around 70,000 students in full-time university-level education). By the aftermath of the Second World War, this number had doubled, and was thus still close to the full-time university-education figure of around 120,000 (Rose, 2002: 265 and 292; Halsey, 2000: 225). Fourteen members of the 1945 Labour government had been W.E.A. tutors or otherwise involved in organising classes, including the Prime Minister, Clement Attlee, and the Chancellor of the Exchequer, Hugh Dalton. Jonathan Rose (2002: 292) notes further that 56 W.E.A. 'supporters, teachers, and students were sitting in the House of Commons', mostly on the Labour side.

The curriculum of adult education

The spirit from the start was consistent with the idea that working-class education should be no different from any other kind of education. J.M. Mactavish—who became secretary of the W.E.A. in 1915, succeeding Mansbridge—summed up the aim in a speech at the conference in 1907 which led to the report on working-class education: 'I claim for my class... as a right wrongfully withheld... all the best that Oxford has to give' (Jennings, 1979: 13). Harrison notes that when 'thinking, moderately inclined Labour men' came into contact with 'sympathetic scholars' from Oxford and the Public Schools, they saw what was required to form leaders, and inferred that such an education was what was required for the leaders of the working class. The principles of liberal education were then firmly embedded in W.E.A. practice: as one student was quoted as having said, 'it has come as something in the nature of a shock to most of us that there are two sides to every question' (Jennings, 2002: 39). The principle was that students were equal participants, since Mansbridge wanted to distance the W.E.A. from Victorian paternalism (Rose, 2002: 276): the pedagogical style, as Wiltshire (1956) later put it, was 'Socratic' in that it was entirely based on small-group discussions, focused on a prior lecture by the tutor but not dominated by it: as we have seen, Tawney said he learnt more from these discussions than he was ever able to give to them. But there was also respect for the liberal canon: the equality of student and teacher as participants did not in any sense imply anything other than humility before the weight of accumulated knowledge.

The W.E.A.—despite its importance in the Labour movement—is best thought of as part of a wider movement for university extension and for adult education. Tawney, for example, though at the heart of the W.E.A.—and an early tutor in Rochdale and in Staffordshire—also cooperated with the Liberal politician R.B. Haldane when they set up the British Institute of Adult Education, drawing on philanthropic financial support from Sir Edward Cassels (Blyth, 1983: 43). Haldane wrote that 'what we aim at is the creation and diffusion throughout the people of the sense of new intellectual and spiritual values.' Education, he believed, is 'a power liberating from the fetters of ignorance'. The aim of adult education was to open up to the whole of society 'the greatest writers and artists that the history of the world has produced' (quoted by Blyth, 1983: 44). A similarly pioneering project was the Young Men's Christian Association, the educational work of which was led from 1915 by Basil Yeaxlee, a Congregational Minister; his first task in that connection was to organise a highly successful programme of adult education for the wartime army, recruiting university lecturers to do this teaching. He wrote in 1920 that 'there is no need to condescend to adult students, from whatever class they come':

> They are supremely interested in the big things that lie at the heart of history, literature, natural science, economics, political theory, philosophy, and theology... The average man is ready for all that justifies us in calling a subject 'humane'. (Yeaxlee, 1920: 33)

Students came to Oxford University summer schools as 'a puzzled generation', Blyth notes, hoping to find at the university 'some secret of life that would illuminate' how to 'resolve most of the ills of society' (Blyth, 1983: 10).

These curricular principles in the W.E.A., and in adult education more generally, are best summed up then as deriving from the mainstream of liberal education. Mansbridge, while recognising the important basis of compulsory elementary education in opening up the possibility of engaging with 'the beautiful and true', also noted that the new literacy might lead people to the 'cheap and changing opinions' of the popular press (Jennings, 2002: 21). Although students were to be treated with respect and as equals in the sense of not being patronised, he argued that 'the selection of curricula... must be the duty of the University acting in cooperation with working people' (Jennings, 2002: 54). Similarly, Canon Barnett, warden of Toynbee Hall, which he and his wife Henrietta had founded in 1884 in the east end of London to bring education to that very poor district, wrote in 1905 that working-class people ought to have access 'to the knowledge stored in the National Universities' (Jennings, 2002: 40). Tawney, writing in 1906, said that university extension, though aimed 'at primarily the making of citizens', was to do so by imparting 'some knowledge of the corporate life of humanity which is expressed in literature, philosophy and history' (quoted by Jennings, 2002: 41).

The evidence suggests that these principles of respect for the liberal tradition governed how the W.E.A. classes operated in practice. The Board of Education commissioned a report (published in 1910) on how its grants to the three-year tutorial classes were being spent. The authors were a schools inspector, J.W. Headlam, and the prominent liberal Professor L.T. Hobhouse, who was a sociologist at London University. Their report shaped the character of the tutorial classes henceforth (Jennings, 2002: 75). They asserted that to conform to a 'university standard' the classes ought to aim to be 'scientific, detached, and impartial in character' and should aim 'not so much at filling the mind of the student with facts or theories as at calling forth his own individuality, and stimulating him to mental effort'. But that thinking must also be guided by a canon: it should accustom the student 'to the critical study of the leading authorities', and should be such that it 'implants in his mind a standard of thoroughness, and gives him a sense of the difficulty as well as of the value of truth'. The student must be able to understand points of view other than his or her own, and learn 'to distinguish between what may fairly be called matters of fact and what is certainly mere matter of opinion' (Jennings, 2002: 76).

Recurrent assertion of these principles strengthened them. After the First World War, the Ministry of Reconstruction published a report on adult education that, like the Hobhouse and Headlam report, became a reference point for subsequent practice (Jennings, 2002: 143); the committee that wrote it included Tawney, Yeaxlee and also A.L. Smith, Master of Balliol College, Oxford, who had been closely involved in the extension movement of the previous few decades. It argued that liberal education was a 'universal need', in contrast to technical education, which was not. It was the best preparation for citizenship because it would enable students to 'rise above their original prejudices and limitations' (Jennings, 2002: 143). The aim was to create an education that was 'liberal and humane' (Blyth, 1983: 31).

This was certainly how the students between the wars saw adult education. Rose summarises the conclusions of a survey of students in the W.E.A. classes and at Ruskin College, Oxford, undertaken in 1936:

> One of the most commonly cited motives for pursuing adult education was very Arnoldian: 'Disinterestedness'. This involved not only the effort to overcome bias, though it certainly included that. It meant as well that education should be pursued with no thought of competitiveness or economic gain, that knowledge must be acquired for its own sake in an environment where students helped each other. (Rose, 2002: 283)

Rose describes the typical curriculum as embodying a 'conservative canon' (Rose, 2002: 116), and his definitive, detailed exploration in archives, memoires and correspondence establishes conclusively that liberal education of this kind was what these adult students favoured. The predilection had origins in the nineteenth century. Enthusiasm for Shakespeare, for example, was spontaneous, and not at all in deference to 'middle class tastes': for many working-class people, 'Shakespeare was a proletarian hero who spoke directly to working people… The plays provided a language of radical political mobilisation' (Rose, 2002: 122–3). The tendency towards literature in university extension classes in fact grew, moving away from economics (and never really having engaged with natural science because of the expense of providing equipment). Despite increasing pressure on adult education in the 1930s to contribute to vocational training, liberal education remained firmly established (Blyth,

1983: 69). Blyth notes that even the official pronouncements at that time from the Board of Education continued to commend the liberal approach despite the economic crisis and the rising levels of unemployment: thus the adult-education committee of the Board of Education admired liberal education which it praised as 'this process of training, by which the intellect, instead of being formed or sacrificed to some particular profession, or study or science, is disciplined for its own sake... and for its own highest culture' (Blyth, 1983: 107).

Rose notes then that 'for those at the bottom of the social scale, the most old-fashioned literary canons could be terrifically liberating. What was dismally familiar to professional intellectuals was amazingly new to them' (Rose, 2002: 127). This may explain why those intellectuals who did not despise such conservative cultural tastes were popular, such as Laski, Tawney and Cole. In debates about liberal education as against vocationalism, or about the alleged social elitism of the liberal canon, Tawney on the whole sided with tradition which he saw as a firm bulwark against any reduction of education to economics, proclaiming at the W.E.A. annual conference in 1936 that 'our business is not to be the educational Woolworth of the day' (Blyth, 1983: 119). As Rose says, summing up the appealing conservatism of such taste, 'generations of liberal critics, from Matthew Arnold to Lionel Trilling, recognised that literature, by suggesting a wealth of alternative perspectives on the world, would inevitably subvert ideology' (Rose, 2002: 8). It was in practice the extension and radical interpretation of the Leavisite view of literature, expressed in 1934 by the Archbishop of York (in the journal of the W.E.A.) as responding to the 'tension between mechanisation and humanisation'. Unfashionable though that view later became (as we shall see in Chapters 5 and 6), the record of the most popular curricula in adult education up to the middle of the twentieth century suggests that Arnold, rather more than his critics, better understood 'the experiences of common readers in history' (*ibid.*: 9).

Rivalries on the left

At that time—the inter-war years—a central feature of this liberal practice was opposition to Marxism (Fieldhouse, 1983: 11). For a while, the W.E.A.'s main rival for working-class students were the Labour Colleges. They had their origin in a militant break-away from Ruskin College in 1909, over how much control the students would have of the curriculum. The Labour Colleges subsequently claimed to provide an 'independent' working-class education, and based their curriculum on Marxist ideas. They alleged that the W.E.A. was an agent of capitalism, because it accepted funds from the state and because it adhered to a liberal curriculum. Much subsequent academic criticism from the left has repeated this allegation. Fieldhouse, for example, claimed that 'the adult education movement was welcomed by the establishment as a bulwark against revolutionism, a moderating influence and a form of social control' (Fieldhouse, 1985: 123). His only real evidence is an often-quoted statement from Lord Eustace Percy—President of the Board of Education—in 1925, but since Percy was actually making the case for increased expenditure on the W.E.A., he is as likely to have been politically exaggerating as engaging in a conspiracy. Since the W.E.A. made no secret of its aim of ameliorating class conflict, the criticism does in any case rather miss the point. The intellectual leaders to whom the W.E.A. looked—the people whose ideas we discussed in Chapter 2—were, as we have noted, liberals and democrats to the core, and therefore explicitly interested only in reform. Indeed, Temple, Tawney and Lindsay warned the Board of Education and the local education authorities that withdrawing financial support from the W.E.A. would strengthen the new Labour Colleges and, with that, the Marxist left (Jennings, 2002: 111).

The Labour Colleges recurrently attacked the liberal curriculum. Frank Horrabin, for example—who was close to the Colleges—wrote in the W.E.A. Yearbook in 1918 that there was no such thing as a neutral curriculum, since all ideas were class ideas:

> The Labour movement has its basis in the antagonism of interests existing between Capital and Labour—this being the central, fundamental factor in present-day society. It

> accordingly insists that the education with which the Labour movement is concerned must be based upon a recognition of this antagonism. It urges that this antagonism of economic interests is inevitably translated into an antagonism of ideas. (quoted by Harrison, 1961: 294–5)

Education, he said, is inevitably propaganda, 'the only question for the working class being: what kind of propaganda? Propaganda based upon the ideas of the ruling class outlook upon society, or propaganda based upon the point of view of the working class, and designed to equip the workers for their struggle against capitalism and capitalist ideology.' Such ideas remained a minority current for the next half-century, but—as we shall see later, in Chapters 5 and 6—then mushroomed to become the dominant view on the radical and academic left from the 1960s onwards, for whom the ideas of liberal education came to be seen as merely the hegemonic expression of the power of various dominant social groups. But, between the wars, the British Marxist response to liberal education was not the only one which Marxist thinking produced: as Entwistle notes, the educational programme of the Italian communist, Antonio Gramsci, was of the same kind as the mainstream of non-Marxist educational programmes in Britain (Entwistle, 1979: 123). Basil Yeaxlee of the Y.M.C.A. commented on the Marxism of the Labour College type that 'it is as foolish to accuse the universities of deliberately, or even unwittingly, giving a "capitalist bias" to their teaching as it is to suggest that the working-class educational movements approve of a "trade union education".' The whole criticism was based in a kind of childish resentment. With the wrong kind of 'working-class control in education... you have mob-government in education offered because snob-government was once suffered' (Yeaxlee, 1920: 75). Rose, noting that 'the weakness in this argument [about the class bias of liberal education] is that it focuses on the controllers rather than the ostensibly controlled', quotes the comments from numerous W.E.A. students at the time on how they felt about such attacks, and sums them up:

> W.E.A. students found these assaults enormously condescending, and their responses should make anyone think twice before using the word 'hegemony'. (Rose, 2002: 267)

Nevertheless, in the heated political context of the period, the W.E.A. had to respond, and the reply was in effect in two phases. Until about the 1920s, the tendency was to insist that it was working class in the origins of its students, and so was quite different from the universities: it served that class by providing a liberal education to them. For example, George Thompson, who was district secretary of the W.E.A. in Yorkshire from 1913 to 1945, wrote in 1918 that the W.E.A. aimed to provide, from among working-class students, 'the personnel of a political governing class' (quoted by Harrison, 1961: 291). The aim was always to 'help those active in the working-class movement to serve it better'. It should 'exercise a steadily-growing cultural influence... on the students in the class' so as to 'give a clear conception of what are the essentials of a democratic society'. In that sense, therefore, he said, it was a workers' movement rather than a general adult-education movement. Although the University of Leeds was suspicious of this at first as risking left-wing bias, Harrison comments that their 'fears were overcome by the energy of a group of enthusiastic professors... and the fine work done in the first tutorial classes' (Harrison, 1961: 288). Strongly committed to working-class education though he was, Thompson did not question any aspect of the curriculum on class grounds. What mattered in class terms, according to these early W.E.A. leaders, was the political outcome, and as Rose notes of summer school students at Oxford, 'even if [they] fervently embraced the university, they did not change their minds about capitalism' (Rose, 2002: 269).

In the second phase, the W.E.A. was forced by student interests to move away from an unambiguously working-class clientele. The initial response to student choice was in fact an intensification of the liberal inclination, the shift towards literature and away from, for example, economics. But the W.E.A. classes started to appeal to people who were not working class and were not being prepared for working-class power. Harrison (1961: 273) suggests that this 'turn[ing] away from its primary function as a workers' education movement' was unavoidable if the W.E.A. was to avoid becoming 'a narrow sect': it had to attract people who had no particular interest in social reform. In that sense, it was joining the much larger and more diffuse provision of liberal education. Thus 'classes in literature, psychology, music, local history, elocution, folk dancing, gardening and French followed' (Harrison, 1961: 274). The W.E.A. became in effect part of a general project of social enlightenment, democratic and liberal certainly, but not revolutionary. Nevertheless, such general courses were not new for the W.E.A.; what had changed was the balance between them and economics or economic history (Rose, 2002: 274). In any case, to be democratic in the 1930s, in a European context, was to insist on fundamental principles that were under grave threat. The response by the W.E.A. to what students wanted did ensure that it flourished whereas the Labour Colleges were already in steep decline by the late-1930s: as the W.E.A. was growing towards 60,000 students, the Colleges passed their peak of 30,000 in the mid-1920s, and had fallen to 13,000 by 1937 (Rose, 2002: 292).

So, in summary of the curricular philosophy of adult education up to the Second World War, we can say that (in Blyth's words) it was 'a belief in the value of liberal education for an earnest minority' (Blyth, 1983: 347). Harrison describes 'the antithesis between liberal and vocational education' as 'harden[ing] into a dogma' (Harrison, 1961: 325): 'in the socially dominant tradition... the emphasis was literary, philosophical and cultural; education for usefulness (technological, commercial, practical) was socially inferior.' This position was reinforced by the conditions attached to grants from the Board of Education, but was also 'greatly strengthened by the pronouncements and writings of influential friends of adult education, nearly all of whom belonged to the great liberal Oxbridge tradition'. Yet it was not a useless curriculum: in that sense it was also firmly in the tradition in which a liberal education prepared people, shaping their character and enabling them to engage with social issues. H.C. Wiltshire—of the department of extra-mural studies at Nottingham University—noted retrospectively (though arguing for its continuance) that within the adult-education curriculum of the pre-war period

> particular concern is shown for the social studies and for those aspects of other studies which illuminate man as a social rather than a solitary being; its interest is not in

> learning for learning's sake but in learning as a means of understanding the great issues of life. (Wiltshire, 1956: 88)

The aims were utopian, in that they rested on 'what may seem to us [in 1956] to be unwarrantably optimistic assumptions about the educability of normal adults' (*ibid.*: 89). They also then seemed from the point of view of the world of the 1950s 'to add up to something which is essentially nineteenth century and desperately unmodish'. It may also, he thought, have been transient, in that it might have been thought to cater only for a society where many able working-class people had been denied access to a proper secondary education, a position that had been ended, many believed, by educational reforms in the 1940s (to which we return).

A tradition under threat: the 1950s

Responding to such incipient concerns about the relevance of the tradition, there was a vigorous reassertion of the liberal ideal in the early 1950s, exemplified in the influential writing of S.G. Raybould, who was director of extra-mural studies at Leeds University. This understanding of liberal adult education then contributed to the slightly later thinking of Richard Hoggart and Raymond Williams, whose work we shall consider in Chapter 4. In a book published by the W.E.A. in 1951, Raybould reflected upon the meaning of 'university standards' for adult education:

> The idea persists that a university education should be a liberal education, an education, that is, through which the student becomes accustomed to reflect about ends, and not simply means, in human life. (Raybould, 1951: 2)

Such learning ought to be academic in the sense of encouraging each student to 'organise his knowledge, to assimilate new knowledge to it, and to use what he has learnt'. The student then learns the value of knowledge in a practical sense: as well as 'the capacity to think in abstract terms', academic learning includes—rather than being antipathetic to—'the ability to relate abstractions to the concrete phenomena to which they properly refer'. The overriding principles are disinterestedness and objectivity, which Raybould traced in unbroken sequence back to the 1910 report by Hobhouse and Headlam. By meeting other students who have a variety of points of view, 'with different interests and working in different fields of knowledge', the adult student is able to develop

> the synoptic mind, a recognition of the limits of his own and other people's knowledge, and an attitude both critical and tolerant. (*ibid.*: 17)

Raybould argued that adults are better able to benefit from liberal education than school pupils. Although the humanities may provide students of all ages with 'a thorough intellectual training, that is a training in the capacity for logical analysis and reasoning', it is only adult students who can relate them to life as they have already experienced it (*ibid.*: 6–7). Seeking after such insight may indeed be why adult students come to classes in the first place (*ibid.*: 8). The proper attitude, Raybould believed, should be disinterestedness—as much in social science and aesthetic judgement as in natural science or mathematics—and that could be encouraged by breadth (*ibid.*: 3). 'Prejudice', he said, 'is the greatest obstacle to progress in adult studies.' What is required is 'not simply a more rational understanding of one limited field of study, but a general disposition towards, and capacity for, rational thought, feeling and behaviour' (*ibid.*: 11). Tutors had to work at this, since the disadvantage of being a student after years of experience was holding preconceptions (*ibid.*: 12).

In order that the students may achieve the rigour, breadth and objectivity that are aimed for, the adult-education tutor must exemplify 'in his own work the qualities which it is part of the purpose of the class to strengthen' (*ibid.*: 18). By this he meant that the tutor

> must demonstrate in all his work that he himself has accepted, and continues to accept, the discipline he asks of the students—the patient acceptance of criticism, the admission of error, the confession of ignorance, the tolerance of difference, the arbitrament of reason, the consistency of conduct with profession. (*ibid.*: 18)

Similar views were expressed by Tom Kelly, who was director of extra-mural studies at the University of Liverpool. Writing in 1953, he said that universities have three equally important roles—being repositories of knowledge, teachers of it to others, and inventors of new knowledge. Tutors in adult classes had to take part in all three activities, and 'will carry something of the university with them wherever they go' (Kelly, 1953: 103). Thus in some sense the custodial task is twice as important as that of creating novelty. Universities had a duty to disseminate what they held in trust, since 'the body of knowledge and the cultural values which the universities possess are the inheritance of mankind and should not be limited to the privileged few' (*loc. cit.*). This then links the democratising of access to knowledge to the very idea of a liberal education.

Kelly, more than Raybould, saw this task for liberal adult education as even more urgent in the changed circumstances of the 1950s:

> The contemporary world, bedevilled by slogans and slick generalisations, torn by rival creeds and passions, needs... the knowledge, the critical faculty, the power of dispassionate judgment for which the universities pre-eminently stand. (*ibid.*: 100)

Once again, he links that to a wider social project: 'in the present social context... a university should be not only a centre of learning but a centre of light in the region where it dwells, and... it should deliberately set out to spread the knowledge and values of the university outside its walls.' Extra-mural work would have no place in universities if they were mainly concerned with research or professional training, but they ought not to be, and the aim—with Newman and the whole tradition of liberal education—is rather to contribute to the urgent task of 'embody[ing] and transmit[ting] a common culture'.

Yet in the 1950s there was felt also to be a threat to this tradition, one which was to intensify over the ensuing half-century. A source of change was indeed the expansion of education more widely, so that fewer people missed out on it when children: Labour's slogan of secondary education for all had become a reality in the 1950s. Even though it was still divided into academic and non-academic streams (as we shall discuss further below), it might be thought that the 'earnest minority' would have found its way into the academic courses and thus would have had its intellectual curiosity properly stimulated in the teenage years. This might be glossed optimistically, but at the price of detracting from any distinctively radical purpose of adult education, as had already been felt in the 1930s. At the 1947 annual conference of the W.E.A., Tawney rejected criticism of middle-class participation in the Association's classes: 'are they not also the children of God?' (Blyth, 1983: 259). Kelly argued that, as the nature of social class changed, the W.E.A. needed to have a new kind of purpose: 'the old dichotomy between the working classes and the middle classes, which used to provide a foundation for the distinction between university extension work and the classes of the Workers' Educational Association, has now become blurred and uncertain' (Kelly, 1953: 101). Wiltshire noted that 'the working-class intellectual deprived of the university education from which he might have benefited will become a rarer and rarer figure' (Wiltshire, 1956: 90). Kelly also hoped that having a 'vocational interest' does not prevent a subject's being dealt with 'in a liberal spirit' (Blyth, 1983: 308).

But that optimism was challenged by two pressures. One was that people seemed to be less interested in sustained study. Blyth suggests that full employment and new affluence reduced the motive to study hard over three years. Raybould had noted of extra-mural classes between 1924–5 and 1948–9 that there was a trend towards short courses, mostly elementary and not requiring written work (Blyth, 1983: 216 and 249; Raybould, 1951: Appendix). Kelly's interpretation was that this was a consequence of students' having had a sound grounding in the new academic courses in a widened secondary schooling, or as undergraduates in the expanding universities, and thus having a need as adults only 'to supplement their existing education, to open up new interests, and to provide light... on important questions of the day' (Kelly, 1953: 102). But that could seem like wishful thinking, and there began to grow in adult-education circles a sense that there was a more general loss of seriousness. The W.E.A. was then faced with a dilemma. It said in a report on this in 1958 that it was not in favour of 'uncritical acceptance of "mass culture"' (W.E.A., 1958: 9), and yet it tried to avoid seeming disdainful or nostalgic, saying that it

> does not seek to condemn 'mass culture' wholesale, to deny the need for popular entertainment, to ignore the growth of

> mass media of communication, to seek relief from the present in shadowy golden ages in the past.

It aimed to stimulate 'active as well as passive leisure', and hoped therefore that 'taste and discrimination' and 'continuous and vigilant criticism' could be developed alongside 'popular entertainment'. The central challenge for adult educators who were still seeking to strengthen democracy was to counter the 'widespread apathy and ignorance among large members of the public' (*ibid.*: 8–9), but an important audience remained the earnest minority:

> There is a key place too for small groups of active working people who pursue educational activities which take time, require effort, lead to no automatic material rewards, and raise standards of understanding and appreciation. (*ibid.*: 9)

This dilemma became—as we shall see in Chapter 4—a preoccupation of later writers such as Richard Hoggart with no answer at all to the problem that the W.E.A. struggled with here of how to find a democratically acceptable way of maintaining standards in a culture where popular taste seemed to deny them. Harrison summed up the particular problem that faced socialist thought:

> The traditional doctrines of the left were inadequate for this new twilight world which was neither the capitalism of the classical economists nor the socialism of which the pioneers had dreamed. (Harrison, 1961: 335)

What was more, 'the new generation of intellectual leaders ... did not, like their predecessors, draw their inspiration from R.H. Tawney and G.D.H. Cole' (*ibid.*: 336). The old enemies were no longer so straightforwardly there, but neither were the old ideals, since the old humanist certainties which attached to liberal education were themselves being questioned as part of these same shifts towards a kind of consumerist populism.

The other pressure leading to pessimism was that the growth of secondary education and of the middle class would convert adult education into a form of professional development or even technical training rather than liberal enlightenment. In consequence, 'an educational movement', wrote Wiltshire, 'is becoming an educational service' (Wiltshire, 1956: 91). Merely to assert that academic and vocational study are 'equal' is 'part of the cant of our time', understandable in itself—as an attempt 'to rescue technical and vocational studies from the stupid disdain with which they have been regarded'—but destructive of the great tradition of liberal studies. A report on adult education commissioned in 1953 by the government from Eric Ashby (Vice-Chancellor of Queen's University in Belfast) represented, Blyth notes, 'the partial abandonment of the concept that adult education meant liberal education defined as non-vocational' (Blyth, 1983: 303). Ashby wrote in 1955 that 'the old humanism... has become impotent. We are, whether we like it or not, entering a civilisation of experts and technicians.' In consequence, he thought, 'we need to re-examine the idea of what is a liberal education. I am persuaded that specialisation is the first step towards it' (Ashby, 1955: 7–8). Ashby's report also accelerated the decline of the three-year tutorial class, and thus of the liberal tradition as shaped by official regulations (Blyth, 1983: 315).

The W.E.A. tried to resist this argument based on specialisation, refusing to accept Ashby's view that the best we might aim for would be that experts themselves would be educated in a spirit of 'technological humanism' (Ashby, 1955: 9). The W.E.A.'s 1958 recommendations averred that 'a growing gulf between experts and ordinary citizens' might be overcome by providing 'a growing number of people with the opportunity of forming rationally grounded opinions upon matters of importance' (W.E.A., 1958: 8). While expertise was necessary and could not be spread widely, the expert had a tendency to forget about 'judgment, sensitivity and imagination':

> One of the dangers of our society is that ethical standards, educational activities, leisure activities and attitudes towards work will be far too much determined by occupational and professional groups working not necessarily against the community but too much in isolation from it. (W.E.A., 1958: 8)

Rather more in the spirit of the old liberal adult education than Ashby's, however, was a report from the National Institute of Adult Education in 1955 on technical education. They placed their proposals firmly in that tradition by quoting Tawney:

> Social well-being does not only depend upon intelligent leadership, it also depends upon cohesion and solidarity. It implies the existence, not merely of opportunities to ascend, but a high level of general culture, and a strong sense of common interest, and the diffusion throughout society of a conviction that civilisation is not the business of an elite alone, but a common enterprise which is the concern of all. (N.I.A.E., 1955: 26)

The overall aim was described as being

> to discover [what] can be done to make it possible for the worker to be self-reliant, wise and adaptable and, not least, proud of his calling... How, in short, can it be contrived, in so far as education can influence the matter, that individuals shall have the opportunity of living the good life amid the mechanical complexities of modern industrial society? (*ibid.*: 128)

The Institute thus hoped that technical and vocational education might be imbued with a humanistic spirit:

> There ought not to be any period in the educational process during which the values commonly associated with a general education are dropped for a time because of the intense pressure of vocational preparation. (*ibid.*: 118)

This was true of all levels of vocational education, including that for the professions (*ibid.*: 40), but the report was particularly concerned with the skills training which young adults would receive at technical colleges. Their courses should include studies of 'the social, historical and human implications of the subject', however technical the core specialism might be. Moreover—again centrally in keeping with the liberal tradition—there was also the insistence that these courses should include 'first and foremost English and English Literature' (*ibid.*: 122 and 48). They expanded on this, while noting that 'a liberal education without books is unthinkable' (*ibid.*: 125):

> Turning to English literature, not for passive appreciation, but for active help in achieving self-expression and self-fulfilment, seems to us to exemplify what a liberal education has to offer. (*ibid.*: 54)

But, liberal though this may be, it was no longer conceived with the grand social purpose of the old adult education. It was becoming a mixture of leisure classes, personal therapy and palliatives for all kinds of social problems—covering everything from classes in local history or in learning a language, through building the confidence of unemployed people or women returning to the paid labour force after raising a family, to remedying adult illiteracy (Blyth, 1983: 177). Important socially though all these aims may be, they did not have the conceptual unity of the W.E.A.'s original purpose, nor—further back—of liberal education's ideal of transforming society humanely through a certain kind of intellectually challenging and ethically responsible sustained study. The W.E.A.'s problem was not its alone, because the political context in which it had been born was vanishing, as trade unions became pressure groups, as Labour became just another competing party and as democracy seemed secure for the first time. Jennings notes that 'it was doubtful whether the working-class movement of which the association had been the educational expression still existed' (Jennings, 1979: 54).

There was also emerging at this time a new version of the old Marxist allegation that the liberal tradition offered merely an illusion of objectivity. The case was made with particular force by E.P. Thompson, who was working in the extra-mural department at Leeds University, before later writing influentially on English working-class history. He described the aim of neutrality as a pretence: it claimed to be '"objective", "tolerant", gentlemanly, calm, equitable, wise or a combination of these', but in fact dangerously 'extended from a tolerance of a person's right to hold certain opinions to a required tolerance of actual opinions' (quoted Fieldhouse, 1983: 12). Fieldhouse notes that, in the atmosphere of the Cold War, the hostility to communist tutors became even deeper than it had been in the 1920s, when it was already strong. He suggests of Raybould that 'he could not see that his own Labourist attitude was as much devoid of objectivity in this sense as any other attitudes' (Fieldhouse, 1983: 13). These critical views then were the precursors to the much more general left-wing critique of liberal education as an oppressive myth that we shall examine in Chapters 5 and 6.

So the dilemma remained. In a better-educated society, in which the old class divisions of culture had been somewhat eroded, but in which mass consumerism seemed to threaten seriousness of purpose, was there any longer any point at all in thinking of the old ideals of liberal education? Might everyone learn about the best that has been thought and said at school? In that case adult education no longer would have a particularly reforming role, and no longer would be part of the socialist movement. Even more of a challenge, however, were doubts about the liberal curriculum itself: might that kind of culture, far from being universal, merely be the expression of class privilege, not to be offered equally to all but to be abolished as inimical to democracy?

Reading

Formal adult education was only part of the way in which the ideas about liberal education came to be linked to thinking about social reform, and thus amplified the socialist interpretation of liberal education that we have discussed in Chapter 2. Much more broadly than in organised educational classes, there grew up between the wars a loose association between being generally educated and being of the opinion that capitalism needed at least reforming. The mood and the political effect are summed up well by Laski's biographers. His

> most faithful followers were... the enlarged inter-war literate professional class, the broadened base of people with intellectual interests and pretensions who... unlike high-table academics, took him very seriously as a thinker and a seer. (Kramnick and Sheerman, 1993: 591)

They add that Aneurin Bevan—the minister in the post-war Labour government who is most closely associated with the founding of the National Health Service—was probably right that it was these people who secured Labour's victory in 1945.

The main vehicles for this readership were in publishing, and two ventures, in particular, will illustrate the case. By far the most important was Penguin books, founded by Allen Lane in 1935 and reaching its peak influence after the Second World War. It was described by Lewis (2005: 1) as 'one of the benign monopolies that shaped our lives', an 'estate of the realm' (John Gross's phrase) like the BBC, a uniquely ambitious venture in paperback publishing of immense significance quite unfamiliar to later readerships who have become accustomed to paperback books' being available from multiple publishers. The other example is the Left Book Club, of which Laski was a director, more specialised and yet still also of great (though transient) importance politically, much more influential than left-wing political parties themselves. We consider these in this section, along with some related activities, such as army education during the Second World War and links with formal adult education. Penguin and the Left Book Club, important in themselves, are also best thought of as exemplifying a mood in which reading and radicalism went hand in hand.

Rylance indexes the massive expansion of book publishing in the middle of the twentieth century: for example, the number of books sold rose from 7 million in 1939 to 77 million in 1969 (Rylance, 2005: 52). A large part of the growth was in paperbacks, and for a time paperbacks meant Penguin (Joicey, 1993: 30). The reason why the publishing of good-quality books expanded after the 1920s was ultimately social change, creating a large minority of people with the interest and opportunity to read (Rylance, 2005: 48). There was the growth of secondary education (to which we return later in this chapter), starting before the First World War and accelerating after the Second, creating a larger group of adults with a grounding in something like Arnold's idea of culture. There was the slow growth of the middle class, with more income, more leisure and an inclination from their education to take ideas seriously (Lewis, 2005: 72). And there was the extension of the vote to all adults (after 1928), creating a new public sphere in which educated citizens had a duty to think about the state of society, a sense of responsibility that was intensified in the immediate aftermath of the Second World War. By the 1930s, two thirds of adults in Britain claimed to read regularly, and the new BBC had stimulated, through the creation of radio Listeners' Groups, in effect a new form of adult education (Rylance, 2005: 51).

Lewis points out that the audience for new publishing tended to be Fabian socialists, to read Wells and Shaw, to attend university extension classes and the W.E.A., and to have already subscribed to smaller-scale predecessors such as Everyman's Library. Marghanita Laski (Harold's niece, born in 1915) gave a similar characterisation in 1956 of the audience for Penguin books—readers of the *Observer* newspaper, users of public libraries, members of local film societies, who attended concerts for serious music, visited educative exhibitions, were interested in architecture and were fascinated by ornithology (Lewis, 2005: 274). Alexander Goehr, interviewed in the 1990s, recalled similarly the audience for the BBC's Third Programme (for which his father had worked, and on which his own compositions often have been heard)—typified by a 'hard-working, Labour-voting schoolmaster in (say) Derby' (Carpenter, 1996: 14). These people, before and after the Second World War, were the 'young, radicalised middle classes' (*ibid.*: 134), the new publishing pushing them further to the left. The apogee of this mood was the late-1940s, though with a lasting influence well into the 1960s, as all such activities had come to belong to the 'war to win the war' (Summerfield, 1985: 446). Summerfield encapsulates them as relating to the writing of Orwell and Priestley (the successors to Wells and Shaw in this respect), to the *Daily Mirror*, to the Army Bureau of Current Affairs (to which we return), to the Commonwealth Party—the short-lived, left-wing but non-communist opposition to the party-political truce during the war—and Mass Observation, the pioneering project in early social science that sought to record ordinary people's experience of war and its aftermath (Summerfield, 1985: 446).

The ideas that led Allen Lane to launch Penguin books were responses to these trends, but also were linked explicitly to a fear that mass culture was potentially inimical to standards. Penguin was thus also in part following the Leavises—especially Q.D. Leavis—in a defence against cultural decline (Joicey, 1993: 54). Lane insisted, as Lewis puts it, on 'making the best available to the many, without dilution or simplification' (Lewis, 2005: 4). The topical series of 'Penguin Specials'—launched in 1937—was described by Lane as promoting interest in topics 'that people should be informed about, should be interested in, although they don't even know it yet' (Joicey, 1993: 31). Norman Angell—in a book for Penguin in 1940 on 'why freedom matters'—said that the goal was to combat 'the evils of triviality, one-sidedness, emotionalism and hysteria' (Angell, 1940: 134). Intellectual freedom, he said, is not comfortable: 'freedom of discussion... [is] an extremely unpleasant discipline that offends some of our deepest instincts.' Freedom 'unsettles... convictions, creates doubts where before there were none, compels difficult intellectual effort', and forces people to pretend 'to like being told that [they are] wrong'. But without intellectual freedom, totalitarianism of the left or of the right would flourish (*ibid.*: 130).

Though Penguin's commercial aim was crucial to its success—what Rylance describes as its being 'topical, modern, and very directly engaged' (Rylance, 2005: 54)—the commercial and educational purposes could co-exist because of cross-subsidy (*ibid.*: 52). Orwell was in two minds about this: if book prices drop, he said, people may buy more books but spend in total less on them, and so 'in my capacity as reader I applaud the Penguin Books; in my capacity as writer I pronounce them anathema' (Orwell, 1970 [1936]: 191). But Orwell's democratic instincts overcame his scepticism: 'the average intellectual level of the books published has markedly risen', he said on the BBC's Indian Service in 1942, attributing this to Penguin above all (Lewis, 2005: 156). Lane saw the purpose of Penguin and the associated Pelicans (on non-fiction topics) as intrinsically educational: 'good books cheap', he wrote in 1938, but

> the clue to the success of the Pelicans and Penguins resides in the first word of this slogan. There are many who despair at what they regard as the low level of the people's intelligence. We, however, believed in the existence in this country of a vast reading public for *intelligent* books at a low price. (Lane, 1938: 969; his emphasis)

It was the success of such publishing with an educational aim that could lead H.G. Wells to describe Lane as 'one of the greatest educationalists alive' (Lewis, 2005: 113). Joicey notes that, whereas the *Times Literary Supplement* ignored Penguin's launch in 1935, in 1969 it described it as having the 'educative zeal' of the BBC (Joicey, 1993: 30).

Alongside these educational aims, indeed as part of them, the whole enterprise also had a generally left-wing air to it, but—as with the W.E.A. and the other strands of liberal adult education—this was combined with an overriding commitment to objectivity and truth. Lane described himself as a socialist (Joicey, 1993: 35), but Penguin authors were not expected to conform to any political line (Lewis, 2005: 136). Core to the educational aims of Penguin—and a firm advocate of its seeking to promote general liberal education—was W.E. Williams, editor-in-chief from 1935–65, who (rather remarkably) combined that role with being secretary of the British Institute of Adult Education (1934–40), editor of the W.E.A.'s magazine, *Highway* (1930–41), director of the Army Bureau of Current Affairs (1941–45) and its peace-time extension (to 1951), and secretary-general of the Arts Council of Great Britain (1951–63). He was born in Manchester in 1896, and grew up speaking Welsh in Wales. He was a school teacher after studying English literature at Manchester University, moving into adult education in 1928 as an extramural tutor in literature at the University of London, where he remained until 1934.

Williams combined what Rylance called the views of the missionary and the merchant: 'for Williams, Penguin was in many respects comparable to the BBC. But it was also comparable to Marks and Spencer's' (Rylance, 2005: 57). When he was at the Arts Council, but also in the late-1940s, he represented the populist view of art, in opposition to the legacy of J.M. Keynes and the ideas of Kenneth Clark, for whom the Council's commitment to excellence outweighed any attachment to participation (MacArthur, 2013; Lewis, 2005: 160–1). Williams opposed this on the grounds we have discussed repeatedly from left-wing proponents of liberal education—that commitment to wide participation did not preclude attachment to the best that has been thought and said. In the increasingly affluent world of the 1950s, that inevitably meant linking liberal education to commercial means of dissemination, hence the importance of Penguin books. Williams was thus part of that same world of radical supporters of liberal education—for example being on the National Executive of the W.E.A. with Tawney, Richard Crossman (a Labour MP after 1945), William Temple and A.D. Lindsay (Lewis, 2005: 117). Lane was close to Williams, because he was not from the metropolitan élite, the same reason that he later took to Richard Hoggart, from the next generation of adult educators after Williams (*ibid.*: 119).

The Army Bureau of Current Affairs (usually referred to as the A.B.C.A.) was also part of this general purpose, and in practice depended upon Penguin. More widely, it might be thought of as the educational instance of the general developments during the Second World War which led to the 1945 Labour government, to the fully developed welfare state and to the idea that many more people than had previously been thought possible could benefit from access to liberal education. Williams was the main instigator, and his role as director was nominally on secondment from the British Institute of Adult Education (Summerfield, 1981: 142). Within six months of its founding in 1941, over half the units in the army had A.B.C.A. discussion groups (Lewis, 2005: 162). The idea was to bring to the forces the best practices of liberal adult education as it had grown up in the previous four decades, but also using the managerial and commercial acumen that was being newly developed at Penguin (*ibid.*: 153). The belief of the army command was that (as quoted by Summerfield)

> if we can employ men's minds and stimulate their interests by promoting knowledge, discussion and thought about the affairs of the world in which they live, we go far to maintain their morale and thus to make them better soldiers. (Summerfield, 1981: 141)

Despite there being political questions at home—including from Churchill himself—about the left-inclined ethos of the resulting discussions, this principle that army education would strengthen the work of the forces was consistently defended by the military leadership (*ibid.*: 150). If nothing else, it passed the time: in the words of one corporal, 'as far as the desert was concerned there wasn't anything else to do except have political discussions' (quoted by Summerfield, 1981: 154).

This leftish bias was influenced by Williams's own views, and by talks from many of the socialist intellectuals whom we have discussed: for example, in Britain, Laski gave 'almost weekly talks to army and RAF camps' (Kramnick and Sheerman, 1993: 421). But it was not propaganda so much as exposing the participants to the kind of liberal education which adult education had developed, and thus encouraging them to apply the ideas they had read about, or heard in lectures, to think for themselves about what the war was for, and to imagine what would happen in the post-war world. Richard Hoggart much later recalled how the A.B.C.A. pamphlets pushed soldiers to the left not because they were propaganda 'but because they helped reduce the power of the mandarin voices' (Hoggart, 1990: 62). Analogies were then drawn with the highly politicised army of England's revolution in the seventeenth century. In his outline for the War Office of what the A.B.C.A. would do, Williams quoted Cromwell to define the citizen-soldier: he should 'know what he fights for and love what he knows' (Summerfield, 1981: 155). A.D. Lindsay went further in an article in the *Times Educational Supplement* in 1941, comparing the A.B.C.A. classes which he had seen with the most radical discussions in Cromwell's army:

> I got the impression that there had not been an Army in England which discussed like this one since that famous Puritan Army which produced the Putney Debates and laid the foundation of modern democracy. (quoted by Summerfield, 1981: 155)

More explicitly socialist than any of these activities—adult education, Penguin or army education—was the Left Book Club in the 1930s, but here, again, despite the overarching ideological aim of engaging a wide readership with left-wing politics, the underlying educational idea was predominantly that of liberal education. The Club was formed in 1936 by the already successful publisher Victor Gollancz, with the goal of stimulating debate on the left by means of high-quality books, not propaganda. Gollancz had been a school teacher at the ancient and highly selective Repton School, which developed his interest in the value of liberal education (Neavill, 1971: 198). His own publishing house flourished from the late 1920s. The Left Book Club was a direct response to the rise of fascism, seeking to encourage in Britain the sort of non-sectarian left-wing politics that brought the Popular Front to power in France in 1936. It was the first book club in Britain of the kind that became common later—supplying reduced-price books for members. The selections were made by Gollancz and two other socialist intellectuals—Harold

Laski and John Strachey. At its high point, just before the Nazi-Soviet pact of 1939, membership reached 57,000, and so it was rivalling the W.E.A. in its extent. It disowned the communists after that event, and this, along with paper rationing during the war, led to its eventual demise in 1948. (Allen Lane, more astute commercially, had managed to secure quite reasonable rations of paper for Penguin.)

The purpose was always educational, and Neavill notes that 'it is primarily to Gollancz's credit that the Left Book Club remained, on the whole, a serious educational movement and did not degenerate into a simple propaganda machine' (Neavill, 1971: 214). He held to the fundamental tenet of liberal education that 'only by the *clash* of ideas does a mind become truly free' (quoted by Neavill: 207; Gollancz's emphasis). Like the socialist intellectuals whom we have discussed, he believed that reason itself was an enemy of fascism (Lewis, 1970: 91). One of the ways in which the Club sought to realise its educational aims was by organising local discussion groups (and so it prefigured not only later book clubs but also much later book groups). These then stimulated a speaking circuit, so that local groups could be addressed by authors of Club books—and others—and could enter into discussion with them. In the late 1930s, there were as many as 1,200 local groups. The organiser of these, John Lewis, wrote that the aim was not actually to establish a Popular Front, but rather to create the conditions in which the role of reason in defeating fascism might be encouraged. The sole object, he said, 'was to enlighten, to educate' (Lewis, 1970: 13). The work of the Club was thus analogous to the intellectual activities which, he pointed out, had contributed to the American and French revolutions:

> The Left Book Club, undeterred by those who were coming to believe that reason was powerless, returned to the principles of 'enlightenment' as the ultimate defence of democracy and popular rights, in the belief that there can be no effective democratic government when the people are not informed, and where rational discourse does not sift truth from error. (Lewis, 1970: 13)

There was indeed very broad support, from prominent members of the Labour and Liberal Parties, from the Communist Party and even—though this caused controversy, which

Gollancz resisted—from anti-fascist Conservatives. It is true that it was not as eclectic as the W.E.A. had become by the 1930s, and had nothing like the appeal to many millions of readers which Penguin rapidly acquired (Joicey, 1993: 36). Orwell dismissed the Club as purveying 'dishonest pamphlets' of propaganda. But that was generally unfair, and indeed in seeking to combine the eventually irreconcilable liberals, socialists and communists, it might be said that Gollancz was more thoroughly pluralist than any rival, worrying all the time that he was becoming too much of a propagandist (Neavill, 1971: 207). Even though doomed to eventual failure in the face of Marxist hostility to the very idea of liberal dialogue, he was, at worst, naïve. The Club therefore added another, and highly distinctive, dimension to the practical development of liberal education by socialist thinkers. As Woodhams notes (2003: 75–6), writing about the W.E.A.'s *Highway*, there was a common project of radical thought between the wars, and especially in the 1930s, which developed diverse practical activities to fight the threats to democracy. What these activities shared—Penguin, Left Book Club, adult education—was a belief in culture as an agent of progress.

Labour policy and its effects

Though adult education was the main practical way in which the political left tried to extend liberal education to new audiences, the scope for authoritative policy change from the left in this respect lay with the Labour Party, first during its two periods of minority government in 1924–5 and 1929–31, and then with much greater power when it gained majorities in parliament in 1945–51, 1964–70 and (though much more weakly) 1974–79. On the whole, however, in contrast to the work with adults, the conclusion is that the party did very little to affect the curriculum, although by the time of the fourth of these periods there was the beginning of a different approach—a greater attention to vocational and economic purposes for education—that became very much more prominent in the party by the time it formed its sixth government from 1997 to 2010. The period since the 1960s is dealt with in Chapter 7. Here we look at the party's earlier ideas. Two general points may be made about its attitude to questions of what was to be taught in schools. One was that it appeared not to be interested, not out of indifference but rather out of respect. Its implicit definition of a worthwhile education was a liberal education of a quite traditional kind. If the problem with capitalism had been that it prevented working-class people from having access to the best that had been thought and said, then Labour's task was to ensure that they would no longer be denied that right. There was nothing intrinsically controversial about what 'the best' was, and indeed the respect that there was for such socialist intellectuals as Tawney, Laski and Cole tended to reinforce the valuing of inherited knowledge. Thus, for example, a secondary curriculum for workers would be almost no different from that which had graced the most selective and expensive of elite schools since Thomas Arnold had reformed Rugby in the 1830s.

But then the second general feature, until the 1950s, was that the selection of the best for the curriculum came to be inseparable in the minds of most socialists with selection of the best students. Partly following the professional consensus of the day, it was assumed on the left that the most worthwhile aspects of the inherited liberal curriculum required a quality of intellect that was simply not possessed by everyone, and they assumed also that to dilute that curriculum to enable all pupils to take part in it would be to risk the loss of an entire civilisation. So there had to be selection of people. Indeed, the idea of selection by measured merit came to be thought of as a socialist policy, the only fair and educationally respectable response to invidious selection by wealth or nepotism. Since the difficulty of devising a measurement system that would be truly fair and truly free of class (or other) biases was not evident until the development of social scientific research on these questions between the 1930s and 1950s, the socialist aim was to set in place the conditions by which working-class people could take advantage of any meritocratic opportunities they were offered—above all, not having to pay fees to attend the academic schools, and also having bursaries available to compensate for earnings forgone. Even when the apparent inseparability of cultural and social selection came to be seriously questioned on the left in the 1950s, the aim remained for a while the widening of access to a quite traditional liberal curriculum: the new non-selective comprehensive schools would be the means by which everyone would gain access to the best. Only when that in turn proved very much harder than the more optimistic reformers of that time had supposed was the old curriculum finally challenged, but by then the main intellectual impetus to its demise came from elsewhere—from lines of argument (as we shall see in Chapters 5 and 6) which, for the first time in any extensive way, claimed that liberal education was itself one of the main obstacles to a democratic system of education.

Policy in the 1920s and 1930s

What, then, was said about the content of school education in Labour circles in the early years of the twentieth century? Barker notes that the most which can be found is occasional mild criticism of the existing curriculum, and sums up the record:

> The general acceptance throughout the party's history of the existing character of the school curriculum meant that even the belief in the role of education in promoting citizenship played no significant part in Labour's educational programme. (Barker, 1972: 139)

Common schools would serve the purpose of creating a common life by how they were organised and how children were given access to them, and what went on inside the classroom was in that sense irrelevant: socialism was for the playground.

G.D.H. Cole noted that the socialist movement had 'had remarkably little to say about the curriculum' (Cole, 1952: 49). He contrasted this with the attention that Robert Owen had given to socialising children into citizenship in his pioneering schools in New Lanark in the first couple of decades of the nineteenth century. Socialists since the late-nineteenth century, Cole said,

> did not, like the Owenites, stress the significance of the school as a place in which the children should be taught the social values appropriate to a Socialist, or even to a fully democratic, society. They were much more concerned with demanding more education and better, in the sense of better-equipped, schooling than with criticising the positive con-

> tent of education for any fault except its low level of quality. (Cole, 1952: 49)

Socialists now concentrated on alleviating material poverty, so that people might have full access to 'the traditions of bourgeois liberty and religious equality'. The aim was that 'these good things... be rapidly extended to more and more of the people and given fuller content by relief from under-nourishment of mind and body' (Cole, 1952: 51–2).

Similar comments were made by other contemporary observers of the growing Labour movement. Percy Nunn noted in 1920 that what was pushing schools in a vocational direction was the conversion of venerable institutions into training grounds for the new professional classes:

> Schools which have been the stronghold of 'liberal culture' are hastening to fit their curricula to the needs of modern industry and the professions. (Nunn, 1920: 204)

Socialists, in contrast, were now the defenders of the liberal tradition against these economic pressures: 'the strongest opponents of vocational training are among those who speak for labour.' He explained the reason for socialists' views here in terms that are similar to those we have noted from the W.E.A.:

> On the one hand, they claim for the poor the heritage of culture from which they have so long been unjustly excluded; on the other hand, they think they see behind the proffered gift of vocational education the hand of the exploiting employer. (*loc. cit.*)

Nunn himself had come round to this point of view by 1918 – of seeing liberal education as the properly radical policy – under the influence of Tawney and of William Leach, a radical newspaper editor in Bradford, who was active in Labour debates about the curriculum in the 1920s. Leach wrote in 1918 that that 'not until a groundwork in languages, sciences, literature, and the arts is the common heritage of all the population should we tolerate the idea of specialising for anything at all' (Brooks, 1991: 248).

There was not in fact any notable discussion of the curriculum in Labour debates before the 1920s. A new organisation founded in 1923, the Teachers' Labour League, expressed essentially the same kinds of criticisms of the existing curriculum as the Labour Colleges and the Plebs' League were making of the W.E.A. curriculum, insisting (as the Plebs' League put it in 1917) on an unresolvable 'antagonism of interests existing between Capital and Labour' (Barker, 1972: 155). The Teachers' League attempted to argue at the 1925 Labour Party annual conference that the party should be committed to reforming the curriculum, but the motion was lost and, as Barker notes, even its advocates gave greater attention to the aim of making secondary education free.

There were some further attempts by the League over the next few years to commit Labour to reforming the curriculum, but none amounted to much. They came closest to success at the annual conference in 1926, where they attacked the 'predominant methods of teaching and disciplining children', which, they said, fostered 'a bourgeois psychology, militarism and imperialism' (Barker, 1972: 149). Labour ought to counter this by inculcating 'a proletarian attitude towards an outlook on life'. This motion was carried, but—in the manner that the Labour leadership always favoured for dealing with awkward issues—was pushed into the relevant specialist group (the party's educational advisory committee) for further deliberation, and had no influence on policy: as Parkinson notes, these beliefs, 'unique in their ferocity', merely showed how impotent the party then was (Parkinson, 1970: 21). Barker comments that 'the Labour Party had no wish to appear as the advocate of an attack on those very traditions of educational impartiality to which it itself adhered' (Barker, 1972: 151).

The advocates of liberal education were influential in the committee. The most forthright exponent of the view that Labour ought not to sanction using schools for propaganda came from Barbara Drake, who was secretary to the committee (Barker, 1972: 151). She had no difficulty condemning militarism (and indeed it might be added that there was a distinguished current within the tradition of liberal education that would have shared her concerns), but (she wrote) 'we should regard as equally reactionary and contrary to the best traditions of public education in this country an attempt to impose on immature young minds a particular labour or socialist creed or any brand of class conscious psychology.'

Others on the committee were less confrontational in their rejection of socialist propaganda, including Tawney and also Charles Trevelyan, the former Liberal who had been chair of the Board of Education in the 1924 Labour Government, but in the wording that was agreed in the response to the conference resolution the socialist interpretation of liberal education was emphatically expressed: 'the necessary foundation of a Labour and Socialist Commonwealth' would be laid by what Barker summarises as 'a broad and critical education'. That was quite consistent with the tradition of liberal education in which reason and learning were seen as the most effective means of creating responsible citizens, more consistent with liberal principles than anything more deliberately intended. This rejoinder was, then, a reassertion of socialist faith in the social efficacy of Enlightenment reason. That marked the end of any sustained attempt to commit Labour to an explicitly socialist curriculum. At the 1927 annual conference the reference to bias in the curriculum in the 1926 resolution was removed, and the Teachers' Labour League had been expelled because it had become a front for communist infiltration of the Labour Party. Barker concludes that, thereafter, 'what little interest there had been within the party in the ideological character of school curricula disappeared' (Barker, 1972: 152).

Thus policy on the curriculum in the 1920s moved forward largely on a trajectory that owed little directly to Labour thought, and to which Labour discussions related in a largely uncritical fashion. The general question of curricular change arose in the context of the expansion of secondary education between the early years of the century and the eve of the Second World War. Essentially three models for the curriculum of post-primary education were available. One was that in the English Public Schools; at the other extreme was the curriculum in the low-status extensions of elementary education; and in the middle, but closer to the first than to the second, were various attempts to widen access meritocratically to a liberal academic curriculum.

The classical liberal curriculum in the Public Schools was of the kind that had been created by Thomas Arnold and by the report of the Clarendon Commission in 1864, leading to the addition by the end of the century of modern languages, science and mathematics, but with the focus still on Latin and Greek (Gordon, 2002: 187). On the whole, the academic grammar schools in England conformed to that pattern, as the Public Schools became what Steedman (1987) has called the 'defining institutions' of secondary education. The way in which that came about was essentially the report of the Taunton Commission in 1868, shaping the curricula for various kinds of professional career, but ultimately drawing on the Public School model. These grammar schools were academically selective, in a process which gradually became more formalised up to the 1930s, and were a mixture of schools that had been created by public authorities and those which existed outside public management but which did not have the financial endowments (or indeed the status) to develop in their own way (McCulloch, 2002: 33). Modelling the curriculum of both the grammar schools and these endowed schools on that of the Public Schools was encouraged by the influential Robert Morant, at the Board of Education, whose own classical education at Winchester (one of the Public Schools) and Oxford had encouraged him to see a traditional kind of liberal education as the model for any kind of properly secondary education, an education in leadership (Gordon, 2002: 189–90).

At the other end of the spectrum were the short, vocationally oriented courses for pupils who had not been selected for the academic schools or classes. These courses were mostly added as post-primary departments of elementary schools. They never achieved the educational status of the academic curriculum, and eventually—by the 1950s—were coming to be wholly discredited in socialist eyes; we return to this below. But in the inter-war years there was never any serious doubt in the mainstream of socialist thought that selection was necessary.

The third model—a modernised as well as democratised liberal curriculum—was closer to the academic than the vocational, and in England and Wales was in effect brought to an end by a legal judgement in 1901 that local authorities were not entitled to spend public money on gradually building up academic courses in what were called the 'Higher Grade' schools, which were short-lived attempts to create secondary education out of the unsatisfactory post-primary departments of elementary schools. However, this restriction on the academic development of Higher Grade schools did not apply in Scotland, where that policy attracted such official endorsement (and funding) that by the 1920s the size of the academic secondary sector had quintupled from two decades before. The characteristic curriculum of this sector in Scotland was a reformed liberal programme, centred on English, gradually replacing Latin by French, and bringing in science seriously (Paterson, 2004; 2011). In important respects this Scottish practice was what most socialists were aiming for. The Scottish model was highly meritocratic, and further expansion was restricted by cuts in public expenditure in the 1920s; moreover, the non-academic parts of the Scottish system were as undemanding as their counterparts in England and Wales. But none of the previous Scottish expansion was rescinded, and the selection by merit was thought to be consistent with a Scottish tradition of competitive access to higher learning. In particular, it was not thought necessary to change the character of the curriculum in order to provide such competitive opportunities: liberal education of this modern kind was, in principle, thought suitable in Scotland for everyone who was judged to have the intellectual capacity to benefit from it. Education in the public parts of the Scottish secondary system was inexpensive, and there were enough free places to meet needs; so the mainstream socialist goal that educational policy meant ensuring that there were no non-educational barriers to an able pupil's progress had to some extent been achieved (though there were nothing like adequate bursaries to compensate for deferring entry to the labour market). These new schools were much broader in their social intake than the older selective schools (Paterson *et al.*, 2011). It was often then thought that the reason why Scotland did not have so well-developed a record of liberal adult education as England was this socially wider base of academic secondary schooling and the concomitant wider base of the universities (Cooke, 2006; Paterson, 2003: Chapter 6).

The complexities of the process of expanding post-primary education are not of direct concern here. What matter are two points. One was that liberal education of an academic kind commanded the highest status even when the post-primary system was expanding. The second was that a form of democratisation and modernisation of that academic tradition was available in Scotland, showing that such widening was feasible without fundamentally restricting the quality of what was on offer—without detracting from its being the best that has been thought and said. In such circumstances, it is not surprising that Labour did not seriously dissent from the liberal tradition, and did not try to interfere with its curricular content. The curricular developments of the 1920s and 1930s were driven by the characteristic British means of reports of independent commissions. The best-informed in these years, and the most subsequently influential, was the Hadow Report of 1926, which was technically a report of the Consultative Committee of the Board of Education chaired by Lord Hadow, vice chancellor of the University of Sheffield (and including Tawney and Mansbridge as members). Commissioning this report was one of the few educational actions of the 1924 Labour government, although it owed as much to moves already under way, and it thus indicates Labour's respect for non-partisan thinking in this respect (Gordon, 2002: 194; Simon, 1974: 116).

On the one hand, Hadow recommended a sharper break between elementary and secondary education, so that secondary education would simply be the name for 'the education of the adolescent' (the title of the report). They also recommended therefore replacing the word 'elementary' by 'primary'. The main division in secondary education would be between academic and non-academic. The staffing ratios of these two should be the same, and the latter should emphasise practical work. On the other hand, the report paid almost as little attention to the details of the academic curriculum as did the Labour Party, and so in effect that curriculum was believed to be the property of academically trained school teachers, constrained only by the syllabuses of external examinations and—more fundamentally—by the academic consensus in each subject of the liberal curriculum. That was even more true of Scotland, to which the Hadow Report did not directly apply, and where there was no analogous official report at all: the newly expanded secondary system there was entirely in the hands of teachers, school inspectors and examination syllabuses, and so the curriculum was very strongly shaped by the character of liberal education as understood in the universities where these educational professionals had been formed (Paterson, 2004; 2011).

Labour's policy on secondary education was then implicitly shaped by its rejection of any interference in the curriculum and by the curricular assumptions which came from the contexts of the recent history of secondary education and by the Hadow committee's report. The document which became the basis of the party's policy for the next half-century was *Secondary Education for All*, ostensibly the work of the education advisory committee of the party but actually written by Tawney. It argued that the opposition to educational expansion was based on five grounds, four of which had nothing directly to do with the curriculum—that it would reduce the supply of cheap juvenile labour, that it would reduce social and economic inequalities, that it would induce people to forget their place in society, and that education 'is a luxury invented by faddists for the advantage of teachers and administrators' (Tawney, 1922: 141–2). The remaining reason did refer to disagreement over the content of education—ignorance of 'what education is and means'. Although the document did not go into details of the curriculum—in keeping with the general disinclination of Labour to do so—it was quite clear that education for all ought to mean something like a liberal education for all. Taking its definition of secondary education from official regulations, it sought merely to extend the 'broad foundations of knowledge' to everyone, which in the terms of these regulations meant that education 'must, in short, be liberal in spirit, must develop so as to keep pace with the development of the pupils, and must retain them sufficiently long to enable the course not merely to be a truncated fragment' *(ibid.*: 29). All that it had to say about any details beyond that was to endorse current curricular requirements (*ibid.*: 30). Praising moves in Kent and in Darlington to strengthen technical education, it insisted nevertheless that making the curriculum more 'realistic' ought not to interfere with these liberal principles: 'in all cases the basis of the curriculum will consist of English, history, geography, mathematics, science, handicrafts (for girls domestic subjects), and physical education' (*ibid.*: 106–7). It was not acceptable to argue, as London County Council did, that commercial and technical education should be designed 'with a view to enabling the pupils to pass direct into commercial or industrial pursuits' (*ibid.*: 109). This would lead, the Labour document argued, to 'a cheap and mutilated alternative to secondary education' (*ibid.*: 111). Whatever the future employment of pupils, they ought to follow a broad, general education: their eventual economic place in society 'is very largely irrelevant to the question of the curriculum suitable for them' (*ibid.*: 112).

All this widening of access to liberal education would take place within a largely undisturbed hierarchy of schools and of courses, since it was from the highest end of this range that such a curriculum derived its meaning:

> The demand of Labour for the democratising of secondary education implies no wish to sacrifice the peculiar excellence of particular institutions to a pedantic State-imposed uniformity, still less to forgo the amenities of culture for the sake of a utilitarian efficiency. (*ibid.*: 30)

Like Percy Nunn (and echoing Matthew Arnold), the document argued that the working class have been less philistine than 'many whose educational opportunities have been greater'. The aim in secondary education should be accessibility not uniformity: 'what is weak in the higher [i.e. secondary] education of the country should be strengthened and... what is already excellent should be made accessible to all' (*ibid.*: 30).

In this we see the emerging link in Labour thinking between cultural selection and social hierarchy, the latter thought to be essential to maintain cultural standards. Labour's policy was for equal opportunities, not even remotely for equal outcomes, support for which would have been regarded as utopian naïvety. The main mechanism was to make secondary education free (Francis, 1995: 325). Until much later, there was not even any firm commitment to common schools for all. Francis (1995: 325) notes that Tawney was particularly influential in this respect:

> The popularity and influence of the 'patron saint of British Socialism' on a whole generation of labour intellectuals and activists cannot be over-estimated.

If Tawney was the apostle, *Secondary Education for All,* with its commitment to a liberal education defined by an inherited structure of knowledge—and given dignity by a hierarchy of educational institutions—was the bible.

In the public debate which followed this and Hadow, Labour had to respond to the accusation that they were trying to impose an inappropriately academic curriculum on pupils for whom it was not suitable. Stanley Baldwin, for example—newly chosen as leader of the Conservative Party—said in 1923 that it is unwise 'to give everybody a secondary education. It is no good forcing every kind of ability into one form of education if the result is going to be to lower the standard which it is the interest of the country to maintain' (Simon, 1974: 127). So one reason why Labour came to be committed to a variety of kinds of school and of courses was in response to this criticism: they had still not found a way of developing a version of liberal education that might suit everyone, and in the meantime they did not want to undermine the quality of the academic interpretation of liberal education which predominated. To have weakened it, after all, would have been to have removed from working-class pupils who might be given access to selective academic courses the very cultural prize which, Labour believed, ought to be spread to many more people who could benefit from it. In consequence, support for what Lawson and Silver (1973: 392–3) call 'diverse forms of secondary education for all children' prevailed 'in the labour movement until after the middle of the century'.

Respect for liberal education thus persisted through two minority Labour governments and the very great turmoil of politics in the 1930s. Apart from commissioning the report from the Hadow Committee, the only significant educational action of the 1924 government was to introduce new, liberal guidelines for adult education, which enabled the W.E.A.'s approach to be strengthened through its underpinning by state grants (Blyth, 1983: 50). There was also some progress on creating the material conditions that might help to make a reality of equal opportunity—moves towards raising the minimum leaving age, and some funding for free places in secondary education, better buildings, smaller classes, better school meals and scholarships for able pupils to remain in school beyond the leaving age (Simon, 1974: 78–84).

Much the same was true of the 1929 government before the crisis of 1931 which split Labour, with the Prime Minister and the Chancellor of the Exchequer leading a minority into an unprecedented National Government, in coalition with the Conservatives and the Liberals. Before the Labour government collapsed, Trevelyan, as President of the Board of Education, managed to get an increase in the number of free places available in secondary schools in England and Wales, and outlined ideas for what it called 'a unified system of post-primary education' (Simon, 1974: 154). There was some curricular debate about this, in that officials at the Board (as Simon puts it) displayed 'the rooted belief that the main task [was] to maintain the academic curriculum inviolate which in turn necessitates a separate institution' (Simon, 1974: 156). The Chief Inspector for Secondary Schools had said that providing courses for all children should not be allowed 'to weaken the quality of the secondary schools' (Simon, 1974: 155). Again, though, the most revealing point about this disagreement was Labour's attachment to that curriculum and its principal vehicle in the secondary schools, as well as its belief that access to it could be democratised. The MP James Chuter Ede, who led the development of Labour's policies when the party was in opposition in the 1930s, said in 1929 that

> if we are to have a democracy capable of shouldering this great burden [of responsibility for decisions that used to be relegated to the few], I am quite sure that it can only be done through giving to the children of all classes of the community a greater opportunity of entering into those great heritages of literature, of art and of beauty that should enrich the lives of the community. (quoted by Barker, 1972: 139–40)

The Labour government of 1945

The majority Labour government of 1945 gave the party an opportunity to implement its ideas relating to education. Its actions have generally been seen by later commentary as a betrayal of socialist principles, in that it did not introduce comprehensive education, and if anything entrenched a selective system in which the main division was between academic and non-academic courses. In England and Wales, these were located in grammar schools and secondary modern schools. In Scotland, there was an analogous division between senior secondary and junior secondary schools, although it was in one sense less rigid insofar as there were non-academic streams in most of the senior secondary schools, where all pupils thus benefited from the generally academic training of the teachers there (Paterson, 2011; Paterson *et al.*, 2011). Such schools, when they took all the children from a neighbourhood, were referred to as 'omnibus schools'. In England there were also technical schools, but they were never adopted to any widespread extent.

It was true that, in endorsing such a division into streams, Labour was following a policy that had been endorsed by all the major official reports on secondary education since the First World War. Hadow essentially evaded the issue, as Simon puts it (Simon, 1974: 127), re-labelling all post-primary courses as 'secondary' without seriously thinking through what that meant. A report in 1938 of the Board's Consultative Committee on Secondary Education led by Sir Will Spens (vice chancellor of the University of Cambridge) argued that

> a single liberal or general education for all is impracticable, and... varying forms of both general and quasi-vocational education have to be evolved in order to meet the needs of boys and girls, differing widely in intellectual and emotional capacity. (Board of Education, 1938: 2)

Nevertheless, it did recommend common standards of finance, and of teachers, an end to fees and a raising of the leaving age to 16 (from 14) (Simon, 1974: 261). Moreover, as we have seen in Chapter 1, it began to foreshadow a role for English, as a subject, that might provide a humane centre of the curriculum—the kind of cultural focus that F.R. Leavis encouraged. This committee included among its members Shena Simon, who was emerging as an influential figure in Labour debates about education. An even stronger endorsement of a divided system came with the report of a committee chaired by Sir Cyril Norwood, who had been headmaster of Bristol Grammar School. It rather rigidly discerned three types of mind for which would be required three kinds of school—those 'interested in learning for its own sake', those 'whose interests and abilities lie markedly in the field of applied science or applied art' and those whose mind 'deals more easily with concrete things than with ideas' (Norwood: 2–4). Lawson and Silver (1973: 422) point out that the report, unlike Spens's, 'was concerned not with evidence but with assertion'.

In this context, Labour's decision to opt for a selective system might seem cautiously conservative, merely acquiescing in a consensus that had been created before it came to office: the major piece of legislation that sanctioned the tripartite system in England and Wales was in fact passed in 1944 by the wartime coalition, and steered through parliament by the Conservative President of the Board of Education, R.A. Butler (though also shaped strongly by his under-secretary, Chuter Ede; Morgan, 1984: 174). And yet that was not how it was seen by all but a tiny minority of Labour activists at the time. The way to understand this is not in terms of betrayal of socialist principle but rather because socialist principle, as then interpreted, meant offering liberal education to working-class children who were judged to be capable of benefiting, and—prior to that—maintaining in existence a rigorous liberal education so as to make such access worth having. As Francis puts it:

> The great majority [of members of the Labour Party] believed that Labour's decision to implement a tripartite, rather than a comprehensive, system of secondary education would secure the achievement of both 'free secondary education for all' and 'equality of educational opportunity', which they felt were far more vital components in Labour's education policy than the idea of a 'common school for all'. (Francis, 1995: 319)

The shaping set of principles remained *Secondary Education for All*, with its tacit assumption that there would continue to be different kinds of secondary-school course providing for different kinds of pupil: it had said that 'equality of educational provision is not identity of educational provision' (Tawney, 1922: 66). Insofar as there was any pressure on the government for specific aspects of educational reform, it had little bearing on the structure of schooling or on the curriculum: these were taken as given. For example, one forum for such pressure was the Council for Educational Advance, set up under the auspices of the Workers' Educational Association in 1942 (Brooks, 1977). It was chaired by Tawney, and included among its members Richard Crossman (later MP) and Shena Simon. It had influential public support from notable left-wing figures, such as William Temple (now Archbishop of Canterbury) and Sir Walter Citrine, General Secretary of the Trades Union Congress. Among its active members was the Labour MP Arthur Creech Jones, who was parliamentary private secretary to Ernest Bevin, Minister of Labour in the coalition government (and Foreign Secretary in the 1945 government).

The main aim of the Council was the extension of opportunities, described as 'immediate legislation to provide equality of educational opportunity for all children, irrespective of their social or economic condition in order to equip them for a full life and democratic citizenship' (Brooks, 1977: 43). It expanded this to 12 specific objectives, which are firmly within the Labour tradition of seeking to remove practical obstacles to working-class pupils' capacity to take advantage of any opportunities that might be offered:

> 1. The raising of the school leaving age to 15 without exemptions by the end of the war and to 16 not more than three years later. 2. Free education under a single secondary code for all children after the primary stage. 3. Common standards of staffing, equipment and amenities in all schools. 4. Adequate provision of nursery schools and classes. 5. Free medical services and school meals. 6. Maintenance allowances for children in all post primary schools. 7. Day Continued education for all between 16 and 18. 8. Prohibition of employment below the school leaving age and control by education authorities. 9. The licensing and inspection of any schools outside the national system. 10. A unified system of administration to replace the dual control of schools. 11. Free access to universities and Higher Technical Colleges for all who can benefit thereby. 12. Ample provision for adult education. (quoted by Brooks, 1977: 43)

Its specific lobbying in connection with the Bill that became the 1944 Education Act was based on these goals (Brooks, 1977: 46). There are a few implicit references to the curriculum in the list, but they would tend to strengthen the tendency towards endorsing a liberal curriculum of a traditional kind: for example, the point about common staffing standards would ensure academically qualified staff in all kinds of school, and thus would tend to move the non-academic streams towards those of the grammar schools. In their lobbying for the 1944 Act, the Council also pushed for a strengthening of the requirements that young people who had left school must be enabled by employers to attend junior colleges providing vocational education. But in a sense this, too, might have been expected to have strengthened the scope for schools to base their curriculum on liberal principles, since the expectation that all young people who were not destined for the universities or the professions would attend technical colleges after they had left school would free the schools from having to provide such training. In none of these deliberations in this influential body of Labour activists was there any interest in challenging the status or nature of the liberal academic curriculum, nor in questioning the selective system of schooling which was believed to underlie its integrity. In taking that position, they were close to mainstream Labour opinion for which the grammar school was the route to that intellectual accomplishment which was believed necessary for effective government. Morgan notes 'Labour's instinctive faith in the grammar schools, the bright working-class child's alternative to Eton and Winchester' (Morgan, 1984: 174).

Something the same was true of Labour's view of the independent schools, the abolition of which would have been regarded on most of the liberal left as cultural vandalism. The question was not what went on inside them but who got the chance to benefit. Peggy Jay (a prominent Labour intellectual and a councillor in London) argued in 1949 in the left-wing periodical *Tribune*, for example, that

> we are often warned of the dangers of a school composed of high academic children alone. My own view is that if the group were a democratically selected one the dangers would be negligible in practice and the advantages enormous. (quoted by Dean, 1986: 114)

C.M. Joad argued that independent schools should be taken over by the state and used as boarding schools for able pupils aged 16–18 (Joad, 1945: 118). Richard Crossman wrote in the other leading left-wing weekly, the *New Statesman*, in 1949:

> The Public Schools are not merely 'snob' schools; they fulfil the function of educating a responsible elite. This function is necessary in any modern State. What is needed, therefore, is not to abolish them, or turn them into super-State schools for the cleverest boys, but to break the link between elite education and personal wealth, and so make it compatible with Social-Democracy. (Crossman, 1949)

It was important, he said, 'not to level down', because these elite schools provided absolute standards of scholarship in 'the humanist tradition' which had to be preserved if widening opportunity was to mean anything at all:

> Social justice demands that the best education should be available to the best, irrespective of class, provided that the measures taken to ensure social justice do not destroy the quality of education.

Clement Attlee, likewise, said in 1946 (when prime minister) at his old school, the highly selective Haileybury:

> This country changes, but it is our way to change things gradually, and I see no reason for thinking that the public schools will disappear. I think the great tradition will carry on. Maybe they will even be extended. (quoted by Francis, 1995: 335)

The key phrases here for interpreting such admiration for the independent schools are 'great tradition', 'educating a responsible elite' and 'democratically selected': it was the tradition of intellect that was respected, not the socially selective function, which was in fact explicitly deplored.

The main target of subsequent criticism of Labour's education policies in 1945 was Ellen Wilkinson, Minister of Education until her death in 1947. She had impeccable socialist credentials—prominent on the left of the party since the 1920s, MP for north-of-England constituencies, one of the leaders of the 'Jarrow crusade' of 1936 (when unemployed people from her constituency of that name marched the 300 miles to London to protest against the lack of attention by the government to the plight of the economically depressed areas), one of the first female MPs (in 1924) and one of the first female ministers (Parliamentary Secretary to the Minister of Health in the 1929 government, and to the Minister of Pensions and then to the Home Secretary in the wartime coalition). As Minister of Education in 1945 she was only the second woman to have been a cabinet member (after Margaret Bondfield, Minister of Labour in the 1929 government). She was also well-connected on the intellectual left: she was admired by Harold Laski, and had been active in the Left Book Club. Her book about Jarrow—*The Town that was Murdered*—was the monthly selection in September 1939 (thought it was not as popular as less polemically left-wing pieces; Rose, 2002: 252). She was on the board of *Tribune* when it was launched in 1937, and she wrote frequently for it.

Yet equally important in understanding Wilkinson's actions in government are her views about what should be learnt by pupils. She admired liberal education as firmly as anyone we have been examining here. Her biographer comments that 'respect for education was part of the Methodist tradition' in which she was raised. She had that self-directed liberal education which Rose notes of so many able working-class children of the late-nineteenth and early-twentieth centuries: Dickens, Shakespeare, public libraries. In office, some of her strongest resentment was against attempts by officials to exclude working-class pupils from that liberal tradition. Dean notes that 'a vocational, practical schooling which was to contain large doses of work experience angered her' (Dean, 1986: 99), and so, in 1946—as Minister—she wrote what he calls 'a half serious, half mocking memorandum ("Ellen Wilkinson from the standpoint of a backbench MP")' to counter their views. In this, she asked sardonically about what she regarded as the misplaced fears of labour supply that might result from providing a proper secondary education for all:

> What shall we have to do to get miners and agricultural workers if 100% of the children who were able to profit are offered real secondary education? Answer give the real stuff to the select 25%, steer the 75% away from the humanities, pure science, even history. (Dean, 1986: 99)

She continued that the official view 'wants to take away the French and make the child scrub in school as well as at home' (Dean, 1986: 107). In the light of such strong polemic—and of the politically risky path of publishing such a pamphlet while still a Minister (a move inconceivable today)

—it is also hardly plausible that the reason she accepted a divided secondary system was her being in awe of the permanent officials in the ministry, and indeed she also successfully challenged their opposition to raising the school leaving age to 15 (which happened in 1947).

So the most plausible interpretation of Wilkinson's policies is the same as for Labour's attitudes in the whole period since the 1920s. Liberal education was admired, access to it had to be widened, but if anything was done to weaken its integrity—such as by abolishing the selective academic track altogether—it would cease to be worth having. Wilkinson continued to insist—as many of the socialist intellectuals whom we discussed in Chapter 2 insisted—that what a pupil learnt and where they would earn their living as an adult were quite different things. Thus, on the one hand, the Labour government could be pleased that it was removing obstacles in the way that the Labour movement had always sought to do. Wilkinson said in 1946 that

> by abolishing fees in maintained schools we have ensured that entry to those schools shall be on the basis of merit. No one can truly say that grammar schools are being filled with children from a privileged social class.

On the other hand, this was about opportunities, not compulsion: 'not everyone wants an academic education', and it was unconnected to any personal economic benefit:

> Coal has to be mined and fields ploughed, and it is a fantastic idea that we have allowed, so to speak, to be cemented into our body politic, that you are in a higher social class if you add up figures in a book than if you plough the fields and scatter the good seed on the land. (quoted by Rubinstein and Simon, 1969: 38)

In the context of the preceding sentence about merit, that has to be read as implying that the intrinsic worth of the education that was offered must not be judged by the class position of those who benefited culturally from it. In her 1946 polemic, Wilkinson asked if school might not be the source of a cultural awakening which could compensate for the drudgery of the work that most children were destined for. She was contemptuous of wasting time on ostensibly vocational skills in schools for those who would leave at age 15, what she described as '[boys'] building pig styes, or making beehives and wheelbarrows and... girls' doing laundry work or catering' (quoted by Vernon, 1982: 222–3):

> Can't their three precious years of secondary school be at least a relief from all *that*? [Wilkinson's emphasis]... Can't Shakespeare mean more than a scrubbing brush—can't enough of a foreign language be taught to open windows on the world a bit wider—I learnt French verbs saying them as I scrubbed floors at home.

Though education as a route to upward social mobility came to be a commonly accepted aim of the left in the post-war years, and became almost the only goal by the end of the century (as we will see in Chapter 7), such a criterion would be anachronistic if applied to perceptions in or before the 1940s. Indeed, as we noted, it had attracted Tawney's derision as the 'tadpole philosophy'.

Wilkinson's ultimate aim—thoroughly in keeping with the tradition of liberal education—was to use it to create a new democratic civilisation. In a speech in Parliament in 1946 praising the founding of the United Nations Educational, Scientific and Cultural Organisation, she said that

> we are trying to build up out of poverty and misery... so that U.N.E.S.C.O. shall raise the banner of what I believe is the essential thing... the sense that there are such things as standards, that there is a difference between right and wrong, that intellectual needs are not luxuries. Unless we can put standards of values into the minds of youth we cannot have a great civilisation or a great country. (quoted by Vernon, 1982: 213)

To her and her generation this was more than merely a partisan socialist project, and indeed their understanding of socialism was as the means by which everyone could be enabled to take part in these general human debates. That meant raising the cultural standard of the whole electorate, as Matthew Arnold foresaw and as George Tomlinson, Wilkinson's successor as Minister of Education, put it in 1947: 'if we want an alternative to the football pools, we should fill people's minds with something worth thinking about' (Barker, 1972: 154). There was a sense at this time, too, that the shared experience of war had made people more aware of the shared heritage of liberal civilisation, so that the thinking of T.S. Eliot or of F.R. Leavis ought not to be ignored merely because they were not socialists (Dean, 1986: 116).

There are three points to be made about the retrospective critique of Wilkinson and the attitude towards education of her generation of Labour politicians. The first is that there is a tendency to exaggerate the importance of the far-left opposition at the time. As we have seen, Wilkinson was in the mainstream of the Labour Party, and also on its left. Fenwick notes that at most half a dozen (of nearly 400) Labour MPs then supported comprehensive schools (Fenwick, 1974: 58). The left-wing opposition was visible because of the highly vocal MP W.G. Cove, whose attacks on Wilkinson were so 'savage' and 'spiteful' (Fenwick's and Vernon's terms) that they alienated some of his own potential supporters, such as those MPs who were former teachers (Vernon, 1982: 221). She was attacked also by a small organisation of which Cove was a prominent member, the National Association of Labour Teachers, a direct descendent of the Marxist Teachers' Labour League of the 1920s. At a Labour Party conference in 1950, one of its members argued that

> it would be a supreme tragedy if in the years of socialist government we threw out the devil of class snobbery and allowed the worse devil of intellectual snobbery to creep in in its place. (quoted by Francis, 1995: 323)

But that was wholly untypical when Wilkinson's policy of not introducing comprehensive schools was supported not only by nearly all Labour MPs and by the Council of Educational Advance, but also by the Fabian Society, the Workers' Educational Association and the Trades Union Congress (Francis, 1995: 323–4). As Francis notes, indeed, the National Association of Labour Teachers was itself ambivalent, accepting in 1947 that grammar schools had set the standards in the state system and were 'the means whereby the gifted children of the common people have broken into the fortresses of educational privilege' (quoted by Francis, 1995: 329). They thus argued that the grammar school ought to form the model on which a comprehensive-school curriculum would be based.

The second problem with the later criticisms of Labour's education policy in the 1940s and earlier is related to this last point—the allegation that, in largely ignoring the curriculum, Labour was culpable as opposed to admirable for not interfering with the liberal tradition. For example, the Centre for Contemporary Cultural Studies argued in a book published 1981 that the Labour Party's view of the content of education, based on 'Tawney's discussions of content, control and context[,] were... cursory' (Centre for Contemporary Cultural Studies, 1981: 43). They continued in a vein that is not dissimilar to the Marxist analysis that came from the Labour Colleges:

> No positive conception of education was forthcoming to place in opposition to capitalist imperatives, only a conception of culture, which Tawney inherited from Matthew Arnold, which was presented as being outside or above classes. (*ibid.*: 44)

What was certainly absent from Labour views was any sense that the cultural tradition of liberal education was in itself the problem. That critique is telling, however, only if its premises are accepted—only if liberal education is indeed inimical to the kind of liberation which socialism sought. We discuss this view—and in particular the educational views associated with cultural studies, which emerged in the 1960s—in Chapter 6, but what can be said here is that, when Wilkinson entered government, it was such a minority view that it would have been utterly eccentric of her and her colleagues to have pandered to it. As we have seen, respect for liberal education was the very essence of socialist understanding of the curriculum throughout the first half of the century.

The third aspect of the later criticisms of Wilkinson is in a sense the most trivial, in that it is (like Cove's attacks) *ad hominem*, but it reveals a deeper point about the descent of later left-wing thought into relativism—into the belief that universal truths do not exist and that everyone is a prisoner of their upbringing or social position. These views are close to the belief that no culture is universal and that cultural practices—such as a curriculum—are inevitably tied to social-class or other vested interests. Typical of these later comments on Wilkinson is this:

> Being a successful product of the system it is possibly not surprising that Ellen Wilkinson believed in it; like many other Labour politicians of all periods she thought in terms of equality of competition rather than equality of access. (Rubinstein, 1979: 161–2)

He extends this to her personal morality:

> Large numbers of children languished in secondary modern schools because of the Minister's belief in fighting one's way. (*ibid.*: 163)

Simon, likewise, somewhat cynically attributes Wilkinson's views to her individual experience of gaining power: 'even Labour politicians may be recruited to support selective schooling of the kind which started them on the way to ministerial posts' (Simon, 1974: 284). Chitty (1989: 25) then repeats that.

Francis responds to Rubinstein that 'such a remark is both unfair and misleading', and notes that George Tomlinson, Wilkinson's successor, was not a product of a grammar school and yet believed in their worth (Francis, 1995: 328–9). The critique of Wilkinson is largely beside the point, like all attempts to discredit a position by discrediting its supporters: the possibility of truth independently of who makes the claim is something that even the critics implicitly accept, unless their claims, too, are to be reduced to their own personal trajectories. But more serious than that debating point is that these Labour politicians would never have accepted the relativist premise, and indeed that they had learnt the principle of universal reason from the liberal education which they admired. Their faith in that education was based on premises which they believed could be shared, and which—as we saw from the socialist intellectuals of this same period—were believed to be the very essence of civilisation. They may have been wrong in believing that only a selective system could maintain the liberal education that inculcated these principles into each succeeding generation, but, if so, they were wrong for reasons of evidence and reason, not for reasons of identity and emotion.

Chapter 4

Liberal Education and Mass Society

Two post-war socialist intellectuals had something of the same stature in debate about education as Tawney, Laski and Cole, and reached somewhat the same kind of audience: Raymond Williams and Richard Hoggart. They belong to the same intellectual tradition as these predecessors, and indeed were shaped in significant respects by reaction to the same cultural milieu—the ideas of Leavis and of Arnold, and the ethical socialism deriving ultimately from T.H. Green. Their writing, starting in the 1950s, was infused with post-war idealism which then merged into the beginning of the utopian radicalism of the 1960s, and was grounded—as had been Tawney's, Laski's and Cole's—in the experience of teaching classes of adult education. In the words of Collini (1999: 255), 'the enabling circumstances owed much to the conjunction of the idealism of post-war adult education and the optimism of the early New Left.' Yet their development can provide a general introduction to the eventual demise of that tradition on the left, and indeed the contrasting ways in which these two men responded to the social change and changing character of politics in the half century after 1945 are an indication of the tradition's fracturing. That they had—as we shall see in later chapters—an influence on left-wing thought about education as great as their inter-war forebears is reason enough to examine their ideas. That they also—again like these earlier thinkers—were significant far beyond the left is a mark of the vitality which socialist thought continued to draw, in the 1950s, from the wider intellectual culture.

Raymond Williams

Williams is often described as a literary critic or a social historian (Smith, 2009), both of which he was, but the tradition to which he belonged—the one that we have been analysing here—interpreted both of these ways of thinking about society as being centrally concerned with education, with deciding who was to be taught what. He was born in 1921, near Abergavenny on the border between Wales and England. After graduating from Cambridge University, he worked as an adult-education tutor in Oxford University's extra-mural department. In 1961 he became a lecturer in English at Cambridge, and was appointed professor of drama there in 1974. He published widely—books, chapters, newspaper reviewing, contributions to broadcasting. In the words of Smith (2009): 'the whole corpus... established him, in his own lifetime, as a major socialist thinker.' He was, Collini (1999: 219) noted, a 'general intellectual of the Left'.

His first book, *Drama from Ibsen to Brecht* (1952), created his reputation as a literary critic drawing on Leavis but on the left of that movement, proposing that cultural understanding is dependent upon the opportunities with which audiences are provided (Smith, 2009). His next two books developed the analyses of cultural and social change with which he became identified: *Culture and Society* (1958) was an examination of the social basis of those ideas which Arnold and his successors had made the central focus of debate about education; *The Long Revolution* (1961) explicitly placed the development of ideas about culture in the context of educational reform in Britain since the industrial revolution. His combination of social and cultural criticism was summed up by Smith (2009): 'the techniques of modern technology, advertising, and mass communications were, in a number of suggestive books, analysed as carefully as poems and novels had once been.' As a result, his work 'can be seen now as the main progenitor of the cultural studies which would flourish from the late 1960s'. We return to this point in Chapter 6 because cultural studies eventually departed sharply from the tradition to which Williams was heir.

Williams's premise was shared with all the socialist intellectuals whom we have discussed—that a common culture was desirable and feasible, and indeed was one of the main aims for which socialists should work. 'The practical liberty of thought and expression', he wrote, 'is less a natural right than a common necessity' (Williams, 1963: 320). No social class, he said, ought to arrogate to itself 'the right to determine' how understanding is to advance. The very idea of culture implied action and thus politics, not the mere passive acceptance of a tradition: 'the idea of a common culture brings together... at once the idea of natural growth and that of its tending.' Imagining that culture would be acquired spontaneously—merely grow naturally—was 'romantic individualism'; supposing that it was solely a product of politics or of specific policy led to 'a type of authoritarian training'. The challenge was thus to understand both that culture developed quite independently of political programmes, but also that, without deliberate political intervention, it risked being tied to the privileges of a dominant class. The premise, though, was that the cultural inheritance was common, and the indictment is that it currently is not, in an echo of Arnold:

> The whole tradition of what has been thought and valued, a tradition which has been abstracted as a minority possession, is in fact a common human inheritance. (Williams, 1968: 32)

So Williams's intellectual project may be understood as an attempt to disentangle the two—the valuable tradition from the accretion of social characteristics that prevented its being available to all, and indeed which gave to culture the aura of being intrinsically rather than contingently inaccessible. Thus, he said, 'the most difficult task confronting us, in any period where there is a marked shift of social power, is the complicated process of revaluation of the inherited tradition' (Williams, 1963: 309). This was, he noted, an extraordinarily difficult task, one that admitted of no simple political slogans. Consider, for example, the matter of linguistic register, readily thought of in left-wing debate as being about dialect as against a standard literary form which owes its power only to class and economics. 'Yet, while this is true, the matter is complicated by the fact that in a society where a particular class and hence a particular use of the common language is dominant, a large part of the literature, carrying as it does a body of vital common experience, will be attracted to the dominant language mode', not constrained by it but expressing common experience in a language that is not spontaneously common to everyone (*ibid.*: 310).

Williams thus found the work of Matthew Arnold recurrently fascinating and challenging. Arnold had set the terms of the debate that commanded attention even from those who did not share his hostility to socialism. Williams agreed with Arnold's distaste for any tendency to reduce education to mere training (*ibid.*: 121). He admired Arnold's critique of laissez-faire liberalism, 'of the deficiencies of the gospel of "doing as one likes"' (*ibid.*: 127), and, socialist though he was, Williams saw this not only as a disagreement with an ephemeral state of affairs—'a period in which the freedom of one group of people to do as they liked was being challenged by that much larger group who were being done by as others liked' (*ibid.*: 127)—but also timelessly, what Williams referred to as 'the traditional idea of man's business as the "pursuit of perfection"'.

The liberalism of Arnold was 'humane', following his father's goal that the 'object [of society] is to provide for the common good of all' (*ibid.*: 124). Thus, although Matthew Arnold was reacting with alarm to working-class agitation, his response was optimistic rather than contemptuous, because he, too, found the existing capitalist order insufferable. Williams reminds us that 'getting to know... the best that has been thought and said', if truncated at that point, is not an adequate summary of Arnold's position, 'as if perfection were to be striven for merely by "getting to know"': 'Arnold intends this only as a first stage, to be followed by the re-examination of "stock notions and habits"' (*ibid.*: 124). Such a liberalism also was open to the idea of the State as the embodiment of 'our best self', institutions created by 'persons who are mainly led, not by their class spirit, but by a general humane spirit, by the love of human perfection' (quoted by Williams from *Culture and Anarchy*). The means to that end would be 'education, poetry and criticism' (*ibid.*: 130).

All of this, though presented as an account of Arnold's thought, is also a declaration of belonging to that tradition. Williams's dissent was not from fundamental ideas but on account of the changed times: in that sense, the Marxism which Williams also espoused gave him an understanding not that ideas were mere epiphenomena of class or of the stage of economic development, but more subtly that one of the prime tasks of the critic was to distinguish between those ideas which transcended such limits and those which were among the 'stock habits' that Arnold astutely questioned. Culture is not at all to be reduced to material circumstances, but is rather our response to these: 'the history of the idea of culture is a record of our reactions, in thought and feeling, to the changed conditions of our common life' (*ibid.*: 285). The socialist Williams, as much as the Victorian liberal Arnold, valued the autonomous realm of ideas, capable of being shared by everyone.

'Arnold', Williams thus argued, 'was caught between two worlds.' He accepted reason as the basis of all valid political debate—'the critic and destroyer of institutions.' Yet Arnold also wanted something beyond this: 'he not only holds to this, but snatches also towards an absolute' (*ibid.*: 136). Williams's response to the dilemma is inescapably in terms of what education might achieve in the way of generating a common culture, which he takes from Arnold too. 'Others had argued for a new national education, but none with the authority or effect of Arnold', in large measure not because of any aspect of Arnold's theory but simply because Arnold was an experienced educational professional of the Victorian age: '*Culture and Anarchy*, in fact, needs to be read alongside the reports, minutes, evidence to commissions and specifically educational essays which made up so large a part of Arnold's working life' (*ibid.*: 128).

Williams points out that Arnold's apprehension of anarchy from the assertion of the working class as a full part of democratic society had been, in the long run, misplaced:

> The most remarkable facts about the British working-class movement, since its origin in the Industrial Revolution, are its conscious and deliberate abstention from general violence, and its firm faith in other methods of advance. These characteristics of the British working class have not

> always been welcome to its more romantic advocates, but they are a real human strength, and a precious inheritance. (*ibid.*: 133)

Arnold's fears owed too much to Burke, in his expectation of what Williams paraphrases as 'the trampling down of learning by the irruption of the "swinish multitude"' (*ibid.*: 313). The attachment of British working-class politics to the idea of a common culture transcending class is seen most prominently, Williams says, in its view of education, especially since the very large growth of the resources and power of the state in the middle of the twentieth century:

> The working-class movement... has never sought to destroy the institutions of this kind of culture; it has, on the contrary, pressed for their extension, for their wider social recognition, and, in our own time, for the application of a larger part of our material resources to their maintenance and development. Such a record will do more than stand comparison with that of the class by which the working class has been most actively and explicitly opposed. (*ibid.*: 314)

Williams and education

Williams's most sustained analysis of the history of educational policy therefore sought to distinguish between those motives for expansion that were tightly tied to the existing social order and those which were open to appropriation by radical socialist politics. He noted that there had been three main motives for reform since the middle of the nineteenth century, linked to what he saw more fundamentally as three purposes of education that have been held throughout the ages—'training for a vocation, training to a social character, and training a particular civilisation' (Williams, 1961: 148). The first two are indeed products of 'a particular system of values', training for acceptance of the existing social system and for the economic roles which people might be expected to play. The social interests furthering these two aims were labelled by Williams respectively as the 'public educators' and the 'industrial trainers'. In that sense, Williams believed, the story of educational reform since the late-nineteenth century was about its being used to avert anarchy, and to contribute to the productive capacity of the economy in such a way as perhaps even to have saved capitalism from collapse. So far, the story might be taken to be a sort of reductive Marxism, although insofar as both camps accepted mass democracy they could not be said to be unyielding defenders of the existing social order. But Williams's third purpose moves away from such easy interpretation: educational reform recurrently also, even when under no direct influence from socialist thought, aimed to pass on 'general knowledge and attitudes' of a kind that would constitute the very essence of being educated, not contingently, not specific to any particular moment in capitalist development, but as 'the best that can be offered to anyone' (*ibid.*: 147). The proponents of this view were labelled by Williams 'old humanists', not necessarily democrats but unable to avoid the general human implications of the culture that they sought to pass on.

What is more, Williams says, the idea of 'general' in the social sense of for everyone ran alongside the changing meaning of 'liberal education' (*ibid.*: 161). In practice, therefore, the public educators were often in alliance with the old humanists. The former gave the latter an awareness of democracy; the humanists held democracy to an awareness not only of tradition but of the democratising potential of tradition. Yet the eventual and still evolving outcome was influenced always by all three. Williams notes, for example, that the old humanists refused science, against the pressure from Huxley (and, we might add, Arnold), but the industrial trainers forced it onto the curriculum in the name of efficiency, and so the concept of a liberal education changed. But the problem remained (in the 1950s) that the full force of the public educators' argument towards democracy had not yet been felt, and the separation between the cultural and the social meaning of 'general education' remained, so that the schools experienced by most pupils provided no access to a full liberal curriculum. That was meant in the sense that pupils who were outside the academic tradition had only very limited access to the liberal tradition, but was true also in that neither the vocational nor the academic curriculum was being modernised, neglecting social science and 'with hardly any attempt to begin either the history and criticism of music and visual art forms, or the criticism of those forms of film, televised drama, and jazz to which every child will go home' (*ibid.*: 172).

Williams therefore adhered to the ideal of a common culture—and to education's potential role in creating and sustaining it—as strongly as anyone in the tradition we have been examining, whether liberals such as Arnold, Huxley and the Leavises or the socialist humanists who were the main focus of our earlier chapters. Williams saw compulsory basic education as providing grounds for what might come next: 'to be able to read and write is a major advance in the possibility of sharing in the general culture of a literate society' (Williams, 1989 [1983]: 212). What he refers to as 'required levels of general culture' ought to be available to all:

> We cannot in our kind of society call an educational system adequate if it leaves any large number of people at a level of general knowledge and culture below that required by a participating democracy. (Williams, 1961: 174)

His outline of what such a culture might mean in detail is then familiar from all the earlier debate: fundamentals of English language and mathematics, 'knowledge of ourselves and our environment' (thus including both social and natural science), the history and criticism of literature and of other arts, practice in 'democratic procedures' and in sources of information relevant to these (such as libraries and the news media) and 'introduction to at least one other culture', partly by visiting other countries (*ibid.*: 174–5). To achieve these goals, Williams had a faith, learnt, he said, from F.R. Leavis, in the 'combination of close verbal analysis and intense moral argument' (Williams, 1989 [1984]: 22). If 'children of only moderate ability' find this difficult, 'the only sensible answer is to give more time, not to dismiss some of the essentials with a resigned regret' (Williams, 1961: 174).

One reason why Williams did not doubt that most people were capable of responding to general culture in this sense was his belief, shaped by experience, that 'culture is ordinary', the title of an essay written in 1958, in which he pointed out that 'talking to my family, to my friends, talking, as we were, about our own lives, about people, about feelings'—the ordinary working-class community in which he grew up—he 'found as much natural fineness of feeling, as much quick discrimination, as much clear grasp of ideas within the range of experience as I have found anywhere', including in the Cambridge in which he was educated (Williams, 2002 [1958]: 99). This then was also his response to the necessary changes to liberal education which he saw 'mass society' as requiring—the society of mass media, mass consumerism, mass democracy. His lessons of close analysis from Leavis remained: 'there are in fact no masses; there are only ways of seeing people as masses' (Williams, 1963: 289). The techniques of mass culture were 'at worst neutral', and could be put to good use; they were not themselves demeaning or harmful to a modernised form of the intellectual rigour and distinction which the tradition of liberal education had bequeathed. He did not accept that the story was only of cultural decline: in an expanding culture, the good and the bad both grow:

> More people than a hundred years ago now listen to bad music, read bad novels, see bad dramatic works, and look at bad visual art, because all of these things have become technically easier to distribute, and leisure to receive them has greatly increased. Yet, also more people than a hundred years ago now listen to good music, read good novels, see good dramatic works, and look at good visual art.

He cites in support 'attendances at concerts, galleries and theatres of all kinds, or the sizes of publishers' editions' (Williams, 1989 [1958]: 95).

Yet he also noted that these new forms of communication and entertainment had changed the context irrevocably. An old conception of 'working-class culture' was dying:

> We can not fairly or usefully describe the bulk of the material produced by the new means of communication as 'working-class culture'. For neither is it by any means produced exclusively for this class, nor, in any important degree, is it produced by them. (Williams, 1963: 306–7)

He could not side unreservedly with the defenders of the tradition from Leavis, absorbed in it though he was, because he believed that they had no sense of the changing material conditions of cultural production—the new mass media as much as the changing economic and social position of the audience, as society democratised but also became subject to new commercial forces. He acknowledged the power of threnodic accounts, noting a 'general sense of a great literate tradition now under major threat', a process breaking the association of 'literacy with high liberal virtues and aspirations'. Any 'simple adhesion to what they call the "classical", a simple affiliation to what they significantly call the "canon"' was, he thought, inadequate to the task now in hand, which was to find new ways of defining liberal education for new times (Williams, 1989 [1985]: 45–6).

Therefore the task of discrimination remained, in a new form, as did the task of distinguishing between invidious social distinction and necessary cultural selection. On the one hand,

> a common culture is not, at any level, an equal culture. Yet equality of being is always necessary to it, or common experience will not be valued. (Williams, 1963: 304–5)

The aspiration to a common culture did not depend on the achievement of material equality, and indeed to see education as having anything directly to do with such more basic kinds of common life would be to distort the value of what is learnt. To achieve a common culture, the educational system, he said, would have to stop 'sorting people... into "educated" people and others, or in other words transmitters and receivers' (Williams, 1968: 30–1). In a passage saying much the same as Tawney's image of struggling tadpoles, Williams says that an 'alternative to solidarity' has been offered in 'the idea of individual opportunity' conceived of as a ladder. 'Yet the ladder is a perfect symbol of the bourgeois idea of society, because, while undoubtedly it offers the opportunity to climb, it is a device which can only be used individually: you go up the ladder alone' (Williams, 1963: 316–7).

The challenge is then, on the other hand, to avoid this individualising of experience while also recognising that 'some activities are better than others'. The teacher has to teach 'the skills of discrimination alongside statements of the conclusions and judgements which have been received, and which have, provisionally, to be used'. Without that sense of discrimination, 'insistence on equality may be, in practice, a denial of value' (Williams, 1963: 305). That will often entail a reversion to standards that have been accepted for centuries: there are continuities which

> do not relate to some unchanging pre-given human nature... —some of the most important based in a relatively unchanged human biological constitution; others in persistent experiences of love and parentage and death, qualified but always present in all social conditions; others again in the facts of human presence in a physical world—with which certain works connect... often apparently beyond the limited fixed ideas of any particular society and time. (Williams, 1989 [1983]: 220)

The task of distinguishing the best may be difficult but is also necessary: Williams was never of the view that 'the major part of our culture, in the sense of intellectual and imaginative work, is to be called, as the Marxists call it, bourgeois' (Williams, 1963: 307). That is partly because much culture comes from a period long before the present class structure came into being, but also because 'even within a society in which a particular class is dominant', people from other classes can 'contribute to the common stock'. The class categories are too crude anyway: those 'who share a common language share the inheritance of an intellectual and literary tradition which is necessarily and constantly revalued with every shift in experience' (*ibid.*: 308).

Richard Hoggart

Hoggart, too, is sometimes thought of as a literary critic, and he was professor of English at Birmingham University from 1962 to 1973. But more than Williams he was primarily an empirical social scientist, of a kind that would probably now be called ethnographic, and the impact of his *The Uses of Literacy* (1957) owed a great deal to its closely observed account of the working-class community in Leeds in which he grew up. He was born there in 1918, and was educated at Leeds University. He taught at Hull University from 1946 to 1959, at Leicester University from 1959 to 1962, and then, during his decade at Birmingham, founded there in 1964 the Centre for Contemporary Cultural Studies, remaining its director until 1969. He, like Williams, was thus one of the sources of ideas about cultural studies, to which we return in Chapter 6. Hoggart became an Assistant Director-General of U.N.E.S.C.O. from 1971 to 1975, and then Warden of Goldsmiths College (in London) from 1976 to 1984. In retirement he continued to write prolifically and to contribute in many other ways, having always been active in diverse public committees such as the Pilkington Committee on Broadcasting (1960–62). He was a member of the Arts Council of Great Britain (1976–81), an adviser to Penguin books and a member (1977–81) of the company which published the *New Statesman*. As well as *The Uses of Literacy*, however, the event that increased his public prominence most markedly was probably his appearance for the defence in the *Lady Chatterley* trial of 1960, when Penguin were prosecuted for alleged obscenity in publishing the novel. Hoggart was judged to be the most effective witness in achieving the acquittal, and thus in freeing British publishing thereafter from censorship. His northern-English identity encapsulated his modest public image, as he much later (in 1993) imagined Penguin's director, Allen Lane, suggesting to himself in deciding whom to propose as a witness: 'I'm going to have someone for the defence who is not posh, not middle-class, not Oxbridge—a sort of sub-fusc [i.e. drab] university lecturer from the provinces' (Lewis, 1993: 329). Hoggart died in 2014.

Hoggart always described himself as being 'on the left' (Ellis, 2008: 199), 'a centre and central Socialist' who was 'unwilling to be reassigned towards the Right by those who are further left', a point in particular concerning his rejection of relativism of judgement to which we shall return. He further situated himself as being a 'non-Christian, ethical socialist', believing in a 'non-utopian' politics which rejects 'all absolutisms, ideologies, single solutions, blueprints and dogmatisms' (quoted by Ellis, 2008: 199). Like Williams, he thus belonged firmly to the tradition we are analysing here, as Collini puts it 'out of Leavis by Orwell' (Collini, 1999: 228). Working in adult education, he took from Leavis a sense of a shared 'community of values' (Collini, 2008: 37), and more generally he was a public intellectual 'tak[ing] for granted the existence of an educated, non-specialist audience that was not confined to an academic discipline' (Collini, 1999: 226).

Collini (1999: 221) notes an important difference from Williams: Hoggart was not a theorist, and owed more to Tawney than to Marx. Williams is better-known internationally because of the theoretical tone of much of his writing, whereas Hoggart remained more firmly grounded in a specifically British culture, what Collini calls 'unpretentious, morally serious, reflective, and... decent' (*ibid.*: 230). In that sense, Hoggart more consistently than Williams enacted Williams's idea that culture is ordinary:

> I have thought of myself as addressing first of all the serious 'common reader' or 'intelligent layman' from any class. By this I do not mean that I have tried to adopt any particular tone of voice, or that I have avoided using any technical terms and all but the most obvious allusions. But I have written as clearly as my understanding of the subject allowed, and used technical terms and allusions only when they seemed likely, once known, to prove helpful and suggestive. (Hoggart, 1957: 9)

Collini sums up the difference by contrasting *Culture and Society* with *The Uses of Literacy*, first published in 1958 and 1957 (Collini, 2008: 51–2). Williams 'explored the way in which a long sequence of writers had sought for some kind of alternative to "the logic of industrial society" in values and concerns that were eventually brought together under the label of "culture"'. Hoggart was more pessimistic, examining how 'populist egalitarianism and material prosperity' had fatally undermined 'an ethic of effort and self-restraint'. We might add specifically for education, then, that Hoggart not only remained closer than Williams to the practice, and the eventual decline, of an old system of adult education, but also articulated wider concerns about the changing nature of the school curriculum, as we shall see later in this chapter. Williams never addressed the question of whether comprehensive secondary schooling and liberal adult education had indeed enabled a common culture to be created, noting only the aspirations to that end. Hoggart reflected on both, and was dismayed.

Nevertheless, in a striking sense Hoggart as much as Williams shared a heritage from Leavis, as has often been pointed out (including by Williams, 1989 [1957]: 24). *The Uses of Literacy* is a direct heir to Q.D. Leavis's *Fiction and the Reading Public*, concerned as both are with the maintenance of standards of thought and of integrity in a context of mass cultural production, but, as Collini notes, not sharing its 'intransigent elitism' (Collini, 1999: 226), or—at this stage in Hoggart's career—its cultural pessimism. One of the continuities with Q.D. Leavis was a less than wholly admiring appreciation of working-class forms of cultural life. If culture was ordinary for Hoggart, it was also lacking in discriminative power as a result:

> With little intellectual or cultural furniture, with little training in the testing of opposing views against reason and existing judgements, judgements are usually made according to the promptings of those group-apophthegms which come first to mind. (Hoggart, 1957: 191)

Theories, political movements or explicit traditions of culture were not highly regarded in these circles, but the attention to detail which a Leavisite reading of a text could encourage might fit the cultural style perfectly:

> They are enormously interested in people: they have the novelist's fascination with individual behaviour, with relationships—though not so as to put them into a pattern, but for their own sake. (*ibid.*: 105–6)

His work thus avoided any easy romanticising of working-class educational engagement by choosing mostly (and not only in *The Uses of Literacy*) not to look at 'the "earnest minority" among working-class people', those who, for example, 'take up voluntary trade-union activity, and those who seek adult education through, for instance, the classes run by the Workers' Educational Association', those who use the public libraries, buy Penguin books or listen to the BBC's Third Programme (*ibid.*: 318–20).

As a result, Hoggart was the first person in this tradition to suggest that working-class people might feel uneasy about a common culture based on the ideas which form the tradition's core. Hoggart discussed the uprootedness of the 'scholarship boy', the working-class child who is selected into academic education and thus is gradually distanced from the cultural milieu of the home:

> At the friction point of two cultures, the test of his real education lies in his ability, by about the age of twenty-five, to smile at his father with his whole face and to respect his flighty young sister and his slower brother. (*ibid.*: 292–3)

But neither does such a person fit comfortably into the class to which he moves:

> He has left his class, at least in spirit, by being in certain ways unusual; and he is still unusual in another class, too tense and over-wound... He is clever enough to take himself out of his class mentally, but not equipped, mentally or emotionally, to surmount all the problems that follow. (*ibid.*: 302–3)

Hoggart explicitly notes how this dilemma is never adequately addressed in the tradition about which he is writing: it is true, he notes, that Arnold comments on the difficulties of those whose intellectual interests 'take them out of their class', making 'their distinguishing characteristic ... their humanity' (Arnold, 1960 [1869]: 108). Hoggart's comment is that 'there is an important truth in the passage', but that 'Arnold's undefined afflatus' – such as in the vagueness of the word 'humanity' – 'never did sound altogether convincing' (Hoggart, 1957: 313). By that, we might understand Hoggart to mean that it does not provide a response sufficient to the task of working out how a common culture might be achieved and of what it would consist.

The challenge of affluence

Nevertheless, these difficulties do not detract from the importance of seeking a common culture, or from its feasibility in principle. Hoggart thus differs fundamentally from those slightly later writers – to be examined in the next chapter – who infer from this disjunction of identities that a common culture is, if not impossible, then at least undesirable ethically because of the 'symbolic violence' it would impose upon working-class people (the term is Pierre Bourdieu's, as we shall discuss). Hoggart departed from the Leavises by confronting the cultural consequences of social change – consequences of a mass society and of growing material well-being – as problems to be solved rather than as mere decline.

Hoggart started by noting that material progress was always likely to be easier to achieve than cultural (Hoggart, 1957: 323). Thus poverty as such was no longer holding people back in education: the selection of children for the academic tracks in secondary school 'may be in many things clumsy', but it was fairer than selection based on wealth, and 'does with a fair measure of success select intellectually agile children'. (On the whole, the evidence suggests this was true of the very able of all classes, though also showing that opportunities for the not very intellectually agile children of the middle class were rather better than they ought to be; Douglas *et al.*, 1966.) Yet Hoggart welcomed the opportunities offered by mass culture rather than deploring them. He acknowledged that mass communication does make 'a great many things into objects of consumption', including books and art. But 'culture as "cultivation"' is distinct from artefacts: it is, rather, 'a training of the intellectual and imaginative life'. Provided it is done well, doing it for more people does not dilute it (Hoggart, 1970 [1965]: 103). Part of the challenge in fact was to re-imagine a common culture that would be maintained by means other than the intellectual:

> The strongest objection to the more trivial popular entertainments is not that they prevent their readers from becoming highbrow, but that they make it harder for people without an intellectual bent to become wise in their own way. (Hoggart, 1957: 338)

In this too Hoggart departs from the tradition—in which the intellect was the admired main route to wisdom—but also would dissent from later writers for whom the morality implicit in the culture of the dominant tradition was as suspect as its intellect.

As so often with the writers whom we have been discussing, Hoggart then comes back to Arnold, not so much for the central content of his cultural prescription—his 'best that has been thought and said'—as for Arnold's ethical standards, his attack on 'doing as one likes', which Hoggart interprets to be as relevant in the middle of the twentieth century as it was a hundred years before (Hoggart, 1957: 176–7):

> Tolerance becomes not so much a charitable allowance for human frailty and the difficulties of ordinary lives, as a weakness, a ceaseless leaking-away of the will-to-decide on matters outside the immediate touchable orbit.

He attributes this to 'a fuzzy form of egalitarianism' (*ibid.*: 289), exemplified most blatantly in writing in the popular newspapers which

> depreciates the value of a fine application of intellectual gifts, the courage to take unsentimental and unpopular positions, a disciplining of the self. The word 'discipline', for example, is almost unusable in popular writing, except in a derogatory sense. (*ibid.*: 187)

These are, he concludes, 'the peculiarly dangerous comforts of unreason'. The situation has come about inadvertently:

> Overweening freedom owes much to the idea that we must try to be responsible for our own fate and decisions; the apparent valuelessness of the permanent open mind rests in part on a refusal to be fanatic. (*ibid.*: 245)

Nevertheless, the challenge of worthwhile cultural selection remains, since it is an urgent task for any democracy seeking to govern itself wisely, and looking for the system of education that will achieve that end. When he explicitly considers this, Hoggart finds himself returning to the same tradition of thought that we have been discussing.

> Before we enjoy a ritual laugh at senior civil servants trained only in the Classics, we ought to reflect... that, whatever its limits, Greats [the Oxford study of classical languages and literature] did give the best men the ability to consider issues broadly and disinterestedly. (Hoggart, 1970 [1967a]: 76–7)

Likewise, Eliot's *Notes Towards the Definition of Culture* 'is one of the most formidable modern statements of the conservative case about culture and can't be cavalierly answered' (Hoggart, 1970 [1967b]: 119). He considers what in the middle-class home is or is not consistent with a common educated culture: what is unfair privilege, and what are the universally valuable elements of culture? Buying a private education, for example, is not such a thing: it is, he says, unwarranted privilege. But books, 'articulate conversation', 'the steady encouragement to get on'—in short, the general inheriting of the benefits of having educated, intelligent parents—are not so readily labelled as specific to a class (Hoggart, 1970 [1967a]: 78–9).

More generally, Hoggart rejected relativism, and became more emphatic in this position as absolute standards of judgement seemed to him to retreat generally. There is, he said in an interview in 1982 to mark a quarter of a century after the publication of *The Uses of Literacy*, 'a crisis of values;

or rather a crisis in the idea of values themselves. Very few people working in the high arts can be brought publicly to say that there is a difference in achievement and quality between the Beatles and Beethoven'. This was a particular problem for the left. 'The far Left practices, in the name of a concern for "democratic" art and culture, an aggressive philistinism.' He recommended that they 'reread Tawney and [Richard] Titmuss [professor of social administration at the London School of Economics from 1950], so as to encounter again the right, difficult, socialist mixture of firmness, a sense of history, clear analysis, and passionate clarity' (Hoggart, 1982). Elsewhere he summed up a tradition in a similar way: 'Blake, Cobbett, Wordsworth, Coleridge, Arnold, Lawrence, Forster, Orwell, Tawney and Titmuss' (Hoggart, 1995: 14). The source of the relativism is the market as well as the left: the loss of 'guiding authorities', lay or religious, is 'vastly accelerated, in commercial democracies, by greater and more widespread prosperity, the urge to sell everything from clothes to notions, and so the need to persuade' (*ibid.*: 3). But the same grounds suit left and right:

> Many on the Left accept the same framework either because it allows them, as it allows those on the Right, to flatter people low down in the heap, or because they are muddled enough actually to believe that all really are equal in every possible sense. (*ibid.*: 7)

The consequences are felt throughout society. 'Relativism has had many complex offspring; "post-modernism", for instance. But the trend which runs from relativism-to-populism-to-levelling-to-reductionism-to-consumerist-concentration finds its lowest level in opportunism' (*ibid.*: 10).

The specific consequences which Hoggart saw for education are a need to assert a common standard through a prescribed curriculum, and he responded favourably to the development of such ideas in the 1980s, originated by the Conservative government but eventually drawing on a range of support and evidence. For example, he wrote approvingly of the thinking about English from a committee chaired by Professor Brian Cox, professor of English at Manchester University, who had gained Conservative sympathies by his attacks on comprehensive education in the 1970s but whose work with English teachers commanded wide respect

(Atherton, 2009). After rejecting the criticism from the left that any kind of national curriculum is 'a reactionary Tory' imposition, Hoggart commends that committee which

> thought all children should be introduced to some of the masterpieces of English literature. They believed there were such writings, that their value could not be culturally or historically explained away, that they are among the greatest achievements of this nation and that, properly presented, they can interest and excite children. The search for the best that has been thought and said is worthwhile, though we may all become muddled as we try to define it. (Hoggart, 1995: 35)

Hoggart remained consistently of the view that education was the means to achieve a common culture, based on Arnoldian premises, and that ordinary people were capable of responding. He welcomed comprehensive education in 1967 precisely because it opened the way to the kind of core curriculum that was not in fact developed until the 1980s, and certainly he would have had no time for any proposal to judge comprehensive schools by any other than the standards of the selective system:

> Of course, no one wants to advocate a form of education which will dilute the training of the best minds. Yet what we know by now of comprehensive education suggests that the training of existing excellence need not suffer, and that potential ability can be better developed. (Hoggart, 1970 [1967a]: 79)

To that end, what was required was curricular breadth: 'all subjects and all forms of training have to be seen in the light of larger human meanings' (*ibid.*: 81).

Among adults, there had been a change of expectation, but the aim should be the same:

> In the late-nineteenth century, the impulse to attend adult education classes was, for many students, that kind of moral purposefulness which had established Nonconformity and the Labour Movement... Today it would be truer to say that many come because they feel morally and politically confused. (Tawney, 1973 [1959]: 205)

Indeed, the modern student would have the old Leavisite instinct that 'literature rather than philosophy or psychology

... embodies this questioning [of life] concretely and in particulars, rather than abstractly and in generalisations' (*ibid.*: 212). The aims of adult education should be 'to increase range and depth in reading... I say "increase" because I assume that the capacity to respond to language is possessed by practically everybody' (*ibid.*: 214).

In short, Hoggart's view of education—for all that he might differ in detail from Williams, and for all his pessimism—brings into the highly individualised culture of the second half of the twentieth century a tradition of liberal education which is still recognisably that of Tawney, Laski, Cole and Arnold:

> My own working hypotheses are: that, given better conditions, more people are capable of more than we usually imagine; that, since we no longer live in closed societies with high, dense, local textures, no unselfconscious folk-culture is possible; that, since we are all under a centralised pressure towards... mindless togetherness, we must commit ourselves to the increase of individual knowledge and self-consciousness, to greater self-awareness. (Hoggart, 1970 [1967a]: 104)

As we shall see in the next two chapters, it was that tradition which now came under severe attack.

Chapter 5

Doubts about Liberal Education

Raymond Williams and Richard Hoggart were not the last socialist thinkers to see themselves as part of the tradition of liberal education, and indeed both were still writing for several further decades—Williams to the 1980s, Hoggart to the 1990s. But the dominant approach on the left changed profoundly. This chapter and the next explain the grounds on which that came about in the debate about ideas; Chapter 7 then considers the consequences for education in practice. The final chapter considers the minority current on the left of persisting support for liberal education after the 1950s.

This chapter is devoted mainly to the work of Pierre Bourdieu and Basil Bernstein. They are worth studying in detail because they have been so strongly influential on debate, especially on the left. Bourdieu indeed became one of the central sociological thinkers of the late-twentieth century, with significance far beyond his academic role as professor of sociology at the Collège de France. Bernstein's influence was on a more specialised audience in the sociology of education, the subject of which he was professor at the Institute of Education in London, but for understanding the evolution of radical thought on education his work has been as central as Bourdieu's. The theories of these two were influential because they seemed to provide a means of explaining social inequalities in educational progress that avoided reducing these to mechanical reflections of the structure of social classes: as Jenkins (1992: 84, 115) has noted in his sympathetically critical assessment of Bourdieu, his theories became 'enormously popular in the late 1970s and early 1980s', offering to the left a bridge between determinism and decision, a means by which the shaping of human choices can appear to be conditioned though not determined by social class. His work can be taken to have founded what came to be known as the 'new sociology of education' (Moore and Muller, 1999: 190). Goldthorpe (2007: 2) notes of Bourdieu and Bernstein that their ideas moved away from explanations in terms of 'processes involving economic constraints and incentives to ones grounded in differing cultures and modes of socialisation'. The working-class culture is thought by them to be so different from the world of the school that it harms the capacity of pupils to learn there anything much at all, especially the capacity to engage with the canons of liberal education that used to be accepted by significant thinkers on the left as constituting the very reason for democratising access to education. Comments by Jenkins (1992: 104) on Bourdieu could apply to both men: they 'attempt to specify in theoretical terms the processes whereby, in all societies, order and social restraint are produced by indirect, cultural mechanisms rather than by direct, coercive social control'—what Bourdieu calls 'symbolic violence', which Jenkins describes as 'the imposition of systems of symbolism and meaning (i.e. culture) upon groups or classes in such a way that they are experienced as legitimate.'

Both men sought to have influence on social practice, though in different ways. The work of Bourdieu has been described by one of his long-term associates, Loïc Wacquant, as 'the product of an activist science,... attuned to the burning sociopolitical issues of its day and responsive to the ethical dilemmas these entail' (Wacquant, 2008: 262). The political relevance of Bourdieu is exemplified in a passage from Teese and Lamb invoking his ideas (2007: 293–4):

> Governments frequently fail their poorer citizens because social claims on educational success are determined by cultural systems of curriculum, teaching, and examinations whose demands favour the children of educated families and the schools attended by these children. Governments are the trustees of this culture which is made authoritative through the hierarchical organisation of school programs and university courses, and through statutory bodies, like

> examination boards, charged with codifying the curriculum and administering tests and examinations.

Teese—a recurrent advocate of Bourdieu's ideas—is highly influential, not just on academic debates, but also on policy, since he has been the author of several reports commissioned by the Organisation for Economic Cooperation and Development on specific countries' educational policy, including one on Scotland (Raffe, 2008).

Though Bernstein has been less politically prominent, his academic role at the leading institution for training teachers in England gave him a direct influence on educational practice, to such an extent that his supporters have complained that school teachers have come to operate with an excessively simplified summary of what he said about the contrasting languages—the 'codes'—used by 'working class' pupils and the school. Atkinson (1985: 3) notes that this popular account has taken from Bernstein the belief that working-class children use a 'restricted code', whereas middle-class children learn at home the 'elaborated code' that is the normal form of discourse in the school. The account then explains working-class failure or alienation from school by the inadequacy of the restricted code for abstract thought and other subtleties.

One further thing also distinguishes Bourdieu, Bernstein and most of the writing discussed in the next chapter from the writers whom we have been examining so far: the style in which the debate has been conducted. Whereas the socialist intellectuals earlier in the century wrote clearly and for a general educated audience—a tradition that certainly survived with Hoggart and, on the whole, with Williams—such clarity has been notably lacking from most of the writers whom we consider in this chapter and the next. There is, the reader feels, an almost wilful disregard of accessibility, a sense that clarity of writing, far from being the virtue that George Orwell proclaimed it to be, risks glossing over the depth of response that is required. That is to put it politely. Another way of commenting is that left-wing writing since the 1960s has succumbed to the impenetrable jargon that has always been a characteristic of a certain kind of Marxist polemic. Sadly, that sort of writing will be much in evidence in the excerpts from left-wing theorists quoted here, though not in the words of actual politicians. The linguistic separation between the two—a divide that would not have been evident when, say, Laski, Cole and Tawney were writing for a general audience while also acting as leading figures in the Labour Party—is part of the story that is told here, part of the separation of left-wing thought about education from actual practice.

Pierre Bourdieu

Because Bourdieu's theories are more general than Bernstein's, it is useful to begin with them. Bourdieu's starting point is that education is unavoidably about social class—not just contingently, because of a particular historical state of affairs produced by capitalism, but deeply, in the manner in which the social distinction acquired or learnt in the home or through education is inevitably related to inequalities of power, status and wealth:

> In traditionally defining the 'system of education' as the sum total of the institutional or customary mechanisms ensuring the transmission from one generation to another of the culture inherited from the past... the classical theories tend to sever cultural reproduction from its function of social reproduction. (Bourdieu and Passeron, 1977: 10)

This obscuring of the link between handing on culture and handing on cultural advantages or disadvantages is then described as ignoring 'the specific effect of symbolic relations in the reproduction of power relations' (*ibid.*: 11).

The manner in which this happens, according to Bourdieu, is through the consonance between school culture and middle-class culture, in contrast to the dissonance from working-class culture. (If these terms seem sweepingly vague, that in fact is at the heart of the account, and is a criticism to which we shall return.) Bourdieu appropriated a term for this from medieval scholasticism: habitus. Shorn of the elaborate theoretical equipment which Bourdieu attaches to it, habitus may be initially thought of as habits learnt from a person's social milieu. If a child acquires the habit of reading good books, that would be part of her habitus if the preference was inculcated by her whole social environment. So the middle-class child, it is claimed, picks up such habits from the very fact of being middle class, whereas if the working-class child does so it is through untypical opportunities (which might be through being picked out as promising by a benevolent teacher). In the words of Nash (1999: 178): the concept of habitus refers to 'the reproduction of a class as a whole, with no reference to what happens to particular individuals, which is then regarded as just a matter of chance'. Thus the child imagined to be reading a book is not a real child at all, but an abstract embodiment of the social class to which she belongs.

There is clearly a danger of circularity here, which intensifies the further we look into Bourdieu's style of arguing: if the child is not an individual, but a token of her class, then by definition she has the characteristics of her class, and so inferring her behaviour from her class tells us only that that is how we have defined her nameless identity. So Bourdieu also has to pay attention to the ways in which habitus is acquired. The middle-class child receives at home the 'inculcation of legitimate culture for which the social conditions are only ever given to families whose culture is the culture of the dominant classes' (Bourdieu and Passeron, 1977: 128), and 'pedagogic work' (Bourdieu's term for teaching, informal as well as formal) has to last long enough to 'produce a durable training' (*ibid.*: 31). Jenkins (1992: 107) notes that for this to be an explanation of class differences in learning, informal family education must underpin formal education, which in turn becomes 'the basis for the response to all subsequent cultural and intellectual messages'. Children are then locked into their class habitus early on, mainly because it is informal. Thus Lukes (2005: 140) notes that habitus is 'the embodied dispositions which yield "practical sense" and organise actors' visions of the world below the level of consciousness in a way that is resistant to articulation, critical reflection and conscious manipulation'. The almost ineluctable destiny that is embodied in habitus is summed up by Nash (1999: 184):

> The habitus is thus a system of durable dispositions inculcated by objective structural conditions, but since it is embodied, the habitus develops a history and generates its practices, for some period of time, even after the original material conditions which gave rise to it have disappeared.

As Bourdieu and Passeron (1977: 205) put it (in the impenetrable style which Bourdieu favours): habitus is 'the site of the internalisation of externality and the externalisation of internality', by which they presumably mean that the child takes the habits of her social class into herself and then finds the resulting predispositions to be as inescapable as any sort of external force. In the endless possibilities for interpreting such enigmatic utterances lies much of Bourdieu's appeal.

This is then 'domination through symbolic violence' (Lukes, 2005: 141), which is another central concept in Bourdieu's thought. Informal teaching is 'symbolic violence' because it imposes cultural values upon children without their being aware of it: teaching which revealed the imposition would destroy itself (Bourdieu and Passeron, 1977: 8, 12). What is more, the culture that is imposed is arbitrary in two senses. 'It cannot be deduced from any principle' (*ibid.*: xx), by which is meant any principle of rational thought, and it is imposed by arbitrary power, in the sense of power that is not justified by any principles. It is just the power of the dominant classes, as they happen to be, rather than, say—as in previous ages—as the expression of divine authority. To be able to impose these arbitrary values, teaching must hide 'more and more completely... the arbitrariness of the inculcation and of the culture inculcated' (*ibid.*: 37)—that is, the lack of justification of the power behind its authority, and the lack of any universal rationale for what it teaches. A less inscrutable way of putting the point is in Bourdieu's development of the idea of 'cultural capital', which he says comes in three forms—attainment gained (which he calls 'institutionalised cultural capital'), things that can be read or watched or listened to or otherwise experienced ('objectified') and aspects of a person's identity ('embodied') (Bourdieu, 1997 [1986]). The first and second types are recognisably part of education as conventionally defined, and indeed much educational debate is about how to prevent the first (measured attainment) swamping the second (worthwhile things learnt). In a sense, then, the debate between liberal education and Bourdieu's ideas is about the ways in which embodied cultural capital is malleable. Bourdieu says it is shaped by the home, the class structure, the implicit authority of the school and so on. Liberal education, as we have seen, classically supposed that it could be shaped by the curriculum, and especially by the intellectual curriculum, in ways that enabled people to escape all these invidious influences. The contrast could hardly be starker.

That then brings us to the main point for us here. Bourdieu's ideas cannot be reconciled with the principles of liberal education—of a common, educated culture—that dominated radical educational thought until the middle of the century. The very idea of there being universal cultural values is rejected. Bourdieu and Passeron (1977: 37) deny 'the Cartesian myth of innate reason'. This myth is 'the retrospective illusion necessarily inscribed in education as an arbitrary imposition capable of imposing ignorance of its arbitrariness'. That is, the belief that there is anything that we might call absolute reason is not only a myth but also a means by which people are made to think that the culture that is being imposed upon them (by 'symbolic violence') is universal and thus legitimate. People then fail to see that it is actually an arbitrary class culture which the privileged use to bolster their power. What is described as 'universal' is merely 'the dominant ideology' that asserts that 'the only authentic culture' is what is regarded as 'the legitimate culture' (*ibid.*: 40). That in turn is defined to be 'the culture endowed with the dominant legitimacy' (*ibid.*: 23), which is a legitimacy derived not from any cultural principles but from sheer power.

Bourdieu and Passeron also then reject not only the 'myth of reason', but also the specific features that have come to be at the heart of liberal education, although here, again, the style of argument—general and allusive—results in there being no systematic analysis of liberal education, but merely a dismissal of what are taken to be representative segments. There is the assertion that a neutral syllabus is impossible, in a passage that seems to be proclaiming a rather strong form of ideological determinism:

> The 'neutralisation'… of messages and… of the conflicts between the values and ideologies competing for cultural legitimacy constitute a typically academic solution to the typically academic problem of reaching a consensus on the

> programme as a necessary condition for programming minds. (*ibid.*: 59)

Different forms of authority come down to the same source: 'the same principles directly establish political authority, religious authority and pedagogic authority' (*ibid.*: 66). If this is true, then there would be no scope for using 'pedagogic authority' to challenge political authority.

Similarly, there is a rejection of the whole of liberal education as being more about the style of the ruling class alone than about the conceptual content that it purports to convey: 'it has often been remarked how much an education… concerned to transmit a style, that is, a type of relation to language and culture, owes to the humanist tradition inherited from the Jesuit colleges—an academic, Christian reinterpretation of the social demands of an aristocracy.' The argument moves without detailed examination of historical change to assert that 'the bourgeois language [which it assumes to be the heir to that tradition] can be adequately handled only by those who, thanks to the School, have been able to convert their practical mastery, acquired by familiarisation within the family group, into a second-degree aptitude for the quasi-scholarly handling of language' (*ibid.*: 114–5).

The critique goes further than merely to reject a tradition of liberal education. It also suggests that the 'traditional… mode of inculcation'—by which is meant (*ibid.*: 45) teaching directed only at the limited social groups who are already equipped with the characteristics (the 'habitus') to be able to respond—reinforces not only power but also the legitimacy of power. Bourdieu calls this 'misrecognition', by which he seems to mean that a curriculum (and other educational practices) can induce people mistakenly to attribute legitimacy to arbitrary authority. There is a logical problem with this term, since 'recognise' is what is known as a 'factive verb' (see, for example, Wyse, 2009: 106): it presumes the truth of what is recognised. Just as there logically cannot be 'false knowledge' (though there can be 'false belief'), so there cannot be 'mistaken recognition', though there can be mistaken belief that something has been recognised. This is not just a quibble, because the plausibility of the term 'misrecognition' depends on there being some plausible connotation in the claim that certain cultural content confers authority, which is precisely what Bourdieu seeks to deny. Though there cannot be a word 'mis-know', what would be meant by 'mis-recognition' is not what Bourdieu intends the word to mean: it would perhaps be something closer to recognising the cultural value of the object of the verb, but misunderstanding that value. For example, suppose that it is believed that knowledge of the plays of Shakespeare confers cultural authority, but that Bourdieu says that this belief is a 'mis-recognition' of authority embodied in such knowledge. Bourdieu's term rings true only because the claim of such authority is indeed rather plausible: knowing Shakespeare really does seem to be the kind of thing on which cultural authority rests, but what we infer from that recognition might be more problematic. Thus, though recognising Shakespeare's cultural authority, we might fail to see that the authority has been distorted by Shakespeare's place in those traditional school curricula that have been associated with high-status schools. But that is a feature of actually existing school curricula, not a feature of the cultural authority of Shakespeare. Bourdieu is seeking to deny the plausibility implicit in the factive nature of the verb 'recognise' even while depending upon it surreptitiously.

Cultural authority

Bourdieu's account of power is thus a mixture between overt claims that certain cultural forms falsely purport to confer authority and implicit recognition that they do in fact confer authority. Teaching, Bourdieu and Passeron (1977: 22) say, is merely 'the arbitrary imposition of the dominant cultural arbitrary', and is that which 'corresponds to the objective interests (material, symbolic and... pedagogic) of the dominant groups or classes' (*ibid.*: 7). If this is as arbitrary as is claimed, however, then the whole system is determinist, even mechanical: the working class are trapped in their culture that is dominated by the culture which the education system teaches, and they accept this fate because the teaching has induced them to believe that school culture has intrinsic authority whereas in fact its authority is arbitrary. The allegation of determinism has often been made against Bourdieu. Jenkins (1992: 110) says that 'the habitus remains a "black box"...; the argument is essentially deterministic and institutions remain shadowy and inadequately constituted in theoretical terms.' Bourdieu's own writing tends to confirm such claims, though it is convoluted enough to allow a defence that the reader is mistaken. He says that social reproduction is based on 'processes which tend, behind the backs of the agents engaged in the school system—teachers, students and their parents—and often *against their will*... to stamp pre-existing differences in inherited cultural capital with a meritocratic seal of academic consecration by virtue of the special symbolic potency of the *title* (credential)' (Bourdieu and Passeron, 1977: ix–x; their emphasis).

One of the reasons for the apparent determinism is the methodological shortcoming of Bourdieu's approach to statistical evidence. He tends to move from a statistical description that applies to a social group (for example, 'girls') to attributing that description as an objective fact applicable to every member of the group. For example, he notes the larger proportion of girls than of boys who study languages, which he attributes to 'objective mechanisms which channel girls preferentially' towards languages. That is still a description of a group ('preferentially'), and so is still reasonable. But then the group description becomes a description of girls as such: these mechanisms pushing girls towards languages 'owe part of their effectivity to a social definition of "feminine" qualities', which is then strengthened further to: 'the internalisation of the external necessity imposed by this definition of feminine studies' (*ibid.*: 78). That is, the larger proportion of girls who study languages has come to be attributed to the very definition of 'femininity'. This conferring on individuals of features that properly relate to groups, not the individuals within them, has been described by Jenkins (1992: 96) as the 'subjective expectation of objective probability'. Nash (1999: 178) likewise notes that

> Bourdieu constructs a 'statistical model' of class reproduction in which, by some profoundly inexplicable mechanism, those brought up within the class are supposed to have internalised a habitus with the objective chances of that class built into it.

That is the sense in which what happens to particular individuals is merely a matter of chance.

It is precisely the scope for individual variation that would justify the beliefs in the emancipatory potential of liberal education that were held by radical writers earlier in the century. Yet Bourdieu explicitly denies such potential. Bourdieu and Passeron (1977: 23) say that the idea of 'culture for the masses' is plausible only by being 'blind' to the domination that is entailed in the teaching of 'appropriating legitimate culture', the culture of the elite. They are scornful of 'the Jacobin defence of the teaching of Latin', and of the *Universités Populaires* of the early twentieth century, which sought to disseminate liberal education widely (Premat, 2006), and were probably one influence on the development of the three-year tutorial class in the W.E.A. (Steele, 1997: 138). In fact, Bourdieu and Passeron contradict themselves in this connection, since they are also sceptical of the view that education imposes a 'culture "not made for them" on children of "humble origin"' (Bourdieu and Passeron, 1977: 41), and they try to maintain consistency by saying that the 'symbolic violence' is not in the culture inculcated but in 'the fait accompli of the legitimacy of the dominant culture'. But that distinction between content and method sits uneasily with their claim that 'the arbitrariness of the inculcation' (the method) is inseparable from 'the arbitrariness... of the culture inculcated' (*ibid.*: 37). Education devalues the culture of 'the dominated classes'—'e.g. customary law, home medicine, craft techniques, folk art and language'—in favour of the culture of the dominant in, for example, 'law, medicine, technology, entertainment or art' (*ibid.*: 42).

That exchange was precisely what appealed to early generations of radical thinkers, and Bourdieu and Passeron are not clear, even here, whether it is the rejection of the 'culture of the dominated' that is heinous or the monopoly of access to the high-status culture by those of high status. Jenkins (1992: 148-9) notes that 'the superficiality of [Bourdieu's] treatment of the working class is matched only by its condescension', as, for example, in his belief that the working class lack an aesthetic sense in their homes: 'nothing is more alien to working-class women', Bourdieu wrote (1984: 397), 'than the typically bourgeois idea of making each object in the home the occasion for an aesthetic choice.' Jenkins asks: 'does Bourdieu *really* believe that it is alien to working-class women to furnish and decorate their homes on the basis of aesthetic choices?... In this, as in many other aspects of the book [*Distinction*], he betrays his membership of the French bourgeois cultural networks.'

Yet that ambivalence does distinguish Bourdieu from other sorts of left-wing thought which claims that there is a distinctive working-class culture that rejects putatively bourgeois culture. One form of 'resistance' is associated with the attitude to school reported by Willis (1977)—an aggressive rejection. Bourdieu and Passeron (1977: 24), too, suggest that the working class oscillate between this and 'a sense of unworthiness', and that the response by a certain kind of left-wing political movement has been to celebrate working-class culture uncritically, for example in the old communist idea of what Bourdieu and Passeron call 'proletkult'.

Other writers are less willing to condemn such nihilism. Giroux (1983: 282)—another prominent left-wing thinker on these matters—said that 'the concept of resistance' developed by Willis 'is relatively new in educational theory', a comment that ignored the whole history of left-wing enthusiasm for a common culture. Giroux shares with Bourdieu a critique of high-status culture as arbitrary. Thus Giroux says that 'schools at all levels' draw a 'distinction... between high-status knowledge—usually the "hard sciences"—and low-status knowledge—subjects in the humanities' (*ibid.*: 279). That this inverts Bourdieu's perceived hierarchy is less important than the claim that the cognitive content of the curriculum can be interpreted as relating to social status at all. Michael Apple, similarly, while rejecting what he calls 'a rather vulgar brand of relativism' (Apple, 1978: 377), claims that expertise is not necessary to deciding upon a curriculum, and in fact is an imposition of the kind that Bourdieu would recognise: the 'insistence on technical criteria [of student achievement]... makes both the kinds of questions raised, and the answers given to them, the province of experts, those individuals who possess the knowledge already' (*ibid.*: 384). But there is a difference from Bourdieu in these writers' assertion of a radical epistemological gulf between working-class and dominant-class culture. Giroux refers to 'working-class knowledge as well as knowledge about women and minorities'. Unlike Bourdieu, he does not attempt to explain why or how this supposed 'class' culture would be inimical to a common or universal culture. The absence of explanation is noticeable in the slippage in that comment from a culture 'of' the working class to knowledge 'about' the other two groups he mentions: perhaps the claim of a uniformly oppositional way of thinking is just too implausible to be asserted of women or entire 'minorities'. But even more evasive is Giroux's further point that 'knowledge in the working-class culture is often constructed on the principles of solidarity and sharing, whereas within middle-class culture, knowledge is forged in individual competition and is seen as a badge of separateness.' What is meant by 'the' working-class culture, what warrant there is for the claim that there is a single 'middle-class' culture that always (since there is no qualifying 'often') is individualistic, and how it is known that the two do not interpenetrate each other are rhetorical gaps that, whatever its flaws, Bourdieu's theory of legitimation seeks to overcome. He does not deny that working-class people respect the dominant culture as legitimate: indeed, trying to understand why that is so is, in a sense, the whole purpose of his work here. A comment by Jonathan Rée seems apposite, arising out of a consideration of the view of liberal education held by, for instance, the Workers' Educational Association: 'we [should not] allow ourselves to be deceived by the ease with which the phrase "educated middle class" trips off our sociologically trained tongues' (Rée, 1987: 212).

The more telling critique of Bourdieu is from those who question, not so much his mapping of ideas onto social classes, but rather his understanding of the ideas themselves. Kingston (2001: 90) comments on Bourdieu's views about culture that though 'no set of evaluative criteria is culture-free, *all* criteria are, in some sense, arbitrary. At issue is whether the criteria are relevant to the purported aims ("biases") of a particular society—in this case, a pluralistic democracy with a sophisticated, technologically advanced economy.' If, he says, the practices that the middle class do disproportionately at home with their children are educationally rewarded, that is 'because they directly stimulate intellectual development and engagement, not because socially biased gatekeepers accord them value' (Kingston, 2001: 97). It is then necessary, Kingston says, to take 'the political risk of saying that some practices are "better" than others'.

Moore and Muller (1999: 189) go even further in their criticism. The idea of 'science' in Bourdieu's writing (and in that deriving from him) tends not to represent what science actually does. Such writing tends to reduce claims to truth to merely the 'perspectives' of particular social interests:

> [It] reduces knowledge to experience in order to de-legitimise rational, epistemologically grounded knowledge forms and truth claims that are represented as expressing no more than the 'standpoints and 'interests' of dominant' social groups... [T]hese reductionist, relativistic and perspectival approaches rely upon a simplistic and positivistic caricature of science.

In this view of the curriculum favoured by the 'new sociology of education', strongly influenced by Bourdieu, 'there was a rapid shift away from political universalism to a thoroughgoing celebration of difference and diversity' (*ibid.*: 191). '[T]he voice of reason (revealed as that of the ruling class white heterosexual male) is reduced simply to one among many, of no special distinction.' Rose notes, likewise, that the new sociology of education

> held that the content of education is problematic and socially constructed, that the learner is competent to define the content, that all subcultures are equally valuable, that academic knowledge is not superior to other kinds of knowledge. Rather than offering all classes the kind of education traditionally enjoyed by the elite, schools should value and preserve folk cultures. (Rose, 2002: 281)

In truth, the evidence rather tends to support the idea that culture is not radically divided at all, and also that access to what Bourdieu and his followers would see as a dominant culture is a means to opportunity. Kingston (2001: 92–3) agrees with DiMaggio (1982) that, with appropriately rigorous analysis of evidence, we can see that cultural capital facilitates academic success: knowledge of culture pays off because teachers reward it. Kingston calls this a 'cultural mobility' model, pointing thus to the way in which high-status knowledge is of benefit to people of all social backgrounds, a form of 'strategy' or 'investment' that might reinforce social advantage, but also might challenge it (Lamont and Lareau, 1988). Goldthorpe elaborates this point:

> Differing class conditions do not give rise to such distinctive and abiding forms of habitus as Bourdieu would suppose; because even within more disadvantaged classes, with little access to high culture, values favouring education may still prevail and perhaps some relevant cultural resources exist; and because, therefore, schools and other educational institutions can function as important agencies of re-socialisation —that is, can not only underwrite but also in various respects *complement, compensate for or indeed counter* family influences in the creation and transmission of 'cultural capital', and not just in the case of Wunderkinder but in fact on a mass scale. (Goldthorpe, 2007: 14; his emphasis)

That is precisely the tradition of left-wing support for universal access to liberal education that has been elaborated earlier in this book.

Basil Bernstein

The ideas of Basil Bernstein are more specialised than those of Bourdieu, and there were occasional disagreements between the two men, but both sets of ideas point in the same direction and have probably had similar effects. Bernstein's work is specialised in concentrating on how social classes differ in their use of language. Thus Bottomore (1977: xvi) suggests that Bernstein's ideas of 'linguistic codes' are expressed 'more comprehensively' as 'linguistic and cultural capital', in the terms used by Bourdieu. Bourdieu regretted that Bernstein does not relate language 'to the social conditions of its production and reproduction, or even, as one might expect from the sociology of education, to its academic conditions' (Bourdieu, 1991: 53), but he did not dissent from Bernstein's conclusions. Bourdieu and Passeron, indeed, sum up rather lucidly the essence of Bernstein's thought, describing 'the tendency of bourgeois language to abstraction, formalism, intellectualism and euphemistic moderation', contrasted to 'the expressiveness or expressionism of working-class language, which manifests itself in the tendency to move from particular case to particular case, from illustration to parable, or to shun the bombast of fine words and the turgidity of grand emotions, through banter, rudeness and ribaldry' (Bourdieu and Passeron, 1977: 116).

If this seems sweeping, so too are Bernstein's theories which, though he modified them several times, in essence come down two chains of association (Atkinson, 1985: 42–3; 82; 136–7). One links the ideas of formal language to what he calls an 'elaborated code'. That is more commonly found in a curriculum composed of discrete, academic subjects—what he calls the 'collection curriculum'—and taught by 'visible pedagogy', by which is meant what is sometimes also referred to (by others) as didactic methods delivered formally with the attention on the teacher and the subject rather than the student. The other associations are the opposites of these elements, just as in the contrast drawn by Bourdieu and Passeron: the language is informal, the code is 'restricted', the curriculum is 'integrated' in the sense of emphasising what would now be called cross-curricular themes, and the pedagogical style is 'invisible', meaning facilitative of the student's autonomy rather than directed by the teacher. This description of Bernstein's key idea is too crude, but it captures the essence of the contrast he draws: for example, he never developed any ideas that might cut across the two chains of association (for example, of teaching discrete subjects in a student-centred way using elaborated discourse, even though that might be thought to be the characteristic style of, say, the individualised tutorial system of Oxford and Cambridge colleges). What makes his work controversial, however, is the further association of each chain with particular class cultures, again as surmised by Bourdieu and Passeron: the first (formal) chain is thought to be typical of the middle class, the second of working class.

Bernstein's ideas on social-class differences in modes of thought may have been made more complex over time, but the essence did not change from one of its original statements, in 1958:

> It is contended that members of the unskilled and semi-skilled strata, relative to the middle classes, do not merely place different significances upon different classes of objects,

> but that their perception is of a qualitatively different order. (Bernstein, 1971: 44).

His language became more complex three decades on, but the ideas are the same. In 1990, he wrote that 'class-regulated codes position subjects with respect to dominant and dominated forms of communication' (Bernstein, 2003: 13). In a comment similar to that by Richard Jenkins on Bourdieu, Rosen (1972: 6, 13) noted that Bernstein never examines the actual class system, and presents a stereotyped view of working-class life. Bernstein does indeed seem to have regarded class as destiny, referring in a 1971 work to 'the genes of social class' which 'may well be carried… through a communication code that social class itself promotes' (Bernstein, 1971: 165). Atkinson (1985: 61) comments on this that, in Bernstein's account, 'the biological genetic code and the cultural communication code are formally equivalent in that they are mechanisms for inter-generational transmission.' Bernstein (1973: 181) argues that we can thus find in social class 'the origins of the dominant power and control relations of the school'. Education, he says further, is 'highly efficient in regulating the class basis of the social relations of the mode of production' (Bernstein, 1977: 185). As with Bourdieu and Passeron, and indeed in explicit agreement with them, he concedes that a feature of the education system is its 'appearance of objectivity, of neutrality, and at the same time of altruistic purpose and dedication' (*ibid.*: 190), but that is no more than an illusion: it 'disseminate[s] and legitimate[s] the professional ethic'. Education serves to confirm these professional elites in their self-belief (their 'consciousness'), and this confirms their sense of a right to social leadership ('symbolic control').

The way in which education reproduces class inequalities is a mixture of curricular content, linguistic style and modes of teaching. Thus the formal didactic style operating on traditional subjects alienates most working-class students. With visible pedagogies, a syllabus or programme starts with the concrete and moves to the abstract. That means moving beyond 'the local, context-dependent, context-tied operations' to 'understanding and application of principles' and, even later, to 'the understanding of the principles of the principles'. But 'often the children of the lower working class (including other disadvantaged ethnic groups), are constrained by the local, context-dependent, context-tied skills; by a world of facticity' (*ibid.*: 75). The equivocation 'often' lets him off the hook of having to defend such an apparently strong statement, but since he never quantifies such a putatively quantitative term (or even clarifies whether it refers to 'many children' or 'children many times') we are left with no clear empirical grounds of debate. His explanation then cannot avoid referring to different class cultures: as Atkinson (1985: 47) notes, Bernstein thought of 'social worlds' as distinct from each other, and liked to invoke 'relatively self-contained working-class "communities"', such as in the passage (Bernstein, 1971: 63): 'the vocabulary of the Elephant and Castle is different from the Angel, Islington; is different from the Gorbals; and is different from Tiger Bay.' We might add that there is also here a collusion in a sort of radical sociological mystique, in that no gloss is offered of the names of these working-class districts in two areas of London, in Glasgow and in Cardiff. Bernstein adhered to what is sometimes referred to as the 'Sapir-Whorf hypothesis', by which (as he put it) language determines culture (*ibid.*: 144). That is, linguistic 'codes essentially transmit the culture and so constrain behaviour' (*ibid.*: 143).

Social control

As with Bourdieu, the question then arises as to whether this theory allows much space for freedom to students to escape the allegedly typical culture of their class. Bernstein's own writing about this is opaque, as in his description of codes as 'culturally determined positioning devices' (Bernstein, 1977: 13): that seems to be clear that codes are a mechanical product of culture, and 'position' seems also to be a strong form of influence on individuals (though it has to be said, too, that this description of the causal chain from culture to code is the reverse of Sapir-Whorf). Atkinson—a writer who is sympathetic to Bernstein (and whose 1985 book Bernstein says understands his work almost unfailingly; Bernstein, 1995: 5)—tries to excuse Bernstein by saying that his mode of arguing is 'probabilistic' (Atkinson, 1985: 23) or by analogy (*ibid.*: 36) which he calls 'homology'. For example, there is a homology between a 'stratified' division of labour and 'cultural categories' that are regarded as 'pure' (thus hinting that the 'collection' type of curriculum, by which subjects are clearly defined and separate, is homologous with the style of economy that is often taken to be characteristics of industrial capitalism). 'Homology' in this usage, however – unlike in its precise mathematical version from which it borrows, falsely, a sense of rigour – is so vague as to tell us nothing other than a re-statement of the premise, that middle-class dominance is maintained through a traditional curriculum.

Bernstein's actual empirical practice in research shows little evidence of truly probabilistic reasoning. For example, he describes an experiment in which 'working class' and 'middle class' children aged 8 to 11 were asked to classify foodstuffs (Bernstein, 2003: 18–20; see also Holland, 1981). He does not say anything about how these class labels were defined, but, even leaving that aside, there is a lack of clarity as to how class can explain what was observed. Essentially, a greater proportion of the working-class children than of the middle-class children classified according to 'a specific local context of their lives', such as 'it's what we eat at home', as opposed to concepts that 'related less to the specific, local context of their everyday experience', such as 'these come from the ground'. In his conclusion, Bernstein ignores variation within these class categories, and says 'that the middle-class children showed that they held two principles', organised as a hierarchy. Thus – as with Bourdieu – there is an unacknowledged switch from a comparison of proportions to attributing to a whole group what Bernstein calls 'the modal principle of classification' of that group.

Behind the class differences in ways of thinking, and thus also in ways of relating to the school curriculum, there is a principle of 'social control'. Bernstein argues that 'how a society selects, classifies, distributes, transmits and evaluates the educational knowledge it considers to be public, reflects both the distribution of power and the principles of social control' (Bernstein, 1977: 85). Inequalities of power are maintained by the linguistic codes that are acquired first at home in a way that is related to social class, and then confirmed by the hierarchy of knowledge in the school. Teachers – which he calls 'transmitters' – are the agents of that social control: 'the process of learning how to be a transmitter entails the acquiring of rules of social order, character, and manner which became the condition for appropriate conduct in the pedagogic relation' (Bernstein, 2003: 65).

As Bourdieu, therefore, Bernstein doubts whether there are universal principles that might form a common culture, and the old style of liberal education would simply be the cultural code of the dominant class. Nevertheless, rather more than Bourdieu, he accepts that schools do attempt to convey universal meanings:

> Educational knowledge is... knowledge freed from the particular, the local, through the various languages of the sciences or forms of reflexiveness of the arts which make possible either the creation or the discovery of new realities.

He also sometimes seemed to be fully in tune with the 'new sociology of education' in a kind of romantic endorsement of 'working class culture' as defined by him rather than (say) as having the universalising principles of the early Workers' Educational Association or of the early socialist writers:

> If children are labelled 'culturally deprived', then it follows that the parents are inadequate; the spontaneous realisations of their culture, its images and symbolic representations, are of reduced value and significance. (Bernstein, 1972: 106–7)

In the light of this view of working-class culture, he acknowledges that the question is raised of whether working-class children can ever relate to school knowledge. By being socialised into the 'collection codes' of the school—the formal division of the curriculum into subjects, each defined in relation to theoretical principles—children are discouraged from seeing any relation with 'everyday realities' (Bernstein, 1977: 99). Where knowledge is organised traditionally—'by collection codes'—social order, then, 'arises out of the hierarchical nature of the authority relationships'. On the whole, Bernstein sees such formal organisation as confirming the social status quo, and in that respect his ideas are close to those of Bourdieu. Thus he says that the 'visible pedagogy' of traditional teaching styles is 'capitalist', and is also 'the standard European pedagogic practice, in one form or another, of every elite secondary curriculum, whether in the East or the West', deriving from the medieval university (Bernstein, 2003: 85). In this traditional kind of schooling, 'children of the disadvantaged classes are doubly disadvantaged. There is no second site of acquisition [by which he means such things as a quiet study space at home] and their orientation to language, narrative, is not privileged by the pedagogic communication of the school', by which he means that the characteristic form of discourse of the working-class home is inimical to the kind of learning required by the school (*ibid.*: 78). His view of what might be taken to be the tradition of the best that has been thought and said may be summed up by this:

> Its arrogance lies in its claim to moral high ground and to the superiority of its culture, its indifference to its own stratification consequences, its conceit in its lack of relation to anything other than itself, its self-referential abstracted autonomy. (*ibid.*: 87)

Yet he also acknowledges that there might be adaptations of the traditional forms of pedagogy that could be emancipating. 'It is certainly possible to create a visible pedagogy which would weaken the relation between social class and educational achievement' (*ibid.*: 79). Achieving that would require a 'supportive pre-school structure' but also a relaxing of the pace of learning, the sequence in which it takes place and the curricular structures through which it is taught. This goes rather further than Bourdieu in recognising that there might be a form of traditional knowledge that could be open to all social groups. Atkinson (1985: 133–4), indeed, acknowledges that Bernstein's ideas here have some resemblance to those of Raymond Williams and even to the analysis of tradition by F.R. Leavis, though neither Atkinson nor Bernstein goes further to follow Leavis and Williams in asking how a selective tradition might be widened, in content and in opportunity, while not losing its essential form.

It has also to be noted too, however, that, in practice, Bernstein's theories have not been received in any way that would be consistent with older radical ideas. Harker and May (1993: 175) claim that 'teachers reacted to [Bernstein's] model as if it were a model of reality, a thing of practice rather than a thing of theory', which is a knowing allusion to Marx's injunction not to mix these up. Atkinson (1985: 10) then also suggests that the simplistic version made Bernstein vulnerable to criticism from the left as stereotyping working-class culture. Atkinson believes this to be a misrepresentation of Bernstein's ideas, whereas writers much more hostile to his work see the political ambiguity as intrinsic to its characteristic approach. Thus Rosen (1972: 2–3) noted that, from the beginning, both the left and the right welcomed Bernstein. On the right, Bantock, for example, saw Bernstein's claims about the contrasting linguistic capacities of working-class and middle-class children as requiring separate schooling, while the left saw the same contrast as a reason to reform schooling to make it more receptive to what the theory would represent as working-class culture.

Bernstein is also less strong than Bourdieu in his belief that an 'invisible pedagogy'—child-centred education—would be likely to be even more invidious. In such a style of teaching, Bernstein suggests, the discursive rules are known only to the teacher (Bernstein, 2003: 71). As a result 'the surveillance of the child is total', because more is expected to be on display (Bernstein, 2003: 83). Bourdieu and Passeron (1977: 16) had described child-centred education as a 'self-destructive Utopia', since it does not in fact escape from 'arbitrariness', merely conferring on the teacher a less fettered scope for being arbitrary: the 'insistent appeal to an affective understanding' by the teacher of the child, 'is to gain possession of that subtle instrument of repression, the withdrawal of affection, a pedagogic technique which is no less arbitrary… than corporal punishment or disgrace' (*ibid.*: 17). But Bernstein also says that a curricular organisation which is less strongly related to traditional subject boundaries offers 'a potential code for egalitarian education' (Bernstein, 1977: 110). We return to consider child-centred education more fully in Chapter 6.

In short, the essence of the ideas of both Bourdieu and Bernstein is that they deny the premise on which radical support for liberal education had been based. Far from liberating the working class through knowledge, education was no better than a form of capitalist social control. The concept of the best that has been thought and said was merely an ideological illusion, concealing the intrinsically middle-class nature of such values. Bourdieu's and Bernstein's theories are highly abstract, but they subsequently have shaped very diverse areas of educational debate among left-wing theorists, leading ultimately – in the past three or four decades – to a detailed indictment of the whole legacy of liberal education. We turn now to these various forms of such challenge.

Chapter 6

Relativism and Liberal Education

Cultural studies

The current of thought about education exemplified by Bourdieu and Bernstein is now the norm in left-wing theories, even when not explicitly owing any debt to them. The ideas of a canon, of received culture, of the best that has been thought and said, are anathema. What was previously held to be an invaluable tradition is perceived as the product merely of powerful social groups, what is referred to as an 'academic elitist' curriculum (the term as used by a very influential writer in this connection, Stephen Ball (1990: 102)). One of the most direct responses to the old liberal tradition came in the form of cultural studies, which indeed grew directly out of it insofar as Hoggart was the founder of the Centre for Contemporary Cultural Studies in Birmingham in 1964.

Hoggart himself had no such reductionist intention, seeking instead to apply to the new mass media the same critical techniques as writers in the tradition from Leavis had used to analyse written text in their social contexts. He argued that social science ought 'to read art expressively as well as instrumentally', thus not at all reducing it to being products of social relations; and he said that what was new was that this ought to be done 'with the arts at all levels, mass art as much as "high art"' (Hoggart, 1973 [1959]: 254). It is easy to see, though, how this approach to all art—not starting from any premise that only the best was worth studying—would become what Stuart Hall, one of the most influential and prolific writers in the cultural studies movement, said was the paradigm of 'conceptualis[ing] culture as interwoven with all social practices' (Hall, 1995 [1980]: 198). Culture, he said—following Hoggart's own practice—is 'the lived traditions and practices through which... "understandings" are expressed and in which they are embodied' as well as 'the meanings and values which arise amongst distinctive social groups and classes' (*ibid.*: 199). The latter is the peculiarly cultural-studies mode of referring to what Arnold meant by 'the best', illustrating in its insistently sociological description the refusal of any judgement of value. 'The best' is not the acme in any absolute sense, but only the 'lived traditions' of certain—dominating—social groups, an evaluation as the best which comes to be attached to these traditions only on account of these classes' power.

Cultural studies, according to Hall, did continue to mean the study of cultural artefacts in a traditional sense, the 'internal relations within signifying practices' rather than how these referred to the world, by which is meant, for example, reading a story as a story, and discussing the ways in which its characters relate to each other (*ibid.*: 200). But two further meanings of 'culture' were now prominent. It studied 'the categories and frameworks in thought and language through which different societies classified out their conditions of existence', and thus was an essentially anthropological study of all the diverse ways in which societies thought (*ibid.*: 200). And it studied 'the manner and practice through which these categories and mental frameworks were produced and transformed', and so was interested in the mechanics of cultural production—the film or television studio, the economics of publishing, later the technology of the internet. Tom Steele is more specific, defining cultural studies to include an attention to texts in social context that, in practice, resembles Bernstein's attention to the social context of language use: it is, says Steele, 'the interdisciplinary approach to the arts, involving Marxist sociology, social history, close textual analysis and Leavis's approach to literary criticism.' Leavis would have recognised the motive—the understanding of literature's relationship to society—but not the ideological presuppositions.

Social class was no longer the centre of attention, as left-wing politics itself was forced to change by wider changes in society. Steele notes that 'the model of social revolution based on industrial mobilisation, the general strike and spontaneous mass upheaval was no longer a mobilising myth' (Steele, 1997: 203). The specific effect was to shift attention towards multiple contributions to culture, investigating

> the power of marginalised cultures to contribute to the positive transformation of a 'common culture' since... such cultures are not dens of ignorance which only an enlightened middle-class culture can illuminate but sites of resistance and communal value. (*ibid.*: 209)

Thus nothing in these frameworks by which cultural studies is defined would really warrant any judgement, since all imply a fundamental relativism, and thus nothing would indicate any criteria of value by which culture could form a curriculum.

Cultural studies also then was explicitly hostile to the liberal attempts to create a common culture. The old aims in the Workers' Educational Association of using adult education to create a neutral space of debate were, Steele says in his history of cultural studies, an imposition in an inappropriate sphere of 'the spurious neutrality of the intra-mural university', meaning the claims to objectivity of the main university tradition (*ibid.*: 203). The liberal attempts to create a large audience for good literature, in Penguin books for example, were portrayed as an evasion of class politics: thus W.E. Williams of Penguin and of the British Institute of Adult Education was merely the 'voice of metropolitan radical taste, a moderniser, a publisher, academic and back-room fixer, whose project was to shift adult education away from its "archaic" concern with the working class and the class struggle towards a more popular educational style centred on the arts and closer to the universities' (*ibid.*: 73). Writers such as Orwell, whose aim was an objective radicalism, are accused of 'quietism', of not being sincerely committed to anything, of favouring—in his essay 'Inside the Whale'—a position of detachment for the writer which was an evasion of responsibility (*ibid.*: 166). The very categories of thought on which previous educational approaches had been based were rejected in this way of thinking as themselves an imposition. Thus the school curriculum was merely 'an externally imposed order, based on the sacredness of subjects', and had to be replaced by cross-curricular projects, 'in which both teachers and students are free to make decisions —and to find areas of common interest which they can explore together' (Hunt, 1972: 32).

This reluctance to judge value was central to the tenor of cultural studies, its equating of culture with class in a manner that is recognisable from Bourdieu and, in its attention to modes of expression, from Bernstein. And yet cultural studies is also illiberal, as Collini notes, retaining from its evaluative roots in liberal education the capacity for polemical invective against that very tradition. Collini (1999: 256) contrasts the sensitivity of the originating thinkers in cultural studies with the later developments. Writers such as Hoggart and Raymond Williams had open minds in engaging with concrete details of the past. But cultural studies now was 'chilling and distancing' in its 'lack of imaginative sympathy with those who have lived and died before us (especially if they lived comfortably)' (*ibid.*: 257). Cultural products from social groups who have benefited from inequalities of power are rejected as merely expressions of that power, and more specifically 'in the frequently incanted quartet of race, class, gender, and sexual orientation, there is no doubt that class has been the least fashionable in recent years' (*ibid.*: 257). The old canon could not survive such a critique, since none of the authors contained in it did not benefit from at least one of these social inequalities (nearly all being at least one of white, middle-class, male and heterosexual).

There was then—as in Bourdieu—a systematic rejection of the very idea of a common culture, and thus of any possibility that there could be an agreed cultural basis of a curriculum. There was the rejection of what Giroux called 'traditional humanistic education', the rationale of which was 'that it offers students assured access to a storehouse of cultural materials that is constructed as a canon' (Giroux, 1995 [1985]: 650–1). He acknowledged the 'flexibility' of this approach:

> The values that are operational here do fluctuate according to specific ideological needs—witness the now quite secure incorporation of a women's studies canon or even a literary theory canon into some university curricula.

But he cannot accept that this justifies such an approach because of the implicit hierarchy of value: 'there is an always implicit "gold standard" by which these provisional incrementations and fluctuations are regulated.' For example, although in the old liberal curriculum, 'students would have access to a wealth which is "humanising" in its effect', that is to be rejected because this humanism is in 'complicity with the economy which has produced that wealth for humanity'. His scepticism of hierarchy as such extends even to the core of the traditional canon:

> The humanist rationale for the canon is based upon an hierarchical economy where cultural objects are ranked. Certain of those objects (Shakespeare's writing, for example) are assumed to be 'the best' of western culture; they thus represent... the *essence* of the culture. It is exactly this symbolic view of culture against which Cultural Studies should fight. (*ibid.*: 651; his emphasis)

In considering the implications of its work for educational curricula, cultural studies has focused particularly on literature (and in that sense, if in few others, it is heir to the literary tradition we have been discussing). The view here is that 'English studies may well have been invented by the liberal educators to incorporate the colonised masses into the new national settlement of Englishness', although there is also an acknowledgement that 'labile texts' might be interpreted in new ways (Steele, 1997: 201). Because of this view of literary studies, the inclination of earlier socialists to accept an inherited canon is seen as having a 'deeply conservative... approach to liberal education'. In noting that the typical topics of adult education classes in the earlier part of the twentieth century were 'history, philosophy, political economy and social science', but that 'English studies' dominated, Steele concludes that 'what had to be established was: what did it mean to be English?' (*ibid.*: 43–4). That is a view shared by many writers in this vein, for example Doyle who sees English studies as 'a strategy of "classification, pacification and cultivation"' (Doyle, 1986: 90): 'any shadows of socialist organisation were to be dispersed by the radiance of a common culture and heritage.' Wallis and Allman (1996: 164–6), likewise, regretting the 'elitism' of the tradition of adult education deriving from Arnold, Eliot and F.R. Leavis, and associated with H.C. Wiltshire (whose admiration for liberal education we noted in Chapter 3), said that emancipation through education could be achieved only if 'excluded groups' such as those 'defined by race, gender, class, etc.' achieved 'control over the curriculum'.

Such interpretation of the earlier motives is to make two mistakes. The obvious one, though it is minor here, was to conflate the national identity with the language. The deeper misunderstanding is to misjudge the motives. As we have seen, people wanted to study literature to gain insights into perennial concerns, into questions of moral philosophy that transcended time and place. Adult students also did that on their own account, not under instruction from what Steele calls the 'hegemonic order'. If, as he says, 'English literature was seen as *the* vehicle of the "civilising process"' (Steele, 1997: 44; his emphasis), that was a hope shared not only by the students (as we have seen from the evidence assembled by various researchers, and discussed in Chapter 3), but also from the leading socialist intellectuals of the first half of the century.

Liberal education as a conspiracy

The tendency in cultural studies is thus to see liberal education as a conspiracy, but reality keeps intruding to disrupt this glib assumption. Steele quotes the nineteenth-century liberal advocate of adult education, Lyon Playfair, as saying that 'the main purpose is not to educate the masses but to permeate them with the desire for intellectual improvement' (Steele, 1997: 44; Playfair, 1894: 8), and interprets this—with the heavy sarcasm which is typical of this genre of writing—as meaning that 'it is possible that the "vulgar" minds so readily conjured up by the cultural elite were cowed by contact with the creative genius of the race.' Playfair said nothing of the sort. He interpreted the growth of adult education in the nineteenth century as seeking to break down the 'high impassable wall' that had come to separate 'the learned class and the working class', and his tone, far from being condescending, indicates his intrinsically democratic impulse: 'the learned linked themselves to the past, and separated themselves from the present[,]... while the people went on their way without caring for the pedants' (Playfair, 1894: 2–3). Most strongly of all, he sees the very future of learning as lying in widening access to the opportunity for trained thought: 'it is chiefly among [the mass of the people] that great discoverers in science and great inventors in industry arise', citing the lowly origins of, amongst others, Humphry Davy, Michael Faraday, John Tyndall, James Watt, Alexander Graham Bell, George Stephenson and Richard Arkwright (*ibid.*: 12–13).

Steele—attentive to the evidence as he is, despite the ideology—does not fail to notice that adult students did indeed take great inspiration from what they read:

> Students found radical heroes and impressively free-thinking women in the pages of George Eliot, theological subversion in Milton, moving descriptions of the inhumanities of capitalism in Dickens, and weak and frivolous aristocrats and monarchs in Shakespeare.

For liberals such as Playfair (or Arnold or Huxley), such learning was not 'indoctrination' and these consequences were not straightforwardly 'unintended' (Steele's words). Steele thus has to acknowledge that literature was 'bearing the torch of humanism', offered in the name of 'class harmony' but interpreted by the masses as showing their own human dignity (Steele, 1997: 45). 'The "truth" of English studies', he concludes, 'was always cultural studies' (*ibid.*: 202), presumably though only when liberated from 'hegemony'.

The objects of the critique by cultural studies also include the founding fathers, Raymond Williams and Richard Hoggart. They are of course first of all praised. Hoggart was 'disquieted by the patrician tone adopted by Mrs Leavis' (Steele, 1997: 28), countering to her 'peg on the nose' approach 'ideas from the non-academic arena of serious journalism', such as Orwell's essays. He is also praised for following Tawney's lead in teaching adult classes as a dialogue about serious ideas (*ibid.*: 138). But the faint praise is also damning: 'Hoggart's... dogged commitment to ploughing a furrow between academic specialist "detachment" and an overly constraining political commitment… has attracted political criticism from both left and right' (*ibid.*: 140). Thus Hoggart's insistence on belonging to the liberal educational tradition is referred to as part of an 'ideological contestation over cultural meanings' with 'communists': Hoggart and others (such as Raybould), it is claimed, 'argued that workers' education in the class sense was incompatible with the larger or "true" ends of adult education' (*ibid.*: 132 and 123). The sense that he might belong to a different tradition—to that stemming from Arnold—is lost, as also is the much more pragmatic point that Hoggart was simply a teacher, a motivation not much approved of in cultural studies where his lack of interest in 'literary theory' is 'notorious' (*ibid.*: 136). To that misdemeanour is added his empirical realism: 'socialists have not found in Hoggart's work the heroic class of myth' (*ibid.*: 28).

Williams could not have been accused of evading theory, and so is more accepted, but there is an insistence that he was not truly part of the tradition from Arnold to Leavis, even ambivalently. Stuart Hall notes that there are two ideas of culture in Williams's *The Long Revolution*. There is the anthropological, a description of what people do and the beliefs they have about these activities, in which, Hall says, 'the purpose of the analysis is to grasp how the interactions between all these practices and patterns are lived and experienced as a whole' (Hall, 1995 [1980]: 197). In this connection, Williams's rejection of Marxism is welcomed by cultural studies—'against a vulgar materialism and an economic determinism.' But more problematic is the other meaning, which is evaluative, what Hall describes as Williams's interest in 'the giving and taking of meanings, and the slow development of "common" meanings—a common culture'. Hall insists on a disjunction from Arnold, for whom, he claims, 'the "best that has been thought and said" [is] regarded as the summits of an achieved civilisation' (thus ignoring what Williams himself reminded us to notice, Arnold's immediately following enjoinder to use these ideas to cast a fresh light on stale practices). But what Steele calls Williams's 'marriage of Leavisism and left politics had failed because it had not taken into account that Leavisism, despite its oppositional standpoint, was unhappily also hostile to socialism' (Steele, 1997: 24). Indeed, Williams himself could appear to be 'conservative' because he insisted 'on the priority of the written word', treating 'literature as literature and not as a branch of history or sociology' (*ibid.*: 186).

If Williams nevertheless was ideologically acceptable to cultural studies, that was because he was saved from the anthropological sin of interpreting 'culture as a common way of life [rather than] culture as the product of class struggle' (*ibid.*: 177) by the criticisms which the social historian E.P. Thompson had made of *The Long Revolution* in a lengthy review in 1960 (Thompson, 1961a,b). Thompson later—in the 1980s—came to deplore 'the poverty of theory' (Thompson, 1978), but in this early piece his Marxist invective was unrestrained. He indulges in that ad-hominem denunciation that the left has always favoured. Williams, the 'scholarship boy', is implicitly Thomas Hardy's Jude, shut out from Oxford:

> It may be that the 'scholarship boy' who comes to Christminster undergoes quite different intellectual experiences from the middle-class intellectual who enters the socialist movement. In the first, there is a sense of growth *into* the institutions of learning, with less of a crisis of allegiance than is sometimes suggested: the sense is that of Jude entering into his inheritance on behalf of his own people. The dangers besetting the middle-class socialist intellectual are well enough known. But he may, nevertheless, in joining the socialist movement experience more sense of intellectual crisis, of breaking with a pattern of values: there is still a rivulet of fire to be crossed… [T]he working-class scholar may tend to persist in the illusion of Jude: the function of bourgeois culture is not questioned in its entirety, and the surreptitious lines of class interest and power have never been crossed. (Thompson, 1961b: 37; his emphasis)

The condescension is not only striking—Thompson the enlightened middle-class socialist telling the originally working-class Williams what to think—but is also in stark contrast to the actual middle-class socialists of earlier in the century.

Thompson rejected the claimed objectivity and independence of the intellectual tradition which Williams endorses, though critically. 'At times, in *Culture and Society*', Thompson said, 'I felt that I was being offered a procession of disembodied voices—Burke, Carlyle, Mill, Arnold—their meanings wrested out of their whole social context, the whole transmitted through a disinterested spiritual medium' (Thompson, 1961a: 24–5). This is inaccurate, taking no account of what Williams had said in criticism of Arnold's liberal attack on 'stock notions':

> The worst harm done by the 'stock notion' of class, a notion receiving constant assent from the material structure of society, was that it offered category feelings about human behaviour, based on a massing and simplifying of actual individuals, as an easy substitute for the difficulties of personal and immediate judgement. Arnold had many useful things to say about class, but it is one of the 'stock notions and habits' whose influence he did not wholly escape. (Williams, 1963: 126)

That in turn is somewhat unfair to Arnold, for example in the point—which we noted Hoggart quoting—that able individuals, drifting free of class through a liberal education, are thereby unsettled, although Williams would extend such a perception of unease through cultural aspirations to many more people than Arnold would have acknowledged. What Thompson and the cultural studies critics fail to see is the honesty of Williams's engagement, the taking of Arnold (and the whole tradition) seriously and respectfully as themselves honest attempts to create a common culture through education, rather than something axiomatically to be presumed to be merely a matter of class 'hegemony'.

Thompson, as polemical Marxist rather than the fine historian that he also was, might not accept the validity of the effort at understanding. He accused Williams of 'a concealed preference—in the name of "genuine communication" —for the language of the academy', which 'has seemed less than disinterested to those millions who have inhabited the "shabby purlieus" of the centres of learning', such as Hardy's Jude and Sue (Thompson, 1961a: 25). That claim is rather belied by the history of liberal adult education, where Oxford was precisely the model to be admired. More to the point, however, is Thompson's denial of the central project of the liberal tradition, of the aspiration to create a common culture through education: 'the "reading public" is another misleading term', because 'undifferentiated' (*ibid.*: 29). Social class could simply not be overcome by education: 'it is not clear to me how "universal participation" or a "common culture" can "dismantle the barriers of class" which are also barriers of interest' (Thompson, 1961b: 36).

If Williams excused himself in the eyes of the cultural-studies theorists by heeding Thompson's advice never again to be so warm as in *Culture and Society* to the idea of a tradition, Hoggart remained unreconstructed. He never ceased to address a very wide audience, learning through it the idea that a common culture might reside in the debate itself:

> It took me years and the acquaintance of some intelligent, imaginative and humane Conservatives—whose Conservatism was not based on self-interest but on a feeling for the importance of history, tradition and duty—to learn to be hospitable to the idea of the good Conservative. (Hoggart, 1988: 130)

That not only indicates an abiding openness of mind, but also—despite its main point—a recurrent contact with people who were not of his own political point of view. But then Hoggart himself has been described as a conservative, Miller (2004) for example denouncing his 'ranting hostility towards relativism and anti-elitism'. Hoggart certainly unapologetically rejected relativism, what he referred to in 1996 as 'the obsessive avoidance of judgements of quality, or moral judgement' (Hoggart, 1995: 3). Ellis notes that, in consequence, 'the charge of cultural elitism [against Hoggart] has been made not only by those... on the left, but also by "market populists" [on the right]' (Ellis, 2008: 205).

Reading the criticism of Williams and Hoggart, it is easy to feel that writers in cultural studies do often seem to be addressing only an audience of 'socialists', a contraction from the cultural breadth of those earlier socialists whom we have discussed. The audience is indeed often even narrower still, a form of sectarian Marxism. Thompson complains that 'for a socialist thinker Mr Williams is extraordinarily curt with the socialist tradition—and indeed in his reference to *any* minority radical tradition' (Thompson, 1961a: 30; his emphasis). The reply from the standpoint of what might be called the liberal humanism of the dominant liberal education would be a curt rejoinder that it does not matter, in rather the same manner as teachers in the tradition of the Workers' Educational Association responded to the sectarian attacks from the Marxist Labour Colleges. If writers such as Hoggart and Williams address a general audience before they appeal to socialist sectaries, then so much the better for education, it might be thought, since their analysis will then reach the social mainstream. We might add, half a century after their main works, that their lasting relevance might thereby be rather better ensured than if they had written only for contemporary orthodoxies that now are no more than those of a fundamentalist fringe.

The debate fostered by cultural studies thus may seem rather peculiar to outside observers, or to those who have read Williams and, especially, Hoggart on the actually democratising features of education and society in Britain in the second half of the twentieth century—the decline of deference, the prolonging of the compulsory phase of education, the construction of a common curriculum. Williams's recognition that we can see all this without supposing that change has all been in the one direction—without ignoring the consumerism and bad taste and persisting inequality—seems quite at odds with the notion that no common culture is possible at all. As the possibility of a common culture has come closer, the dominant parts of what we might call the academic left exaggerated the ideology of class divisions in culture, and also exaggerated the multicultural divisions in other dimensions—ethnicity or gender, for example—and so erected on the basis of what Freud called the narcissism of small differences a project that denied the very possibility of a liberal education of an old kind.

A comment from C. Wright Mills in 1954 on earlier generations of post-war left-wing thinkers seems apposite for cultural studies too:

> 'Left establishments' have often been as confining in their values, and as snobbish in their assignment of prestige, as any national establishment. In fact, often they have seemed more restrictive, first because of their usual pretensions not to be, and second because dogmatic gospel is often more needed by minority circles than by those secure in major institutions. (Mills, 1954: 213)

It is, he said, quite false to suppose that the left alone is capable of exercising a forward-thinking imagination, though it is characteristic of the left to think that it has:

> I think it naïve to assume that the major divisions among the cultural workmen of a nation are those who are established and accordingly somehow unfree and those who are of an advanced guard, creative in culture and radical in politics. (Mills, 1954: 214)

It is of the essence of the socialists in the tradition we have been examining that they never entertained the kind of narrow self-assurance which Mills notes. Socialism, for them, entailed always a debate with everyone.

New Left critique

Cultural studies may be a matter largely of academic debate, as may the ideas of Bourdieu and of Bernstein, important ultimately in shaping a whole climate of opinion, but not of immediate public concern. But the different meanings and interpretations of multiculturalism enter right to the heart of educational policy. If one thing most strongly distinguished the liberal education tradition it has been an adherence to universalism, to the belief that all people not only have the same liberal rights but also belong to the same culture, in the sense that any cultural variation that is to be observed—much of which may well be desirable—has to be judged by the same absolute standards everywhere and at all times.

Multiculturalism as a state of affairs cannot be denied, and liberals have not sought recently to deny that society is composed of multiple cultural traditions (Barry, 2001: 22). The question is rather whether education should promote it rather than the common culture that the liberal educational tradition has always sought. The beginnings of doubts came from the Marxist New Left in the 1960s, not yet attached to multiculturalism in the form that it took later, but sharply critical of claims that anything that might be called British culture could any longer sustain a claim to universal significance for socialists, and thus rejecting the strongly patriotic instincts of the socialist intellectuals of the first half of the twentieth century. Perry Anderson, in an essay in *New Left Review* in 1968, argued that 'British culture as it exists today is a profound obstacle to revolutionary politics' (Anderson,

1968: 5). He said that the core of the problem is that 'Britain —alone of major Western societies—never produced a classical sociology' (Anderson, 1968: 7). Anderson might here be thought to be too attached to disciplinary labels rather than ideas, and he does have to acknowledge that 'there were social critics of Victorian capitalism, of course: the distinguished line of thinkers studied by Williams in *Culture and Society*' (*ibid.*: 13). In not accepting this as real social criticism, he rejects the central literary component of the liberal educational tradition which previous socialists had adopted enthusiastically: 'but this was a literary tradition incapable of generating a conceptual system' (*ibid.*: 13). The British intellectual tradition, he claimed, was inveterately parochial, 'proof against any foreign influences or importations' (*ibid.*: 15). Believing that, he thus has to dispose of the influences which British thinkers did absorb from abroad, for example the Germanic sources upon which the British idealist philosophers drew—the thinkers who, as we have seen, prepared the way for socialists' acceptance of the tradition. But he dismisses them as eccentric in a passage of extraordinary historical omission:

> The curious episode of a belated English 'Hegelianism,' in the work of Green, Bosanquet and Bradley, provides piquant evidence of this. Hegel's successors in Germany had rapidly used his philosophical categories to dispatch theology. They had then plunged into the development of the explosive political and economic implications of his thought. The end of this road was, of course, Marx himself. Sixty years after Bruno Bauer and Ludwig Feuerbach, however, Green and Bradley innocently adopted an aqueous Hegel, in their quest for philosophical assistance to shore up the traditional Christian piety of the Victorian middle-class, now threatened by the growth of the natural sciences. (*ibid.*: 15)

Not only does this equate philosophy with just one kind of philosophy, arguing circularly, in effect, that because Britain produced no Marx it did not found the Marxist tradition of thought. It also, more importantly, neglects the very great practical significance for thinking about the welfare state of the teaching and writing by these British philosophers.

The educational role of Leavis and of *Scrutiny* are seen to be the chief villains here, displacing a properly theoretical development into the metaphysical mists of literature: 'as a critic, Leavis is a landmark that has yet to be surpassed', but he refused to 'justify' or discuss his own 'metaphysic' (*ibid.*: 51). It is true that *Scrutiny* was highly critical of the established social order, so much so, indeed, that the movement could be said to have been 'born in close relation to Marxism' (*ibid.*: 53), but 'Leavis became obsessed with the commercialism of the new media and the corruption of the metropolitan world of letters.' To proclaim 'literacy and humane culture' as the essence of civilisation is to exchange a proper interest in social change for something merely 'inner and spiritual' (*ibid.*: 54). As a result, 'the pages of *Scrutiny* are pervaded by an immense pessimism: a sense of inexorable cultural atrophy, and of a dwindling minority aware of it' (*ibid.*: 53).

Anderson cannot neglect the debt which Raymond Williams owed here, and he is credited with eventually 'correcting' all this vapid idealism (*ibid.*: 55n). Indeed despite his strictures on the British tradition of liberal education, he concedes that *The Long Revolution* passes the ideological test of being a proper work of 'socialist theory' (*ibid.*: 55), arising out of Leavis and 'literary criticism, of all disciplines'. Anderson thus condemns by defining out of real existence the socialist idea of a liberal education. In effect he is saying that because Williams emerged from literary criticism his socialism does not count in making British ideas matter: he matters, Anderson concedes, despite these intellectual origins rather than as the latest socialist flowering of them. Anderson completely ignores any older socialist work in the tradition—the thinking of those whom we discussed earlier, who in turn owe their origins not only ultimately to the idealist philosophers whom he regards as merely 'curious' but also to their engagement with diverse ideas from outside Britain, few of which, though, were Marxist—literary ideas, legal ideas, direct political contact.

Anderson is also, ironically, a prisoner of the tradition he excoriates, ignoring in this essay any attention to natural science, and discussing only the social sciences and some selected aspects of the humanities—'history, sociology, anthropology, economics, political theory, philosophy, aesthetics, literary criticism, psychology and psychoanalysis.' That neglect would have been regarded as rather odd in the tradition of liberal education that stems from Huxley, and in which natural science found an early place.

Marxism of Anderson's kind has not been the only strand of left-wing thought since the 1960s which has denied the universal validity of the core ideas underpinning liberal education. There was a general shift from explaining history in terms of broad categories to distrusting these as themselves oppressive. One of the internationally foremost theorists of this shift, the American political philosopher Iris Marion Young, summarised the change thus:

> Many feminists, black liberation activists, and others struggling for the full inclusion and participation of all groups in this society's institutions and positions of power, reward, and satisfaction, argue that rights and rules that are universally formulated and thus blind to differences of race, culture, gender, age, or disability, perpetuate rather than undermine oppression. (Young, 1989: 267)

We return to this point shortly, but—still on the theme of how late-twentieth-century Marxist thinking relates to the tradition of thought about liberal education stemming from Arnold through Hoggart and Williams—we find, for example, an argument in 1990 from two socialist critics of such change, authors in the same vein as Anderson:

> Feminism's move from class history to 'case history,' and Left history's move from class history to 'personal history,' have played a major part in developments within Left education theory, inadvertently privileging individual selfhood in the classroom in the name of class-consciousness. (Swindells and Jardine, 1990: 125)

They blame this individualising of attention—which they regret—on Hoggart and Williams, whose appeal to socialists they find puzzling since Hoggart 'wasn't even a Marxist' and Williams 'freely acknowledges' his debt to Leavis (*ibid.*: 125 and 127). This indictment is expanded in a general rejection of that tradition of radical liberal education to which Williams and Hoggart certainly did belong. The tradition suffers from what its adherents regarded as its central strengths. For example, there is 'a particularly damaging affinity with Leavis in producing and elaborating a narrative of moral realism' (*ibid.*: 132), in other words a belief in absolute ethical values which liberal education ought to teach.

There is 'a strong assumption that the grammar school *is* education' (*ibid.*: 136; their emphasis), which is indeed the view taken by those who sought to democratise access to the established liberal curriculum. There is 'the "bourgeois individualist" narrative of working-class consciousness, the autobiography, the moral realist account' (*ibid.*: 137), the pedagogical attention to the individual as the ultimate site of any meaningful learning. And there is the belief—which indeed we have seen recurrently—that the values of culture 'are *not* "middle class values", but something more universal' (*ibid.*: 137), by which is presumably meant just 'universal' (unqualified as that adjective has perforce to be), since that in fact was what was claimed. They conclude, as is characteristic of such polemics, with an unacknowledged obeisance to Bourdieu and a glossing over of the subtlety of both Hoggart's and Williams's thought:

> What is lost from sight in these discussions (with the foregrounding of Hoggart and the receding presence of Williams) is the acknowledgement (central to Williams's theoretical argument) that access alone will not suffice, that for the working-class child the encounter with culture itself is an *experience* of inequality. (*ibid.*: 140; their emphasis)

What we have here, then, in this Marxist critique—a critique dating from the 1960s and continuing—is a claim essentially that liberal education is naïve because it places too much faith in the individual and too much trust in the potentially universal qualities of the inherited culture that the liberal curriculum aims to pass on. Liberal education is thus indicted both for being too specific and for being too general.

Rejection of established culture

In practice—as opposed to in academic theory—the Marxist critique of liberal education has had its main impact only indirectly, since debates about Marxism could hardly be said to have been central to actual socialist politics at least since the 1980s. The rejection of 'bourgeois individualism' has been part of a more general critique of established culture—of a more general sense that the culture for which universal claims had been made was just too partial to be anything much more than an agent of oppression. In practice, then, the critique that has had the more general effect on thinking about liberal education has been in the name of an all-embracing multiculturalism in which 'working class' culture takes its place alongside multiple others.

Beiner notes the change in left-wing politics, in discussing the ideas of Iris Marion Young. 'For earlier generations of the left', he says, it was expected that 'the political community [would] pull together in pursuit of social justice and the other goods of a shared political life', but now 'the politics of cultural pluralism has come to seem more progressive than a politics of commonality' (Beiner, 2006: 30–1). Barry explains why 'multiculturalism [has] come to be thought of as a left-wing cause' by reference to the demise of the sort of Marxism that was the first source of critique of the liberal tradition: 'the shift from Marxism to postmodernism and despair at the prospects for wholesale economic redistribution are relevant', and so 'there is a line from the New Left through communitarianism to multiculturalism.' This is not new, he notes, since it was already happening even in the 1960s: 'the turn from Marx to Hegel and from Enlightenment to Herder was already under way more than forty years ago' (Barry, 2002: 205–6). The actual radical individualism of some of this romantic thought is highly ironic, considering that the Marxists had indicted the liberal tradition for its individualism (ignoring liberal education's strong attachment to the universal principle of Enlightenment reason), and we return to it later when we consider child-centred education. But the main romantic strand here is the claim that all cultures are equally valid—the romantic attachment to culture which Herder founded in reaction to the Enlightenment and which subsequently came to inspire mainly right-wing politics until, in the 1960s, it fused with anti-colonial thought to create a new kind of left wing.

Thus we find again Iris Marion Young pointing out that 'the concept of a social group has become politically important because recent emancipatory and leftist social movements have mobilized around group identity rather than exclusively class or economic interests' (Young, 1989: 259). She misses here something about the older practice of class-based socialist thought. It did not 'mobilise around class interests' in the sense of asserting the equal validity of all class cultures: as we have seen, it was, on the whole—

even as late as in the writing of Hoggart—quite critical of many features of working-class culture. The political purpose was to give access to universal values, and if these were perceived as middle-class then that was not an intrinsic limitation but rather an expected consequence of middle-class economic and cultural privilege. The multiculturalism of which Young writes is, by contrast, rather sceptical of any claim to there being universal values:

> Ideally, a rainbow coalition affirms the presence and supports the claims of each of the oppressed groups or political movements constituting it, and it arrives at a political programme not by voicing some 'principles of unity' that hide differences but rather by allowing each constituency to transform economic and social issues from the perspective of its experience. (*ibid.*: 265)

Similar views have been expressed by another influential theorist of the new multiculturalism, Nancy Fraser. The 'struggle for recognition', she said, 'is fast becoming the paradigmatic form of political conflict in the late twentieth century' (Fraser, 1995: 68). In 'post-socialist' politics,

> group identity supplants class interest as the chief medium of political mobilization. Cultural domination supplants exploitation as the fundamental injustice. And cultural recognition displaces socioeconomic redistribution as the remedy for injustice and the goal of political struggle. (*ibid.*: 68)

This is a very strong assertion, and—for educational purposes—could hardly be more different from the assumptions of those socialists who adhered to the classic project of liberal education. The 'fundamental injustice' is, with Bourdieu, now the claims about a universal culture rather than the historically unjust restriction of access to that culture. The overcoming of material disadvantage as a prior step to extending access to a liberal curriculum is now not even seen as important, in its place being not the opening of doors but the 'recognition' of what is outside them. Jude would be turned away from Oxford to be told that what was inside its walls was no better than an expression of upper-class power, and that the culture he already had, and found lacking, was in fact lacking only in not being 'recognised' as important.

A problem associated with these theoretical claims about group identities is the question of what constitutes a group, a matter of practical import if any kind of group-specific curriculum were to be constructed. Young just evades the issue—'I shall not attempt to define a social group here' (Young, 1989: 259)—even though group identity is important enough to affect deeply the manner in which people think, and therefore—for our purposes—presumably also learn:

> A person's particular sense of history, understanding of social relations and personal possibilities, her or his mode of reasoning, values, and expressive styles are constituted at least partly by her or his group identity.

Fraser is somewhat more explicit, but her definition leaves open the possibility that there are no such groups at all, and that liberal culture, and a liberal education in particular, might be perfectly sufficient to deal with the differences:

> Examples [of cultural or symbolic injustice] include cultural domination (being subjected to patterns of interpretation and communication that are associated with another culture and are alien and/or hostile to one's own); nonrecognition (being rendered invisible via the authoritative representational, communicative, and interpretative practices of one's culture); and disrespect (being routinely maligned or disparaged in stereotypic public cultural representations and/or in everyday life interactions). (Fraser, 1995: 71)

It is true that Fraser does see class oppression as somewhat different from the others. Whereas the aim of class politics might reasonably be to 'put the [oppressed] group out of business as a group', the aim of all other kinds of cultural politics is, at least in part, 'to valorize the group's "groupness" by recognizing its specificity' (*ibid.*: 78). Insofar as groups intersect with each other this is not a wholly tenable proposition: what do we make of class-specific aspects of 'gender culture', for example? Is reading highbrow novels middle-class (because it is more common there) or female (because women read more novels than men)? More to the point here, what then is to be done with such novels in the curriculum? That question brings us right back to both Leavises. Nevertheless, Fraser offers a useful clarification of the dimensions of the debate, seeing it as structured along two cross-cutting axes: affirmation or transformation, and redistribution or recognition (*ibid.*: 87). The liberal welfare state, she says, was redistributive but affirmed existing culture rather than challenging it: that view would extend to the socialist thinkers from earlier in the century whom we discussed. She allocates 'socialism' to the categories of redistribution and transformation, which, too, ignores the affirmation of the established culture of that earlier tradition of socialist support for liberal education. 'Recognition and affirmation' she describes as 'mainstream multiculturalism', so that it entails no challenge to existing cultures and no aspiration to have any specific culture understood to be universally valid for all social groups. Then, finally, she interprets the only kind of 'transformation' as being the placing of all cultural values on the mutually critical plane of 'deconstruction', the label she gives to the combination of 'recognition and transformation': there is no acknowledgement here of the idea that recognition might be given only to those —potentially very considerable—aspects of marginalised cultures that might be brought within the universal, nor that 'transformation' might entail the transcending of all particularism in the interests of general values.

Her ignoring of the actual practices of liberal education—what actually happened under the heading Fraser would give of 'redistribution' and 'affirmation' of liberal culture—may be illustrated by considering the curricular implications of her example of 'gender identities' and 'racial identities'. She says that only 'feminist deconstruction aimed at dismantling androcentrism' could unsettle 'gender dichotomies', and likewise only 'anti-racist deconstruction' could disrupt 'racial dichotomies'. That simplistically political view is to ignore, say, Shakespeare, who recurrently 'destabilises' gender identities—consider the multiple layers in *As You Like It* of a woman, dressed as a man, playing at being a woman, and then chided for not being sufficiently manly, complicated in his own day by the fact that the woman would have been played by a boy—a series of gender disruptions that lie at the heart of the play's plot—or consider the questioning of presumed racial identities in *The Merchant of Venice* or of colonial identities in the relationship between Caliban and Prospero in *The Tempest*. 'Transformative recognition' seems in practice indistinguishable from the idea of promoting a common culture, and therefore to be something which the mainstream liberal education has always potentially been able to do.

Rejection of enlightenment

More generally, the way of thinking exemplified by Fraser and Young may be taken to be one instance of the general decay of what John Gray calls 'the Enlightenment project', although arguing also that its rational roots go much further back and that it is really these which are now being challenged (Gray, 1995: 123). For liberal education, the shaping component is humanism. The Enlightenment merely gave modern voice to an ancient rationalism, which is why liberal education, with its roots in antiquity, could be adapted to the modern age. All these sought the universal through 'the displacement of local, customary or traditional moralities, and of all forms of transcendental faith, by a critical or rational morality' (*ibid.*: 123). All these stem from 'Greek logocentrism—which I understand as the conception in which human reason mirrors the structure of the world', but the difference which the Enlightenment made was that scientific knowledge became the paradigm of all authoritative claims (*ibid.*: 152, 158 and 161). It was because of this universalism of the Enlightenment, we might then infer, that socialism could readily share with liberalism respect for an education that was rational. Though liberalism does not deny the existence of different cultures, it treats them as 'chosen lifestyles, whose proper place is in private life, or the sphere of voluntary association' (*ibid.*: 124). Young called this 'an opposition between the public sphere of a general interest and a private sphere of particular interest and affiliation' (Young, 1989: 256). Liberal universalism thus is inextricably linked to an idea of common culture:

> The ideal of the public realm of citizenship as expressing a general will, a point of view and interest that citizens have in common which transcends their differences, has operated in fact as a demand for homogeneity among citizens. (*ibid.*: 252)

To this end, a common educational curriculum is the logical means.

Gray says we must now reject all this, with significance for education since the major implication is for how we regard knowledge:

> The most fundamental Western commitment, the humanist conception of humankind as a privileged site of truth, which is expressed in Socratic inquiry and in Christian revelation, and which re-emerges in secular and naturalistic form in the Enlightenment project of human self-emancipation through the growth of knowledge, must be given up. (Gray, 1995: 155)

If there are no longer any universally valid truths, no agreed criteria of evaluation, then the very concept of a curriculum based on the best that has been thought and said no longer even makes sense. 'There is no view from nowhere which is "the moral point of view"; there are only diverse moralities and value-perspectives' (*ibid.*: 162). In Young's words, 'a general perspective does not exist which all persons can adopt and from which all experiences and perspectives can be understood and taken into account' (Young, 1989: 257).

Therefore, for our educational purposes here, there is no independent standpoint from which we could aim to construct a curriculum that would be valid for all cultural groups. A common culture would be no better than enforced dominance:

> Cultural assimilation should not be a condition of full social participation, because it requires a person to transform his or her sense of identity, and when it is realized on a group level it means altering or annihilating the group's identity. (*ibid.*: 272)

Young meant by 'culture' here almost everything that education might seek to inculcate:

> By culture I mean group-specific phenomena of behaviour, temperament, or meaning. Cultural differences include phenomena of language, speaking style or dialectic, body comportment, gesture, social practices, values, group-specific socialization, and so on. (*ibid.*: 271)

Yet, though all cultures must then be regarded equally, the actual programme of change proposed by these writers makes no mention of the liberal culture itself. As Fraser puts it:

> The remedy for cultural injustice... could involve upwardly revaluing disrespected identities and the cultural products of maligned groups. It could also involve recognizing and positively valorizing cultural diversity. (Fraser, 1995: 73)

In a sense, that neglect of liberalism has to be, partly because its claims are universal and therefore deeply contradictory to these programmes, and partly because, as Gray notes, it is not a cultural tradition in the sense meant by these writers:

> For liberalism to become merely one form of life among others would involve as profound a cultural metamorphosis as Christianity's ceasing to make any claim to unique and universal truth. (Gray, 1995: 177)

This is why the multicultural challenge to liberal education is so profound, but also why it is quite consistent with the ideas of Bourdieu and of the dominant strand of cultural studies, however reluctant these writers might be to admit to such relativism. All these projects would indict liberal education on the grounds of its unwarranted arrogance.

Such ideas deeply shaped a certain kind of left-wing thinking about the curriculum in Britain in the 1970s and later, not so much in mainstream political parties such as Labour—which continued (as shall be seen in Chapter 7) to ignore such theoretical discussion of curricular matters altogether—as among those left-wing thinkers who might be considered to be the fringe except that they came to be the mainstream of academic debate about education. The allegation was repeatedly that claims to universality are spurious, masking an actual exercise of domination. A familiar example was the allegedly intrinsic gender bias in some school subjects. Davies, for example, argued in typical vein in the 1980s that some subjects have 'inherently masculinist biases'. So—like Gray—she rejected the liberal conception of the neutrality of science:

> 'Subjects' like physics are supposed to be neutral, or 'pure.' But the teaching of scientific principles without any parallel discussion of how this knowledge might be applied (the bomb, space programmes) is an incredibly partial and short-sighted stance. (Davies, 1984: 63)

The mixing of scientific and ethical issues here is also typical of the mode of arguing, ignoring one of the fundamental principles of liberal educational thought. In similar style, Bentley and Watts (1986) claimed that 'normal, formal science is masculine', and propose that 'a feminist science would see the philosophy of wisdom as being entirely congruent with views of the purposes of science'; they take the phrase 'philosophy of wisdom' from Maxwell (1984), who describes it as recognising why people do science at all: again, ontology (being) and epistemology (knowing) are conflated. Bentley and Watts complain that

> school science portrays a picture of both the positivist and reductionist tradition of scientific methodology... Positivistic science portrays theories as logically ordered sets of laws which explain reality. Arguably, such theories are examples of masculine logic and explain the reality of masculine science. (Bentley and Watts, 1986: 127)

Leaving aside the caricature of positivism (which, more accurately, is best described as being a philosophy which seeks not to confuse reality with the categories in terms of which we seek to explain the world), of science (which is always tentative in its claims to knowledge) and of men, we might be inclined to say about this that it does not seem to leave much room for women at all, but the response is as reductive as the claim:

> Both the reality and the logic of women is often different to this, and given the opportunity to observe the same events, women may well advance theories that differ. Furthermore, they may look for confirmation of their theories in exactly those aspects of processes that males choose to dismiss.

The caveats 'arguably' and 'often' have been lost, and the attribution of essential differences is rather stark. Davies infers essential gender differences from statistical patterns, trying to add plausibility by appealing to personal experience:

> Girls' reluctance to do science is inextricably linked to the way 'science' is (abstractly) presented in school: I will make the inevitable plea for my own sex and claim that women, for whatever reasons, do show more concern about social issues, do have a greater sense of social responsibility. (Davies, 1984: 63)

Such essentialising based on differences of statistical averages is reminiscent of the similar way of arguing that we noted in Bourdieu and Passeron and in Bernstein. Reviewing some of the British research of this kind, Glover and Fielding (1999: 60–1) note, for example, its 'assumption[s] that women are inherently more careful of the environment and more peace-loving than men', and 'that girls will react positively to the more applied aspects of the sciences and will be turned away by theoretical or abstract aspects'.

Rejection of universalism

We find analogous arguments in connection with race and multiculturalism. David Gillborn, for example, who is a professor at the Institute of Education in London, has rejected a fundamental tenet of both liberalism and liberal education in his view that 'at its heart... pluralism rests on an assertion of one true and superior set of values' (Gillborn, 1995: 9). His expansion of the claim emphatically rejects any kind of tolerance for rival points of view:

> Pluralism, despite its liberal commitment to democracy and power sharing, enshrines a belief in a superior and non-negotiable common framework of values. The selection and definition of school knowledge is legitimated by recourse to a version of rationality that assumes openness and goodwill lie at the heart of what is, in fact, a political process of labelling and exclusion. (*ibid.:* 12)

Aiming to create a common culture through education is thus inherently racist:

> Racism lay at the heart of the Thatcherite project: a racism typified by notions of a common culture and ethnic difference (not the innate superiority and biological determinism characteristic of earlier 'scientific' racisms). A 'new' or 'cultural' racism... has grown in prominence during the period. (*ibid.*: 347)

He referred to this new approach as 'cultural restorationism', meaning 'a concern with "tradition", "heritage", "language" and "way of life"', and claimed that this 'operates as a code for "race"'. A particular target of this rhetoric was Nicholas Tate, chair of the government's curricular agency in England, whom Gillborn quotes citing Arnold: 'Tate clears the way for a programme of further curricular reform expressly concerned with the identification of a 'common culture' that is both bigoted and elitist', and allegedly racist because it deploys 'the same discursive strategy' as Herrnstein and Murray, American authors who caused much controversy by claiming, in their book *The Bell Curve* in 1994, that some part of racial differences in intelligence is related to genetic differences.

This is strong rhetoric, and—as with E.P. Thompson's attacks on Raymond Williams a quarter of a century before—characteristic of the *ad hominem* invective favoured by certain segments of the left in its exaggeration, its lack of detailed evidence to support the attribution of invidious intentions, and the accusation of guilt not even by association but by means of similarity merely perceived by the writer: it need hardly be said that Tate has never expressed any sympathy for any kind of racism. Indeed, when Gillborn's article was published Tate responded in the *Times Educational Supplement* (27 June 1997) firmly: 'it is a long time since I have read such a piece of pretentious, jargon-ridden nonsense. The way to tackle racism is to get across the idea that we are all—I repeat all—part of a common national project.' Tate's support for a national curriculum to be followed by all pupils was based on the same universal principles as characterised liberal education throughout the twentieth century.

Some left-wing critics of a common curriculum were less extreme in their denunciation, but reached similar conclusions based on the belief that a common culture was incompatible with the integrity of group cultures. Troyna and Vincent, for example, implicitly agree with something of the old left-wing support for a common curriculum when they note that 'an "entitlement curriculum"' could obviate 'many of the discriminatory practices' which have prevented 'particular groups of students from having access to all parts of the curriculum' (Troyna and Vincent, 1995: 153). Nevertheless, they are suspicious of what they disparage as 'the ideologies of universalism and individualism which translate into the everyday discourses of: "treat them all the same" and "respond to individual needs"' (*ibid.*: 154). The reasons for their doubts are what happens when the common curriculum clashes with multicultural difference:

> The corollary, of course, is a disregard for group membership,... and the conviction that the professional imperative is to intervene, if and when the 'inadequacies' of the child *qua* child demand.

That is, the teacher's professional judgement would quash the distinctiveness of the child's 'group'.

Gillborn makes similar points. He does not accept that decisions about what should be in a curriculum could be made 'rationally':

> It has been argued, not least by feminists, that 'rationality' is a particularly effective means by which the powerful encode their interests into what can and cannot legitimately be spoken—all knowledge has a political character and is implicated in the exercise of power throughout and beyond the academy. (Gillborn, 1995: 9)

He then concludes similarly to Iris Marion Young that, rather than try to construct a common culture, the aim should be deconstruction of all identities: 'postmodern theories of the decentred subject, where identities are recognised as fractured and changing, offer a way forward' (*ibid.*: 3).

A related but distinct source of critique of a common culture from the left comes from some of those who would promote minority languages through the curriculum. It has long been argued that mass, compulsory schooling from the late-nineteenth century onwards had tended to insist on using a single, dominant language, which in the UK meant English rather than Welsh or Irish or Scottish Gaelic. In the various movements to revive or strengthen minority languages that have grown since the middle of the twentieth century, campaigning to have a more diverse linguistic culture reflected in the classroom is common. The strongest form of that recognition is streams or whole schools in which all or most teaching is through the medium of the minority language. This is thus a linguistic version of multiculturalism, and the anti-racist's rejection of a common culture is echoed in those campaigning for such languages. May (2012), for example, noting that a 'unified linguistic culture was seen as a prerequisite for modernity, a basis of political legitimacy and a means of shared cultural identity', argues that

> given that education accomplishes this for majority group members—whose cultural and linguistic habitus are viewed

> as consonant with the school's—why can it not do so for minority group members as well? (*ibid.*: 176)

The way ahead for minority languages, he argues, is to attach their campaigning to the general project of multiculturalism:

> We see in multicultural education the first glimmer of recognition concerning the historical role that education has played in the *institutionalized* devaluation and marginalization of minorities within the nation-state. (*ibid.*: 182; his emphasis)

Because this linguistic claim is about the medium of teaching and learning rather than directly about what is learnt, he does accept that 'a recognition of minority habitus as cultural and linguistic capital in schools can coexist, albeit not always easily, with an ongoing valuing of a common or "core" curriculum', but he is sceptical as to whether the content really is independent of the medium. He disagrees with Brian Barry's rejection of multiculturalism in favour of 'a difference-blind egalitarian liberalism', and asks:

> Common to whom, one might ask, and on whose terms?... [T]hose whose cultural and linguistic habitus are not reflected in the public realm are more likely to pay a far higher price for their subsequent participation in that realm. In contrast, those whose habitus are consonant with the civic culture and language—and, as such, are regarded as cultural and linguistic capital—have no such difficulties. (*ibid.*: 109)

Like Gillborn, May rejects pluralism fundamentally: 'such an approach may in fact serve simply to reinforce the current cultural and linguistic hegemonies that multicultural education is concerned, at least ostensibly, to redress' (*ibid.*: 183).

The older socialists would have been rather taken aback to find any such association of left-wing rhetoric with a rejection of 'pluralism' and 'egalitarian liberalism'. Attempts to convert such ideas into practicable programmes tend to become confused because of a faint memory of the emancipatory potential of the concept of 'entitlement'. An example from the early 1980s is a discussion by Donald and Grealy (1983: 96–7) of what Labour should do about the question of a national curriculum. They explicitly follow Bourdieu in saying that the central problem is 'the uneven distribution of cultural capital', but they then point to a dilemma: 'in the left's thinking about education, there appear to have been two main responses to this phenomenon.' On the one hand, there is the tradition of seeking to broaden access to liberal education, which these authors describe as 'a guilty defence of high culture'. On the other, there has been a dismissal of 'the national culture as irrelevant, sheer bourgeois mystification'. They say both these positions suffer from positing 'an absolute distinction between a dominant culture and the subordinate cultures which it governs,' which they say is indefensible. So they propose instead teaching 'how language and culture work, not... the nation's cultural heritage as objects of mysterious richness'. Even leaving aside the exclusive concern with the linguistic and literary curriculum here, we might note that this evades the main issue, the question of how to select examples of the best ways in which 'language works' so that students might refine their own linguistic practice and might—more fundamentally—learn some understanding of life from the insights of great works of literature. It also is in the end indistinguishable from one of the classical aims of liberal education, for example as developed by L.C. Knights and F.R. Leavis—the refinement of sensibility through linguistic analysis. This ostensibly radical programme is then much the same as the programme recommended later in the same decade for the National Curriculum in England and Wales by the committee chaired by Brian Cox (which we noted being praised by Richard Hoggart): its central concern was how to ensure that children acquire 'knowledge about language'. The irony is that Cox was also denounced by Donald and Grealy for his earlier criticism of comprehensive education and for being complicit with the allegedly conservative line from Arnold to Leavis (Donald and Grealy, 1983: 88).

A later and similar example of the unresolved tension in recent left-wing thought about the curriculum is in a pamphlet in 1997 offering to 'rethink education and democracy' by offering 'a socialist alternative for the twenty first century', written by 'the Hillcole Group' which included among its authors several academics who have been prominent since the 1970s in socialist debates about education (for example, Caroline Benn, Clyde Chitty and Ken Jones). They shared enough of the multiculturalist instinct to resist central imposition, echoing rhetoric such as Gillborn's in seeking 'to avoid the heavy-hand of government directives and prescription along "nationalist" lines,... whose ostensible objective, some assume, is to return the country to a mythical past when a Christian monocultural orthodoxy held sway' (Hillcole Group, 1997: 65–6). As part of that position, they reject 'outdated and arbitrary academic "subject" divisions', and instead aim to 'encourag[e] literacies and learning of many different kinds as part of the task of encouraging the multiple intelligencies that people possess' (*ibid.*: 88–9). Nevertheless, they also want to retain the idea of 'entitlements in terms of areas of experience, which can then be used as the basis of rational curricular construction' (*ibid.*: 68). The acceptance that there are rational principles which might be the basis of common agreement already differs from the rejection of reason which we have seen in other writers, but the tension remains unresolved and the desire to reject inherited knowledge while retaining some universal principles remains a sharp contrast with socialist writers on a liberal education up to the 1950s.

Multicultural ideas in practice

A striking feature of these left-wing academic positions, however, is that they were more distanced from mainstream politics—even from mainstream left-of-centre politics—than had been their predecessors up to about the 1950s. Equal gender opportunities as promoted by Labour governments became in practice defined to be essentially that of liberal feminism—the removal of obstacles to equal participation (in the Sex Discrimination Act of 1975, for instance) or the encouragement of girls to study subjects—such as the natural sciences—in which only a minority of them had traditionally been interested (Arnot and Miles, 2005; Arnot *et al.*, 1996; Croxford, 1994; Weiner, 1978). The main practical means by which this effect on gender differences has been felt has been through the imposition of various kinds of prescribed national curricula, which—as shall been seen in the next chapter—owed rather more to policy from Conservative governments in the 1980s and 1990s than to any political initiatives from the left (Orr, 2000). The direction of thinking about the curriculum has not been particularly influenced by left-wing thought at all, except insofar as liberal principles have become social norms (a point to which we return in the next chapter). Little has then remained of the old liberal universalism on the left so far as educational curricula are concerned, since the theoretical debates have rejected it, and the practical debates have paid it attention only as a set of abstract principles. In practice that has meant, then, a neglect anywhere on the left of the detailed attachment to a shared culture which left-wing thought earlier in the century took for granted.

The nature of the resulting pragmatic compromise, and the absence of the universalistic principles that were taken for granted earlier, may be illustrated by two particularly influential writers on ethnic multiculturalism—Bhikhu Parekh and Tariq Modood. Both of them are academics and both have been closely involved with policy, especially Parekh who chaired a commission, set up by the Runnymede Trust in 1998, on 'The Future of Multi-Ethnic Britain'. Joppke describes Parekh as 'Britain's "race relations" eminence', and this report as the last official affirmation of British multiculturalism (Joppke, 2004: 249). The report rejects both universalism and particularism. It says that because 'cultural difference has come to matter more,... the claims of community [have been strengthened] over both universalism and culture-free liberal individualism'. But it also rejects the most radical kinds of cultural separation: 'it must be acknowledged that no culture can require that its continuity be guaranteed by the state in perpetuity.'

Parekh and Modood have expanded on the principles behind such a compromise position. Parekh responds first to Brian Barry's view that multiculturalism inevitably entails moral relativism, and thus is (in Parekh's words) a rejection of the Enlightenment tradition. Parekh wants to retain the essence of Enlightenment universalism, and thus favours social integration. He outlines various modes of political integration, all of which he rejects. The model which he dismisses most curtly is straightforward assimilation, the erosion of all cultural distinctiveness in favour of creating a common culture. Modood, likewise, simply notes as an inescapable fact that 'the difference-blind approach to equality... has steadily given ground in recent decades', especially as 'socialist organisations' have departed from their previous fear 'that such forms of recognition and remedial measures are divisive of working-class solidarity' (Modood, 2007: 87–8).

Second, Parekh is sceptical of the other extreme, what he calls the 'millet' model. The term comes from the governance system of the Ottoman Empire, where religious groups were allowed a great deal of freedom provided they did not impinge on anyone else. This model takes the view that not only are 'human beings... above all cultural beings embedded in their communities', but the state also has a duty 'to uphold and nurture its constituent cultural communities'. He rejects this as he rejects that first model, on the grounds that it 'militates against the development of common social and political bonds without which no political community can act effectively and maintain its unity and cohesion'.

The third model which Parekh rejects is merely 'procedural' integration, in which 'our sole concern should be to ensure peace and stability', with no group interfering in any other group's affairs (Parekh, 2006: 199); we saw that this was the position favoured by radical multiculturalists such as John Gray. The commission's report goes further: 'procedural neutrality is not enough, for no political system can be stable and cohesive unless all its members share a common national culture' (Commission on the Future of Multi-ethnic Britain, 2002: 43). A version of this is 'civic' assimilation, in which there is a shared political culture, but in which private lives are to be as separate as cultural difference would require (Parekh, 2006: 200). The commission's report says in effect that this approach is naïve because

> in practice universal values—life, liberty and the pursuit of happiness, for example—are too abstract to guide decisions in particular cases, for they need to be related to, and interpreted in the light of, society's traditions and history. (Commission on the Future of Multi-ethnic Britain, 2002: 52)

The report therefore comments further, in words that have a direct bearing on what would happen in a classroom, that there has to be agreement on 'the basic preconditions for democratic dialogue', including

> people's willingness to give reasons for their views, readiness to be influenced by better arguments than their own, tolerance, mutual respect, aspiration to peaceful resolution of differences, and willingness to abide by collectively binding decisions that have been reached by agreed procedures. (*ibid.*: 53)

Modood is of a similar view specifically in relation to Islam: 'nothing I have said implies that Muslim citizens should not be part of mainstream democratic processes—to the contrary. My argument is about what additional forms of recognition and representation may be necessary to empower excluded groups.' Parekh believes that 'the government... should not be culturally neutral or indifferent but even-handed, empowering all cultural voices to participate in a common dialogue' (Parekh, 2006: 222).

There is clearly a danger here of satisfying neither side. In rejecting radical multiculturalism but also rejecting universalism as arrogant imposition, Parekh is left with what might appear to be a somewhat pusillanimous—and some might say very British—compromise. Multicultural society needs a shared culture to transcend its particular cultures, but 'the shared culture can only grow out of their interaction and should both respect and nurture their diversity and unite them around a common way of life' (Parekh, 2006: 219). Thus 'the interculturally created and multiculturally constituted culture is an unplanned growth' (*ibid.*: 221). There is also some vagueness about the status that is to be accorded to inherited—and still by far the majority—culture, which we might describe as a form of post-Christian liberal universalism. Modood, for example, refers to 'multiculturalism or the accommodation of minorities', and to 'multiculturalism [as] the need to give respect to stigmatised or marginalised identities', which seems a definition that ignores the majority (Modood, 2007: 50 and 121).

The vagueness of the aspiration does at least make this more tolerant than the hard line of the academic left, and its attachment to a tradition of tolerance does provide some continuity with the liberal education of the past. Trevor Phillips, former chair of the UK Commission for Racial Equality (2003–06) and of its successor, the Equality and Human Rights Commission (2006–12), suggested that British 'attachment to democracy, freedom of speech, and equality' should form the basis of multiculturalism in practice. '[I]ndividual choices [are] to be respected as long as they do not interfere with our fundamental values, or our long-cherished traditions' (Phillips, 2005). Taking that sort of pragmatic view, there might seem to be not much at stake after all.

Parekh does at first sight seem quite ready to accept an educational tradition which would be consistent with that sort of pragmatism, and thus which would be no radical departure from dominant traditions:

> The aim of education, as all the great educationists have rightly argued, is to develop such worthwhile human capacities as intellectual curiosity, self-criticism, the ability to weigh-up arguments and evidence and form an independent judgement, to cultivate such attitudes as intellectual and moral humility, respect for others and sensitivity to different ways of thought and life, and to open students' minds to the great achievements of humankind. (Parekh, 2006: 227)

That seems as firmly in the tradition of liberal education as anything we have seen. But he contradicts himself in more detailed ways as part of his criticism of 'Eurocentrism' in education, and the nature of his reservations show that even this pragmatic multiculturalism remains ambivalent about the universalism of liberal education.

What he means by Eurocentrism—the 'monocultural content and ethos of much of the prevailing system of education'—has three parts, the first two of which ignore the plural nature of the European tradition and the third of which contradicts other things which he says about the nature of liberalism. He says, first, that there is the belief that 'European civilisation represents the highest form of life reached by humankind so far and provides the standards by which to judge all others' (Parekh, 2006: 225). Such beliefs were indeed common, even dominant, in the liberal tradition, but they were clearly not shared by many of the socialist critics who were both critical of any kind of dominance and also of the view that the inherited culture was not rich enough to provide resources for that very criticism.

Parekh defines Eurocentrism, second, as entailing the belief that European civilisation 'attained its glory unaided by, and ow[ing] little if anything to, non-European civilisations'. That belief, too, was widespread, but not without dissent from within the liberal tradition. An awareness of cultural diversity grew from the Enlightenment, a fascination with the idea that there were other civilisations which were far older than Europe's. Indeed one of the multicultural consequences of possessing an empire was that it forced its more thoughtful administrators into contact with the non-European civilisations over which some European states ruled for a while (see, for example, Dalrymple, 2002). No educational tradition that paid as much attention to ancient Greece as did the classical tradition in Britain could wholly ignore that all tradition offers an ambiguous legacy, as we noted in Chapter 1 (Campbell, 1968). Plato was as much a source for Islam as for Christianity, and indeed had influence much further afield than that. When Parekh claims that a 'Eurocentric' curriculum was 'unlikely to awaken students' intellectual curiosity about other cultures', he is ignoring the central importance of history in the traditional curriculum, a distancing from students' immediate concerns that was potentially as stimulating as the study of the present day in another culture. That is a historical universalism which has fallen out of fashion.

The third aspect of Parekh's definition of Eurocentrism is not just ambivalent but also ambiguous. On the surface, it resembles the first, in being the claim that there was a belief that only European culture was the source of the 'rise of individualism, secularism, science, technology and so on', and Parekh does not appear to dissent from these values, only from the belief that they are European (Parekh, 2006: 225). But there is a lack of precision in the thinking here, evident in the lazy 'and so on', since it is not clear what the common element is meant to be, and later in the same book he is not at all enthusiastic about what would certainly be a common feature of all these ideas: rationalism. He claims that 'mak[ing] a sharp separation between reason and tradition' is not tenable because 'the realm of culture… gives a society its identity' and is more fundamental than reason, which is akin to just another 'custom': 'reason and customs are embedded and mediated' in 'the realm of culture' (*ibid.*: 356–7). Thus he is sceptical of the liberal claim that reason is 'impersonal and homogeneous in nature, transcending time and place and identical in all human beings'. He even goes so far as to say that 'the liberal way of life is historically contingent and embedded in a particular culture' (*ibid.*: 361).

This is not the place to debate that, or Barry's reply that it is to misunderstand the uniqueness of liberalism's central claim (which is that culture is a private matter, provided it does not impinge on the rights of others to similarly private choices). The point for us here is that such doubts about the universal relevance of liberalism's interpretation of reason are doubts also about liberal education. Thus in considering the components of 'rationalist liberalis[m]' Parekh seeks to distinguish between 'values that are universal—for example, human dignity, equality of worth and rights, and respect for life', on the one hand, and on the other those which are 'culturally specific', such as 'personal autonomy, individualism and individual choice' (*ibid.*: 360). Not only does this seem—when put together with the earlier quotation—to concede that such values are indeed specific to the European tradition; it also, in a more important sense, runs directly counter to classic aims of liberal education. In the words of Kenneth Strike, that aim is to promote 'autonomy and rationality by promoting academic study and undominated dialogue', and requires the student to learn to be separate from any shaping culture—'the appraisal of one's own traditions' that is best achieved by the distancing effect of 'academic disciplines' (Strike, 1991: 475). 'The chief beneficiaries of the world's literature, philosophy and science', Barry (2001: 31) points out, 'are those whom it enables to break out of the limited range of ideas in which they have been brought up.' Rejecting 'autonomy' and 'individualism' as Parekh does is to reject the very basis of liberal learning.

A subsidiary conclusion—expanding that point from Barry—is that nothing which Parekh proposes for a 'multicultural' literary curriculum has been absent from the best of the liberal tradition. Consider what he says about the need for students to study 'works that explore the structures and forms of experiences of historically marginalised groups such as women, slaves, the poor, the oppressed, migrants and colonial subjects' (Parekh, 2006: 229). He gives three sets of reasons to do so, on which the central tradition of liberal education might comment as follows:

> (1) 'They explore new experiences or familiar ones from neglected and unusual angles.'
>
> Is this not what *Hamlet* does with kingship, *Middlemarch* with industrial change, *Tess of the D'Urbervilles* with the experience of a young woman's being exploited by men, and *Heart of Darkness* with the nature of imperialism?
>
> (2) Such works 'reflect a spirit of defiance and playfulness.'
>
> It is difficult imagine anything more 'playful' than *As You Like It, Tristram Shandy, Ulysses* or *The Pickwick Papers*.
>
> (3) And they 'explore the sensibilities, moods and types of pain and pleasure falling outside the experiences of the literary genres of classical writers.'
>
> Unless this is a stipulation by definition—such that nothing which a 'classical writer' has written is deemed admissible—then it may be pointed out that amongst the examples of dealing with unusual experience are: *Merchant of Venice* (the experience of racism), *Othello* (likewise), *Emma* (the experience of a strong, intelligent woman in a misogynistic society), *Heart of Midlothian* (the experience of a working-class woman refusing to accept being silenced by authority), *Jane Eyre* (the experience of women's being silenced in marriage), *Leaves of Grass* (the experience by ordinary Americans of the process of building a nation), *Grapes of Wrath* (the experience of the poor working class in a crisis of capitalism) and *To Kill a Mockingbird* (the experience of racism).

On the other hand, if the nature of multiculturalism requires —as Parekh (2006: 332–3) proposes—that schools teach 'creationism' alongside 'evolutionary and other theories as well, and provide a balanced critical assessment of them all', then the rationalism and the respect for the difference between religious myth and science which lie at the heart of liberal education would seem to have slipped away, and we would have to conclude that even a moderate multiculturalism is simply not consistent with liberal education as it has been conceived traditionally on the left.

Child-centred education

While multiculturalism ended the left's allegiance to old ideas of liberal education by denying the possibility of culture that could be common, child-centred education undermined the very concept of culture in education as anything other than oppressive of individual freedom. The essence of the idea is that children are natural learners, that this instinct may be encouraged only by allowing it to develop spontaneously at first and then—as the child grows—only under broad guidance from the teacher, and that any external structure of knowledge is an imposition which impedes this growth (Darling, 1994; Entwistle, 1970). For these reasons, child-centred education—or 'new education' or 'progressive education'—has long appealed to that segment of left-wing opinion which, at the extreme, becomes anarchism. These reasons are also why the appeal became stronger in the 1960s, when that interpretation of liberation became common. Although the most radical versions of child-centred ideas have never appealed in Britain to the mainstream of left-wing thinking or (even more) policy, the general idea that education should concentrate on the child who is learning rather than on what is to be learnt has become deeply embedded, and aspects of it have been intensified as society has become individualised and as the internet has seemed to some left-wing writers to make the teacher almost redundant. To even the milder of these views, defining education as being to pass on the best that has been thought and said is archaic.

There are three features of child-centred ideas that have appealed to the left. The first, and oldest, is its romanticism. The understanding of childhood as spontaneous growth has a history going back to Rousseau, who has been thought to have first conceived of childhood in its modern form as a distinct phase of life rather than—as in earlier views—a period merely of physical immaturity (Numata, 2003: 247). As an aspect of the more general reaction against Enlightenment rationalism, it came to be believed that metaphors of natural growth were the way in which child development should be understood (Oelkers, 2002). That romantic view attracted much support among nineteenth-century and twentieth-century intellectuals of a dissenting disposition, especially novelists and poets, for example H.G. Wells (Mack, 1941: 266–79), Thomas Mann (who sent his son Klaus to the student-centred Odenwaldschule in Hesse; Mann, 1932) and Tolstoy (as in the discussion of education in *Anna Karenina*). Tolstoy argued that

> to make education fruitful, that is, to help mankind to advance further and further toward happiness, teaching and learning must be free for both teachers and pupils. Education must be more than a mere compilation of knowledge gathered from everywhere, knowledge that is unnecessary, taught untimely, and sometimes harmful. (quoted by Cohen, 1981: 249)

George Bernard Shaw—always mischievous in expressing extremely what he nevertheless did consistently believe—wrote in the preface to *Misalliance* that education should respect the rights of the child

> to do what it likes and can, to make what it likes and can, to think what it likes and can, to smash what it dislikes and can, and generally to behave in an altogether unaccountable manner within the limits imposed by the similar rights of its neighbours. (Shaw, 1910: 32)

The art critic Herbert Read—an anarchist—wrote in *Education Through Art* in 1943 that

> if… the purpose of education is integration—the preparation of the individual child for his place in society not only vocationally but spiritually and mentally—then it is not information he needs so much as wisdom, poise, self-realisation, zest. (Read, 1943: 227)

Although more ambivalent about child-centredness than these others, D.H. Lawrence gave in 1936 a widely quoted maxim for the whole subsequent educational distrust of authority:

> How to begin to educate a child. First rule: leave him alone. Second rule: leave him alone. Third rule: leave him alone. That is the whole beginning… Leave his sensibilities, his emotions, his spirit, and his mind severely alone. (Lawrence, 1936: 620)

The romanticism was rather rhetorical, but of greater effect was the second component, a veneration for new experience over any kind of canon. Oelkers (2002: 681) points out that the very distinction between 'old' and 'new' in education would not have been recognised before the modern period, with origins in the seventeenth century but becoming the norm with the advance of science:

> The past, especially the past of ancient philosophy and science, was no longer regarded as superior to the present because new and better knowledge can be expected in the future as a result of the new methods of observation and research.

Henceforth, there is 'an "open horizon" for learning' such that 'future knowledge can devalue past knowledge in every aspect'. At least so far as the rejection of a canon is concerned, child-centred ideas are fundamental to the modern age. Since the 1960s, they have become part of the revision of socialist ideas to take account of the decay of authority, summed up by the political philosopher Paul Q. Hirst:

> Modern publics have become more demanding, better educated and less deferential. Their attitude to public services has changed from one of gratitude to a consumer consciousness. They demand higher quality and also more diverse services of greater complexity. (Hirst, 1995: 344)

Socialist thought had to reinvent itself thoroughly in order to respond to that, with New Labour as the result in the UK (Sassoon, 1996: 665–706). Challenging the authority of the teacher, and questioning tradition, were the inevitable corollaries in education.

Though there might be room for disagreement in this form of thinking about whether the admiration for new-ness should require that the child discovers novelty (as opposed to learning from those at the frontiers of knowledge who might be better-equipped to invent or discover truly new things), the experience of education—it is believed—ought to prepare children for that kind of innovation because the impermanence of the modern world makes every citizen into a pioneer of new ideas, forced to interpret the world autonomously because no tradition can any longer authoritatively be trusted as a source of meaning. Thus Dewey and Dewey wrote in 1915 that

> the child is best prepared for life as an adult by experiencing in childhood what has meaning to him as a child; and, further, the child has a right to enjoy his childhood. Because he is a growing animal who must develop so as to live successfully in the grown-up world, nothing should be done to interfere with growth, and everything should be done to further the full and free development of his body and his mind. (Dewey and Dewey, 1915: 17–18)

In the development of ideas about child-centred education, therefore, the cardinal principle became that (as Darling, 1984: 167, put it) 'all knowledge can and should be related to the experience of the pupil.' That is the consequence of John Dewey's ideas because, as Darling and Nisbet (2000: 43) explain, his 'concept of "knowledge" is not as a heritage to be passed on but as something which individuals create for themselves'.

In the 1960s, one appeal of this emphasis on experience was to those thinkers on the left who rejected what Jackson called in an essay in *New Left Review* 'the grammar school tradition' of teaching (Jackson, 1961: 8), which he said dominated all kinds of education, whether actually for academic streams or not, and indeed whether for secondary-age pupils or not. It is the practice that we have described here as the dominant liberal tradition, which is not a rejection of freedom as an aim but rather the belief that autonomy is best achieved through immersion in a tradition of academic learning. Jackson favoured instead a style that, he said, was found 'only in junior and infant schools'. He believed that

> it's a style of teaching followed by many men and women who have few academic qualifications but a considerable openness to the rich experiment and advance that has taken place in the last 40 years at the youngest levels of education. What is so impressive about it is the way it draws the whole responsive child into education: the way it makes a total address to the personality. (*ibid.*: 8)

After this child-centredness of the early years, 'education sometimes turns into a narrower and meaner thing as children get older.' The selective system was invidious, he thought, not only because it divides children between streams, but also because it is 'selective in the parts of the personality which it educates'. Thus all pupils, even those who have been judged capable of benefiting from an academic curriculum, and even at the stage when they are fully engaged in that sort of study, would benefit from the style that is common with small children.

There is something more than incipiently intrusive about such surveillance, and indeed some critics of child-centred methods have seen it as a way of socialising children through 'soft psychological technology' (Sharp and Green, 1975) in its aim to make pedagogy scientific (Walkerdine, 1998). Though proclaimed in the name of fostering the natural growth of the child, if science can reliably map that growth then the teacher is as potentially in control of the undeveloped mind as the doctor is of the needs of an ailing body. The eventual outcome of that kind of approach has been described as 'therapeutic education' by Ecclestone and Hayes, a style of teaching that 'focuses on perceived emotional problems and which aims to make educational content and learning processes more "emotionally engaging"' by treating students as perpetually vulnerable rather than resilient and by 'den[ying] the intellectual and privileg[ing] the emotional' (Ecclestone and Hayes, 2009: x–xi). The danger is present in all teaching, but in an approach which venerates tradition the teacher, too—and not just the pupil—is encouraged to be humble before the weight of the past: no honest teacher could fail to be aware of being inadequate compared to the best that has been created by the best minds that have gone before.

The potential contradiction here—between a rhetoric of liberation and a professional practice of domination—has led to the third and most radical element in child-centred ideas: de-schooling. This hostility to the school as an agent of oppressive socialisation also has its roots in Rousseau, for whom society is the source of evil and the human being is never more truly free than in solitude (Oelkers, 2002: 691). The slogan is from a book of 1973 by Ivan Illich, who proposed that the problem lay in schools as institutions and professionals as supposed experts who imposed their speciously scientific ideas on children. Another writer in this vein, Daniel Bell, wrote in 1973 that 'for Illich, schooling creates a new hierarchy of knowledge, in which the [privileged] maintain their position by arcane and technical knowledge that is closed off from the rest of society' (Bell, 1973: 420). Actually deconstructing schools might not have seemed feasible in the 1960s, but enthusiasm for the internet as a source of learning has borrowed from this same source, and, in some recent left-wing thought, has drawn upon the same anti-authoritarian ideas as inspired the original 1960s radicalism. Tom Bentley, for example—an educational adviser to the Labour government after 1997—argued in 1998 that schools ought to become 'learning networks' that would be 'staffed by learning specialists of different kinds', the only examples of which that he gives being not subject specialists but people who know a lot about guidance and assessment (Bentley, 1998: 183). He explicitly associates his programme with Illich, and describes adherence to academic subjects as 'scholasticism', thus—like all the most radical adherents to child-centred ideas—relegating to medieval inadequacy anything which is tied closely to an inherited structure of knowledge (*ibid.*: 124).

Student-centred education has also appealed to some left-wing writers in connection with vocational education. The tenets of student-centredness entered vocational education early, in the various attempts in the 1930s to use education to get unemployed young people into work. It survived as a current in thinking about vocational education in the post-war period. But the full flowering did not come until the 1970s, and has continued to the present. In the 1980s the philosophy of vocational education became student-centred, with an emphasis on students' discovering things for themselves, and with a hostility to any kind of theory (Hartley, 1987; 2003; Standish, 1997).

This vocationalism accompanied a rejection of old styles of apprenticeship: the efficient worker had to be flexible, and so what was required was competence in specific skills, not the induction into a craft. More recently, this ideology has fitted well with fashionable rhetoric about the nature of the economy, requiring flexible specialisation and generic workers. It is suggested that this new economy and the new education preparing for it are associated with the rise to power of a new professional class—software engineers, design specialists, media workers, purveyors of personal finance—no longer gaining its authority from hierarchy and accepted classifications of knowledge, but now much more dependent on flexible careers, more interested in 'identities' and 'lifestyles' than status, and more inclined to see education as being about a sort of playful experimentation than about disciplined learning. Thus some academic writers on the left have welcomed this vocational student-centredness as a challenge to old styles of hierarchical knowledge. Stephen Ball, for example—following some of the multicultural ideas we noted earlier—has argued that the main educational enemies of the left were the 'cultural restorationists' or (following Raymond Williams) the 'old humanists'. He welcomed the sympathy which many larger employers showed for the vocational student-centredness, and saw this as a way of radically reconstructing schooling whether vocational or not: 'vocational progressivism', he said, is 'set over against the elitist conceptions of knowledge proselytised by the old humanists'.

***

The doubts about liberal education on the left thus have taken many forms, but they all are in some sense versions of the ideas most influentially expressed by Bourdieu. All challenge the claim that some version of inherited culture could be universally valid. All assert, in some form (stronger or weaker) that cultural value is relative to specific cultural groups—one class, one gender, one race, one ethnicity, one language, even one individual. All deny that reason could transcend these specific identities, and therefore all deny the core premise of liberal education that reason and the intellect could shape civilised citizens; indeed, some would reject the very concept of civilisation, as being itself relative. Although there are potentially some tensions among these points of view—for example, between a child-centred idea and an attention to a minority culture that education is hoped to revive or sustain—the shared premise is a suspicion or a downright rejection of universalism. 'The best' no longer even makes sense, because a shared context of understanding by which to evaluate the quality of what has been thought and said has been lost.

Chapter 7

Policy and Practice since the 1960s

Comprehensive education and the curriculum

Meanwhile, Labour politics on education were proceeding largely independently of these left-wing academic ideas. After the party lost power in 1951, two developments took place in its thinking about school education that had implications for the curriculum. One was a gradual shift in favour of comprehensive schools, ending selection at the point of entry to secondary school. The other was a growing tendency to see the expansion of education as being an economic matter, providing employment opportunities for its beneficiaries and supposedly also stimulating the economy overall. The economic rationale was used to justify expansion, and indeed also to justify ending selection: not wasting talent became the dominant theme. But with the party's continuing lack of interest in details of the curriculum, thinking about the content of education was confined to debate internal to education, where it had always been. Thus it exposed the tradition of liberal education in left-wing policy on education to being undermined when professional educational opinion—especially academic opinion—shifted against it.

Labour debates gave the idea of comprehensive education much greater prominence in the 1950s than hitherto. Fenwick points out that the party helped to publicise relevant educational research, and its local power (for example on the London County Council) ensured that enough comprehensive schools existed for the research to take place (Fenwick, 1976: 156). The pressure to change policy in favour of comprehensive schools came from below

—above all from the National Association of Labour Teachers (*ibid.*: 61, 108 and 150), and the main leadership came from Alice Bacon (MP for a constituency in Leeds) who persuaded the National Executive Committee to set up a working party on the question, which she chaired. Francis points out that 'Bacon was a more mainstream Labour figure than previous leading advocates of the common school such as [W.G.] Cove' (Francis, 1995: 331), and the support of the committee ensured that, by 1953, the party was officially committed to extending comprehensive schools. The reason why the policy became increasingly attractive to the party leadership, especially from the 1960s onwards, was that it could be linked to their theme of modernising Britain (Fenwick, 1976: 128). When Labour came to power in 1964, it therefore encouraged local authorities to reorganise their secondary-school systems on comprehensive lines, although —still nervous about how popular this would be—the party did not legislate to force this. All local authorities in Wales and Scotland fully reorganised their schools, but a few in England resisted for long enough for the next Conservative government (in the early 1970s) to enable them to retain their selective systems, even though that government did not interfere with those councils that were already in the process of ending selection.

What to teach children in comprehensive schools remained unresolved by Labour. Its previous policy of increasing the opportunities for working-class children to attend academic courses in the grammar schools and senior secondary schools had never been accompanied by any estimate of the proportion of children who would be capable of benefiting from a full liberal education (Parkinson, 197: 48). There was also continuing unease in the party's leadership about the new policy: George Tomlinson, former Minister of Education, said in 1951 that 'the Party are kidding themselves if they think that the comprehensive school has any popular appeal' (quoted by Dean, 1986: 101). The new party leader after Attlee retired, Hugh Gaitskell, sought to resolve this dilemma by proposing that the grammar-school tradition would remain as part of the evolving comprehensives—as separate tracks within it, or as shaping the whole curriculum (Francis, 1995: 332). He coined the slogan 'grammar schools for all' in an interview with the *Times* in July 1958 (Fenwick, 1976: 109), and that in effect became all that Labour had to say for the next twenty years on the matter of the curriculum. They continued to be of the view, first expressed four decades earlier in *Secondary Education for All*, that the problem with the divided system was that the division was based not on educational considerations but on social and economic grounds (Tawney, 1922: 60).

Some attention was given, it is true, to the needs of adolescents from non-academic streams. The party's advisory committee concluded (as paraphrased by Dean, 1986: 112) that 'of all groups, the [secondary] modern school population was in need of a continued liberal education after leaving school.' But such evidence, too, tended to reinforce the predilection for extending the academic curriculum because that was how the party had interpreted liberal education. In the absence of any clear leadership on the curriculum of the new comprehensive schools, it was shaped at first by the teachers of former academic tracks who tended to occupy the highest-status and most influential positions in schools (Hargreaves, 1982: 51). This not only ensured that the highest-status courses in the new comprehensive schools would be those which Hargreaves describes as having a 'heavy emphasis on the cognitive-intellectual skills and abilities of the traditional school subjects' (*ibid.*: 51). It also meant that, even where aesthetic subjects appeared, for example in music, there was a 'bias' towards the cognitive, which Hargreaves takes to be the 'Western classical tradition' with its 'strong intellectual component because it is normally written down in the form of a score' (*ibid.*: 58). If that was so, there would have been no dissent from Labour: it would confirm that the idea of grammar schools for all came for a while to be, in practice, what was actually developing.

The lead education minister in the 1960s Labour government, Tony Crosland, was certainly not averse to that trend. He himself had been influenced by Laski and Strachey in his youth (Kogan, 2006: 73), and he saw the goal of educational reform not as being the achievement of material equality 'but certainly a greater equality in manners and the texture of social life' (A. Crosland, 1956: 85). He recognised that one of the impediments to cultural equality among children was inequality of cultural opportunities at home, but he believed that schools could overcome this: as paraphrased by Susan Crosland in her biography of her husband, the state should enable 'those without money or position or a literate family background to have equal access to the opportunity that a decent education bestows' (S. Crosland, 1982: 141). There was no sense that such an education was intrinsically inaccessible to children from these backgrounds. He had no objection to the separation of children into different streams, since, like his predecessors, he believed that not all children were capable of benefiting from the liberal education that the academic streams would offer, and he accepted also that teachers were best placed to takes these decisions. The purpose of comprehensive schools, indeed, was to transfer decisions about allocation to the hands of those who could judge on educational grounds alone: the problem with the structurally divided system was that it produced 'extreme social division caused by physical segregation into schools of widely divergent status' (A. Crosland, 1956: 202). But Crosland, like all his predecessors in government, kept away from saying much about what children should now have access to: the curriculum was for teachers to decide.

The dominant influence on that curriculum from teachers who had developed their own experience in teaching academic tracks remained strong until the 1970s. In England, and eventually throughout Britain, it was then eroded by the new kinds of left-wing interpretation of the curriculum which we looked at in Chapters 5 and 6. The older, academic tendency persisted for longer in Scotland, perhaps until the end of the 1980s, aided by a more abiding sense that the liberal academic curriculum was not inaccessible and ought indeed to be the main aim of any kind of humanistic education. These developments in Scotland were influenced by the ideas of the philosopher P.H. Hirst (1974), that the nature of knowledge was as important in defining the curriculum as the needs of society or the characteristics of learners. The result was a report commissioned under the Labour government in the 1970s which was the last official proclamation anywhere in Britain of these old views (until the Conservative government in England after 2010): 'socially relevant issues can[not] really be explored without making use of the insights provided by the various traditions of intellectual enquiry.' The overall aim—quite in keeping with the whole history of the belief in the civilising effects of liberal education—was social integration:

> Schools exist in and for a given society, and one of the main functions of schooling is to equip young people with the skills, the knowledge, and the social and moral attitudes which will fit them for full membership of the adult community. (Scottish Education Department, 1977: 15)

It was not to be an education for conformity, however: this official document's somewhat utopian response to that liberal tradition could have been taken straight from any of the moderately socialist intellectuals earlier in the century:

> There are many activities and experiences which do not seem to have any direct bearing on the social realities of pupils' lives, but which none the less have a profoundly liberating effect. (*ibid.*: 17–18)

But even that Scottish persistence in liberal education had weakened by the 1990s, and certainly the Scottish left showed scant understanding or memory of why socialists had previously been so attached to it.

Humanities Curriculum Project

In the general absence of Labour Party interest in the curriculum, the most creative attempts to adapt the liberal tradition to comprehensive schools were made in England by some teachers working with that minority of university educational academics who did not reject the liberal tradition as oppressive. The most sustained such attempt was in the Humanities Curriculum Project, led by Lawrence Stenhouse (Elliot, 1983; Lawton, 1983; Pring, 1999; 2001).

Stenhouse, too, in fact, was influenced by Scottish practices. He attended school in Manchester, and university in St Andrews and Glasgow. Through teaching between 1951 and 1956 in one of the old Scottish omnibus schools, he formed a sense of how the liberal curriculum that was being offered to the academic streams might be adapted to other groups of pupils without losing its essential philosophical underpinning. He developed these ideas after he set up the Centre for Applied Research in Education at the University of East

Anglia which became the focus of the Humanities Curriculum Project. Lawton summed up Stenhouse's inspiration in a manner that is reminiscent of Matthew Arnold's aims acquired from his father's reforms at Rugby just over a century earlier:

> [Stenhouse] once told me that his ideas about 'humanities' were derived partly from the kind of sixth form general studies he had himself encountered as a pupil at Manchester Grammar School. What Lawrence wanted to do was to make that kind of humanities-based learning experience available not just to an élite few, but to all pupils. (Lawton, 1983)

The Project was funded by the Nuffield Foundation and by the Schools Council (a semi-autonomous organisation that was itself funded by government to develop the school curriculum in England and Wales). In the words of a summary of its evaluation, the project was asked to provide 'stimulus, support and materials for schools [that were] teaching the humanities to students aged fourteen to sixteen' (MacDonald, 1971: 163). The aim was to understand 'how to allow adolescents to reach views responsibly without being restricted by the teacher's bias or subjected to undue pressures by their peers'. So they produced curricular material on controversial topics, such as war and sex. The materials were tried out in a few dozen schools in 1968; by 1970, some 500 schools were using them (about one tenth of the publicly financed secondary schools in England and Wales).

Stenhouse set out the magnitude of the task in *Culture and Education*, in a summation of what he thought might be achieved based on his experience in trying to develop such a curriculum for all:

> Sociologists commonly conceive the function of education as the transmission of culture from generation to generation. It is the purpose of this book to outline a theory which suggests some of the implications of this for the practice of education. (Stenhouse, 1967: 1)

His view of culture was unreservedly of the same kind as intellectuals on the left had entertained for a century, and with no hint of the relativism that was then emerging in the academy: 'culture is something desirable, a refinement, the intellectual side of civilisation' (*ibid.*: 2). Culture would liberate, not constrain: 'culture is a prerequisite of freedom rather than a restriction upon it' (*ibid.*: 9).

Neither did Stenhouse have any inclination to place the needs of the child ahead of the importance of cultural transmission, because he believed that these were not in tension. It was through thinking critically about culture as a shared inheritance that people learnt how to be individuals:

> The personal and individual creative act which is made possible by the mastery of symbols is a kind of critical comment upon the culture from which it springs. (*ibid.*: 34)

What was then required was to distinguish between the particular academic forms that liberal education had taken and the principles that underlay it (*ibid.*: 11). Thus the main challenge now was to

> expose the difficulties which arise when the academic approach is attempted with less able pupils, and distinguish some of the valuable effects of academic education which may be preserved in our teaching of those whose turn of mind is less rigorous and systematic. (*ibid.*: 90)

Nevertheless, though the academic tradition was not for everyone, tradition in a more general sense was:

> We... interact with the past through an immense store of written records and works of art. These stored ideas allow us to bring 'the best that has been thought and said' into a dialogue with our contemporary culture. Interaction with the past is an element in our own cultural development; and it is of course a major role of the educational system to keep going this conversation of past with present. (*ibid.*: 18)

What must emphatically not be done is to simplify by 'watering down', replacing the best by ephemera, for example 'instead of "Paradise Lost", Alfred Noyes's "Highwayman", [Southey's] "The Inchcape Rock" or [Auden's] "Night Mail"'. The effect of that does a disservice to those it is meant to help:

> Of course, they have their place. But to make a diet of them is to reduce literature from its status of the best that has been thought and said to a resource for a wet Sunday afternoon. The teacher has simplified by becoming more frivolous, even trivial, and less relevant to life. (*ibid.*: 125)

In practice, therefore, 'the curriculum may most profitably be regarded as a selection of culture' (*ibid.*: 57), in which critical debate is brought to bear on inherited knowledge. He observed that when Shakespeare's range of experience and emotion is considered (*Macbeth, Merchant of Venice, Othello, Lear, Hamlet, The Tempest, As You Like It, The Taming of the Shrew*, the history plays)

> it would almost appear that the traditional curriculum covers fundamental interests of the adolescent adequately; and indeed it does. This is its prime educational justification. Its relevance makes it of serious importance. (*ibid.*: 136)

The left and vocational education

Nevertheless, as we have seen, Stenhouse's ideas were not the dominant ones in left-wing academic discussion of the curriculum. Because Labour essentially left these details to academic and professional debate, in practice the main response was to neglect the tradition of liberal education, and thus in particular to ignore the kind of curriculum which Stenhouse advocated. In place of that, Labour came increasingly to interpret all education as conducing towards the ends of skills, employability, social mobility and national economic competitiveness.

The origins of these vocational concerns in place of liberal education go far back in Labour's history. Indeed, there was always a current of thought on the social-democratic left which questioned the dominance of liberal education. Before the ideas of Bourdieu and others in the 1960s, this was mostly not on the grounds that knowledge was itself specific to particular classes or other social groups, which was a position largely confined to the Marxists of the Labour Colleges whose educational influence was already dwindling by the 1930s. The child-centred ideas, although gaining influence on the radical fringes from the 1920s, did not feature strongly in mainstream left-wing thought until the 1960s. The main early challenge to liberal education therefore came from those who thought that it was useless vocationally, and who believed that what was needed—either by working-class children or by the economy as a whole—was a strengthened and more systematic programme of training for work. This view was present as a minority position on the left throughout the century, and has grown to be the dominant view of the left in government since the 1960s, attracting to it arguments for using education to promote social mobility or other kinds of widening of opportunity. Thus the vocational case against liberal education has been based on three kinds of instrumentalism: that it is not what the economy needs to prosper, that it is not what students need to get a job, and that, even if it is desirable, it is not sufficient for a left-wing programme since the main goal is to give people opportunities for personal advancement. These motives for supporting vocational education were then, almost by accident, quite consistent with the post-1960s academic critique of liberal education as invidiously restricting opportunity.

Michael Sanderson, seeking to explain why vocational education was of low status in Britain, noted five reasons why liberal education was held in high regard. The first was one we have noted several times, the belief that a liberal education was the opposite of a 'menial' education (Sanderson, 1993: 189). This of course was also one reason why early socialists wanted to widen access to it, since they believed that subordinated social groups should have the chance to escape servility. As Sanderson notes, such a view of the social role of liberal education was similar regardless of the particular version of it that was being discussed, whether classics at Oxford, mathematics at Cambridge or philosophy at the Scottish universities. Harris (1992), agreeing with this first point by Sanderson, argued that the philosophical idealism which lay in the background of all these versions of liberal education—the current of thought which we noted in Chapter 2 came from T.H. Green—'was at least partly responsible for the powerful anti-vocational bias that characterised British educational institutions for much of the twentieth century' (Harris, 1992: 138). Asserting the importance of vocational education therefore came to seem inseparable from challenging liberal education in the name of vocational usefulness.

Sanderson's second, third and fourth reasons are all essentially refinements of that first one, casting different sorts of light on the problem and thus each indicating why, eventually, a left-wing policy favouring vocational education emerged. He argued, second, that 'liberal education enjoyed the dignity of mystery', for example by its being associated with the study of ancient languages. This general view underpinned the gradual shift away from Latin and Greek in the twentieth century, and their replacement by, at first, mainly French and German (Campbell, 1968). In the 1980s and after, the left came also to see the learning of modern languages as not only effective for the economy, but also as a means to reflect cultural diversity (Coleman, 2009; Lanvers and Coleman, 2013). Other aspects of the 'mystery' of liberal education collapsed with the decline of religion, and with it the ending of any claim that a curriculum might be justified by ultimate ends: Sanderson's third point was the connection of liberal education with 'Church, State and Empire'. Relentless secularism inevitably tends towards the vocational in a society where certificated skills are increasingly required for any kind of decent employment (Gallie, 2000).

Sanderson's fourth reason why there was British admiration for liberal education was the 'belief that a mind trained in an abstract liberal discipline could apply itself flexibly to any other subject matter'. This may seem to be not dissimilar to the later claims that the economy requires flexibility, but what has changed is the ending of the view that a general liberal education could inculcate it. Where academic liberal education is perceived to be rigidly based on out-of-date knowledge, other ways of educating flexibly skilled workers seem more plausible, and thus what was in fact an old kind of vocational claim—that liberal education would prepare people for leadership—has become the very opposite.

Sanderson's final reason for the dominance of liberal education was that it was cheap, a motive that we have also noted from the record of the Workers' Educational Association. Part of the response to this problem from the left in power has been to try to persuade employers to take on some of the responsibility for specialised vocational training. This was a recurrent issue in later debates about training, for example when thinkers who were critical of British practice argued for a partnership between the state and employers, as in Germany. One left-of-centre report which emerged from that later period—the final report of a 'National Commission on Education' set up by the Paul Hamlyn Foundation—

argued that responsibility for the UK's poor record on training was shared by government and employers. There was both 'reluctance by employers to take a long-term approach to investment in human resources' and also a 'failure on the part of Government to provide the necessary legislative framework'. They believed that lying underneath both of these inadequacies were 'underlying cultural and social attitudes', including a failure by workers themselves to want to undertake training (National Commission on Education, 1993: 245). We return to this report again shortly.

One of the earliest attempts from the left in Britain to question the admiration for liberal education came from Sidney Webb, who—with his wife Beatrice—has probably better claim than any other single intellectual apart from Tawney to have shaped the ideology of the Labour Party, at least up to the time of the 1945 Labour government. Judges notes that 'the Webbs... [believed] that education provided the impulse to the progress of a modern industrial democracy', believing in the economic value of knowledge (Judges, 1961: 34). Sidney Webb argued that 'national efficiency depend[s] on our making the most of the capacities of the whole population' (Webb, 1904: 9).

In helping to reform the various university colleges in London, for example, Sidney Webb saw them not as liberal institutions of the kind found in Oxford and Cambridge but, as Judges puts it, 'a manifestation of municipal service' (Judges, 1961: 40). Webb said that London University, being in the midst of the economy of a great city, could not aim for

> the all-round cultivation of the individual mind, the continuous appreciation of the finest literature that has been written, the balanced judgement due to a scholarly criticism of the past achievements of mankind, the refinement of humour and the sense of perspective. (Webb, 1904: 53)

In any case, even if this were possible, he wrote of the modern irrelevance of the Oxford Greats: 'a "leisured curriculum" of the Greats kind is not suitable for engineers, business men, teachers, solicitors, doctors, civil servants' (*ibid.*: 52).

Nevertheless, Webb was not inveterately opposed to the principles of liberal education, even though he interpreted it differently from his contemporaries and predecessors whose ideas we looked at earlier. Rather in the same way as Huxley misquoted Mill to make the case for bringing science into the liberal curriculum, so Webb paraphrased Arnold in aid of a liberal kind of vocational education, saying it was necessary to train 'the future business or any other man to see life "truly", and to see it "whole"' (*ibid.*: 98). He accepted the importance of education's contributing to the development of character, culture and resourcefulness (*ibid.*: 10–11), and London University could provide 'subtle cultivation of the imagination and generosity of aim', even if it could not have the socially select character of Oxford or Cambridge (*ibid.*: 50): Webb was thoroughly meritocratic.

At this same time, proponents of a liberal education were not opposed to a vocational emphasis. Percy Nunn, for example, argued in the 1920 book which we have quoted earlier that a vocational aspect of school education would be acceptable provided that it was not for occupations that 'meet no trivial or transient needs', but rather served those which 'have behind them a dignified history and a distinctive moral tradition', of which he gave the examples 'a naval officer, a mariner, an engineer, a cabinet-maker, a builder, a farmer'. Such occupations 'have nursed fine characters and given scope to noble intellects and splendid practical powers'. The reason he would admit training for them into a liberal education was that 'they cannot be worthily carried on without scientific knowledge or artistic culture' (Nunn, 1920: 205). He accepted, too, that vocational work could stimulate pupils' interests: engaging with such vocations

> often unlocks the finer energies of a mind which a 'general' education would leave stupid and inert... In short, the 'vocational' training may become, in the strictest sense, 'liberal'. (*ibid.*: 205)

However, even though 'vocational education, if it is conducted in a liberal spirit, is permissible, [it] cannot be made universal', and so more general liberal education is needed to supplement it.

Such ambivalence persisted between then and the 1950s, though the openness to vocational education remained, despite the bias in the general educational culture against vocational education which historians such as Sanderson have noted. The left was always perhaps more likely than people in other political positions to interpret liberal education to include the vocational because the students in whom it was most interested would not have the luxury of not having to earn a living. But what was always resisted until the 1960s was a vocational aim as a worthwhile educational goal in itself. Richard Hoggart, writing later but looking back, saw vocationalism as inseparable from relativism since it invoked no absolute standards of cultural quality or judgement:

> Vocationalism is or seems value-free to those who wish to avoid a definition of education which raises troubling questions about social justice, about the needs of democracy and, an even worse threat, about education as a good in itself, whatever its practical benefits. (Hoggart, 1995: 22)

Deploring the vocational emphasis of the Conservative government of the 1980s and 1990s, he invoked the old leftist support for liberal education as its most telling indictment: '"don't teach my boy poetry. He's going to be a grocer" (or a grocer's daughter) is back with us after a century and a half' (*ibid.*: 23).

Labour and vocational education after the 1960s

Favretto sums up the reasons for Labour's conversion in the 1960s to justifying educational expansion on economic and vocational grounds:

> If technological unemployment was to be contained, the educational system as a whole had to be radically reformed in order to give children a training suited to an automated age. (Favretto, 2000: 66)

He points out that, until the 1960s, left-wing ideas in Britain rarely paid much attention to economic motives for educational expansion, as opposed to what he calls 'status and classless society discourses' (*ibid.*: 68–9). The new view was linked in public statements by Labour to the idea of 'the scientific age', notably in the speeches which Harold Wilson made in the political campaigning which led to the 1964 Labour government. This rhetoric was not only about widening access to education in order to draw on all potential talent for the economy. Even the critique of existing elite schools was newly cast in terms of efficiency: forming elites to rule an empire was not the same as producing managers to modernise the economy. By contrast, Favretto notes, the 1945 Labour manifesto did not even mention technical education and training (*ibid.*: 71).

That economic interest then prevailed in the 1970s Labour government, which had in any case run out of ideological zeal for equality, and was in a precarious position politically. It did not try to enforce further moves to comprehensive schooling, and left thinking about teaching methods and the curriculum to specialist educational debates. Indeed, there is a sense in which Labour had simply lost faith in the old socialist interpretation of liberal education, mainly because of the economic arguments and perhaps also—on Labour's academic fringes—partly because of the allegation that the old curriculum was only for an elite.

The culmination was a speech by James Callaghan in 1976, shortly after he succeeded Wilson as prime minister, in which he set out what he said was Labour's answer to the question 'what do we want from the education of our children and young people?' (Callaghan, 1976). This speech has often been described as being an attack on 'progressive' methods of teaching—the child-centredness that we have considered in Chapter 6—and was indeed to some extent that (Simon, 1991: 447–8). He said:

> There is now widespread recognition of the need to cater for a child's personality to let it flower in its fullest possible way. The balance was wrong in the past. We have a responsibility now to see that we do not get it wrong again in the other direction. (Callaghan, 1976)

The speech is also seen as the beginning of an insistence that there should be a national curriculum prescribed centrally, and it was that too (Simon, 1991: 450), although with the accustomed Labour self-denial on anything curricular:

> It is not my intention to become enmeshed in such problems as whether there should be a basic curriculum with universal standards—although I am inclined to think there should be. (Callaghan, 1976)

Nevertheless, what is really striking about the speech is not those matters for which it became well known (or notorious on that segment of the left which had come to be enthusiastic about child-centred methods and which, with almost anarchist instinct, had come to distrust any state specification of the curriculum). The main point is the prominence given to economic justifications. Education should enable people to gain employment:

> In today's world, higher standards are demanded than were required yesterday and there are simply fewer jobs for those without skill.

Notably in the light of later Labour interest, there is nothing about social mobility. But his concern with the relationship between education and the economy is also true, in a different way, of those who are on a route of upward mobility:

> I have been concerned to find out that many of our best trained students who have completed the higher levels of education at university or polytechnic have no desire to join industry.

Nowhere does Callaghan invoke the old liberal ideals. The speech's concern with standards actually amounted to something quite elementary; the 'essential tools' for today's society are:

> Basic literacy, basic numeracy, the understanding of how to live and work together, respect for others, respect for the individual. This means requiring certain basic knowledge, and skills and reasoning ability. It means developing lively inquiring minds and an appetite for further knowledge that will last a lifetime.

That is very far from the best that has been thought and said:

> The goals of our education, from nursery school through to adult education, are clear enough. They are to equip children to the best of their ability for a lively, constructive, place in society, and also to fit them to do a job of work.

'Lively' and 'constructive' show how much, despite everything, Callaghan too had absorbed the idea that education was about enjoyment more than it was about rigour, difficulty and critical absorption into a tradition.

The practical left—those, like Callaghan, with an aspiration to govern, rather than to debate socialist ideas in the academy—then responded to the experience of the Conservative government in the 1980s by insisting all the more strongly on education as a means of creating opportunities, rather than holding to the older views that learning great ideas was worthwhile even if wholly separated from what people did with them or from whether their education enabled them to gain a good job or to be upwardly socially mobile. Education came to be seen almost as a branch of economics (Wolf, 2002). A characteristic policy document expressing such views was the report of the National Commission on Education published in 1993. Rather than seeking to reform the liberal tradition, it rejected it out of hand, echoing the debates from the academic left:

> At secondary school level the design of the curriculum has been dominated by the needs of the minority who are being prepared for further study at an intensive academic level. (National Commission on Education, 1993: 7)

What was then needed was greater attention to 'studies of a technical, practical or vocational nature'. It claimed, with no real evidence, that Scotland had 'done rather better' than the rest of the UK, thus ignoring the predominantly academic character of the Scottish tradition. The Commission did favour some sort of breadth, basing the school curriculum on languages, mathematics, science and technology, expressive arts and physical education, and humanities and social science, but the merely nominal character of this obeisance to the liberal tradition is evident in the absence of any detailed discussion of these strangely yoked-together labels. There is none of, say, Huxley's or Nunn's different kind of discussion of the distinction between science and technology, no sense that 'languages' might be the disputed heir to an older debate about various ways of conveying an understanding of multiculturalism, none of Tawney's or Hoggart's thoughts about how the 'humanities' might differ from as well as share features with 'social science', and—in the grouping of 'expressive arts' with physical education—a wilful ignoring of the very notion of aesthetics. The curriculum would also have to teach 'life skills' and 'citizenship', with no apparent awareness that these were, in the liberal tradition, assumed to flow from a proper engagement with the central ideas of the central subjects: literature in several languages, mathematics, natural science and the several ways in which society has been organised in different places and at different times, responding in different ways to varying natural environments. If 'life skills' and 'citizenship' are not embedded in human traditions of thought, the liberal tradition held, they could not be inculcated by any more direct means.

The pedagogical approach would be thoroughly directed by features of the students' current lives rather than by any aspect of knowledge: 'the curriculum needs to be so framed as to recognise the different needs, abilities, interests and circumstances of pupils' (*ibid.*: 59). Despite the Commission's strictures on what they saw as the excessively academic character of schooling, any distinction among different forms of knowledge would be eliminated by the fiat of assessing learning solely in terms of outcomes:

> Subjects or fields of study at the later stages will not be formally designated 'academic,' 'technical,' 'practical' or 'vocational': in all cases they will require outcomes with a mix of knowledge, understanding and practical ability. (*ibid.*: 59)

The report of the Commission was endorsed a year later by a Commission on Social Justice which had been set up by the leader of the Labour Party, John Smith, in conjunction with the left-wing Institute for Public Policy Research. This report repeated the insistence of its predecessor that (in effect) the way to deal with the inherited academic curriculum was to ignore it, and to treat the question as one of economic purpose and pupil motivation:

> The division between education and training is damaging because it polarises knowledge and skill into separate courses rather than combining them to promote understanding; it splits theory and practice when the demand from the economy and from society is that they be combined; it reduces the motivation of the majority of young people because it condemns them to a 'silver' and 'bronze' level vocational education while the minority are allowed onto the prestigious academic track; and it forces a false choice between general and vocational education when it is a

> combination that we all need as preparation for a life of change and continuous learning. (Commission on Social Justice, 1994: 131-2)

Thus not discussing the academic curriculum—which earlier in the century had meant implicitly aiming to hand it on as liberal education for all—had now become the aim of abolishing it by vocational take-over.

The report came with an endorsement from the new Labour leader, Tony Blair, following Smith's death, and its ideas permeated Labour thinking throughout the period of government after 1997. There were two overriding concerns, neither of them dealing with the old ideas of what a liberal curriculum could achieve: trying to use education to stimulate the economy, and trying to bring about more equal opportunities to enter those kinds of educational course, or that level of educational attainment, which would lead to upward social mobility.

Blair, for example, said when campaigning for re-election in 2001 that Labour

> is the true Party of aspiration, of opportunity, dedicated to creating a genuine meritocratic Britain where people can get to the highest level their talents take them; where we break down every barrier, every impediment to our big idea—the development of human potential. (Blair, 2001)

Hence, he said, there was the aim of widening access to university and to advanced skills, including the 'New Deal' which was a (very successful) Labour scheme to get unemployed people back into work often by means of training:

> That's why we are committed to fifty per cent of our young people getting a university degree. Why we want the best schools in Europe. Why we want the New Deal extended to all those who can work but don't. Why we will invest in adult skills, science, technology.

In a later speech, he also related this to social mobility: 'I want to see social mobility, as it did for the decades after the war, rising once again, a dominant feature of British life' (Blair, 2004).

These themes of opportunity and the economy could have been expressed by Harold Wilson or Tony Crosland in the 1960s, and they reflected the development of pragmatic left-wing thought in the 1980s and 1990s. Similar ideas were expressed by Gordon Brown, Chancellor of the Exchequer when Blair was Prime Minister, and then Prime Minister from 2007 to 2010. In 1999, he linked investment in education to economic growth:

> The fairer Britain is, the more open Britain is to the talents of all, from whatever class or background, the more enterprising and prosperous all of Britain will be. (Brown, 1999)

Once again, as with Blair, the main concern is with the economy and with economic opportunity. As Prime Minister, Brown said a decade later:

> The new model for education in the 21st century—the biggest step we can take into the future—is to unlock the talents of all young people. Let the new economy be one where social mobility is not held back and in this new economy there must be no cap on aspiration, no ceiling on opportunity and no limit on where your talents can take you. (Brown, 2009)

We might expect that from leaders faced with economic problems, or specifically responsible, as finance minister, for the country's economy. But the same kinds of concern are found from Labour's education ministers too. David Blunkett was Secretary of State for Education between 1997 and 2001. If anything, his rhetoric was even more closely tied to the economic role of education than was that of Brown and Blair. He wrote in 2001 that 'the role of government is increasingly to invest on the supply side of the economy' (Blunkett, 2001: 2). Investing in skills 'pays a long-term dividend for the individuals concerned and for the performance of the economy' (*ibid.*: 3). He praised vocational education and dealt with the distinction between it and academic education in the same way as the National Commission had done a decade before —by ignoring it:

> It also implies a key role for vocational education in schools and beyond, alongside the development of academic skills. In a modern economy we must recognise the value of both forms of education, and promote entrepreneurship and knowledge in all their permutations. (*ibid.*: 4)

In describing 'the full benefits of education' Blunkett mentioned the economic value to the individual, and to the employer, the benefits in better health and in reduced crime, and the value to the country's 'international competitiveness' of having a well-educated workforce. No intrinsic value is mentioned, nor even an effect on, say, democracy or civic awareness.

The attention to vocational and economic purposes affected policy for adult education as well as that for schools and universities. A report commissioned by the Labour government after 1997 recommended an expansion of what was now called 'lifelong learning', but now with a far heavier emphasis on its economic value than even in the Ashby report of the 1950s which we discussed in Chapter 3 (Fryer, 1997). As in these quotations from Blair, Brown and Blunkett, the overriding concern was not with broad enlightenment, but with what Tight (1998: 482) described as the 'narrower perspective on vocational education and training'. Unlike Ashby, the report did not relate its recommendations to the traditions of liberal adult education at all; in Tight's words, 'the more inspirational, emancipatory and individual elements of the vision have been lost or downgraded' (Tight, 1998: 483 and 479–80).

None of these policy aims after 1997 were inconsistent with older socialist concerns: using education to strengthen the economy, and promoting opportunity in education and by means of education, were, as we have seen, as old as the Labour Party itself. What was missing, though, was attention to ideas. That too had been an omission by earlier Labour leaders, but the difference then was that alongside them in the public debate were socialist intellectuals arguing for widening access to that same liberal education as had been available only to the few. Now, if Labour leaders paid any attention to the recondite arguments within the academic left, they would generally find only a variety of claims that the problem of access lay in the curriculum itself, and that defining a common culture through the curriculum was unavoidably invidious. It is not surprising that these Labour leaders turned instead to the economists who at least could help them to follow in the footsteps of Raymond Williams' 'industrial trainers' by telling them something about the utilitarian value of skills and about the economic benefit of drawing upon all available talent in the society.

Chapter 8

Liberal Education Sustained?

Sheldon Rothblatt has remarked on the persistence of the ideas of a liberal education, surviving in some form for two and a half millennia, and in its modern form since the Enlightenment:

> The phrase 'a liberal education'... enjoys an extraordinary continuity and has survived each of the revolutions that should have disposed of it... The words continue to exercise a hold on the imagination, and scarcely any educational change of significant proportions is undertaken without reference to some aspect of its history. (Rothblatt, 1976: 199)

The common element throughout has been, in some form, the belief that 'liberal education [is] the pathway to civilisation' (*ibid.*: 23). This remains true of the views of the left. Through the changes and fashions of the past half-century, the older socialist views have persisted as a memory. More fundamentally than that, the universalism and rationalism that are the origins of modern socialist ideology have not vanished from thinking on the political left about education. It is what socialist ideas share with liberalism, in all its varieties, that matter here, not only because, in Joppke's words, 'the universal creed of liberty and equality that marks all liberal societies' is now ubiquitous, but also because these Enlightenment ideas are particularly relevant to thinking about an educational curriculum (Joppke, 2004: 253–4). The 'universalistic individualism'—as Boli *et al.* (1985: 156) call it—has as its premise that everyone is the same, everywhere and for all time. Modern socialism's original inspiration was to make that abstract claim empirically true, to create the social conditions in which the actual cultural inequalities of capitalist society would be ended. The aim was always individual, though—to enable people to flourish as they might. If education could stimulate that equality mentally and culturally, even when material inequality had not yet been ended, then socialism might help to realise Arnold's dictum that 'men of culture are the true apostles of equality.' If the ground of these political aims is rational universalism, there is always in socialist and liberal thought a tendency towards a curriculum constructed on these same principles. There is also always a tendency on the left to value culture in the manner that Arnold gave us, and not to reduce education to training for employment, far less to take it as 'the best economic policy we have' (the words of Tony Blair in 1998: Department for Education and Employment, 1998: 9).

In fact, even as liberal education was being doubted on the left, there did persist minority currents that attempted to keep it alive. We have already noted the Humanities Curriculum Project of Lawrence Stenhouse, relatively short-lived and not strongly influential on left-wing programmes for education, but unambiguously based on principles that would have been recognised right back through the socialist intellectuals of the first half of the twentieth century, through the activists of the Workers' Educational Association, to Arnold and Huxley as they laid the ground for a liberal education that would stimulate everyone. Before the 'new sociology of education' changed things utterly, there was an old sociology which examined in careful detail the impediments to working-class students' having proper opportunities to benefit from a liberal curriculum. The classic text in that tradition is *Education and the Working Class*, by Jackson and Marsden, much closer when published in 1962 to the older tradition than to the new ideas which followed:

> On the one hand we have the central culture of our society... which must be preserved and transmitted; on the other hand we have institutions which do this for the middle class but not for the working-class majority. (Jackson and Marsden, 1962: 221)

Not only is this part of an older way of looking at the problem; it also explicitly distances itself from what came next:

> It seems to us that what we call our central culture and what the teachers [in their research interviews] call 'middle class values' are by no means the same thing, and the problem is to disentangle one from the other.

To suppose that culture in Arnold's sense is specific to one class, they say, would be to directly contradict what he meant, in preference for 'something provincial and partisan'. The irony here is that the complacent equating of class and culture by some of the grammar-school teachers whom Jackson and Marsden interviewed in the 1950s became the axiom of a later kind of Marxist sociology, as we have seen in Chapters 5 and 6. Their conclusion links the universalism of education with a tradition of aspiration to a common culture, just as the early Raymond Williams saw in the history of socialist thought:

> How are we to interpret Arnold's magnificent prose in our own time? Can it be done at all in an education system which remains 'exclusive' and not 'national'? Or to put it another way, can we not begin by accepting the nation, and rooting our schools and colleges in that acceptance, instead of endlessly improving the amenities and efficiencies of an elite system? (Jackson and Marsden, 1962: 222)

If Jackson and Marsden provide a point of empirical connection between an older tradition and a continuing, though minority, universalism, a corresponding theoretical continuity is found in an essay by the Marxist theorist Hannah Arendt, writing mostly from America (to where she went as a refugee from occupied France in 1941), but influential on socialist debates in many countries. She was not impressed by child-centred or progressive education, describing these practices as

> that complex of modern educational theories which originated in Middle Europe and consists of an astounding hodgepodge of sense and nonsense [aiming] to accomplish, under the banner of progressive education, a most radical revolution in the whole system of education. (Arendt, 1961 [1954]: 178)

What this meant, she said, was that 'all the rules of sound human reason were thrust aside.' She did recognise the appeal of 'the new' in education to all emancipatory thought, based on the new-ness of each small child:

> The role played by education in all political utopias from ancient times onward shows how natural it seems to start a new world with those who are by birth and nature new. (*ibid.*: 176)

Nevertheless, that is to ignore that we are born into 'the old', into the traditions of thought the legacy of which we cannot escape:

> Since the world is old, always older than [children] themselves, learning inevitably turns toward the past, no matter how much living will spend itself in the present. (*ibid.*: 195)

The problem with education as it had become in America (and she saw America as prefiguring more general social change) was that it had undermined the necessary authority of tradition as embodied in the teacher. The 'crisis of authority in education is most closely connected with the crisis of tradition' (*ibid.*: 193). The undermining of pedagogical authority was also a consequence of an artificial and educationally dangerous attempt to erase all distinction, 'to erase as far as possible the difference between young and old, between the gifted and the ungifted, finally between children and adults, particularly between pupils and teachers' (*ibid.*: 180). Education was induction, and required humility on the part of the learners. She was impatient with 'this absurdity of treating children as an oppressed minority in need of liberation' (*ibid.*: 190), and also with any education that was not primarily intellectual: she rejected the

> basic assumption... that you can know and understand only what you have done yourself, and its application to education is as primitive as it is obvious: to substitute, insofar as possible, doing for learning. (*ibid.*: 182)

In particular, therefore, vocational training or any other kind of education towards practical goals was not truly education, and indeed was a betrayal of the traditions of thought that make us rational beings. The intention of such training

> was not to teach knowledge but to inculcate a skill, and the result was a kind of transformation of institutes for learning into vocational institutions which have been as successful in teaching how to drive a car or how to use a typewriter or, even more important for the 'art' of living, how to get along with other people and to be popular, as they have been

> unable to make the children acquire the normal prerequisites of a standard curriculum. (*ibid.*: 183)

Persistence of universalism

Arendt, or Jackson and Marsden, represent minority currents of universalist thought about education which persisted despite the new sociology and despite the insistently vocational tendency of Labour when in power. More recently, there has also been some re-assertion of universal liberal principles as the left has tried to find a way of responding to the political success and ideological cogency of the new right. A few illustrations of this response might indicate why liberal education of an old kind has not been wholly forgotten. Internationally, though mostly not specific to education, there has been for example Brian Barry's forthright restatement of liberal universalism (Barry, 2001). Laclau has argued, similarly, that 'under the banner of multiculturalism, the classical values of the Enlightenment are under fire, and considered as little more than the cultural preserve of Western imperialism' (Laclau, 1996: 47). The inevitable clashes of interests have to be resolved by appeal to greater principles, and indeed 'in actual fact, there is no particularism which does not make appeal to such principles in the construction of its own identity.' Making sure that universal principles are universally applied is the whole point of emancipatory politics:

> It is one thing to say that the universalistic values of the West are the preserve of its traditional dominant groups; it is very different to assert that the historical link between the two is a contingent and unacceptable fact which can be modified through political and social struggles. (*ibid.*: 33)

There is similar re-evaluation of relativist or essentialising ideas in connection with specific political movements. In connection with the position of women, Dietz, for example, has argued that

> despite the best of sentiments in attempting to find something unique in women's identity as (potential) mothers, social feminism distorts the meaning of politics and political action largely by reinforcing a one-dimensional view of women as creatures of the family. (Dietz, 1985: 20)

She says that women cannot be emancipated except by appeal to universal ideas:

> Not the language of love and compassion, but only the language of freedom and equality, citizenship and justice, will challenge nondemocratic and oppressive political institutions. (*ibid.*: 32)

Specifically on ethnic multiculturalism, Alibhai-Brown (a journalist and prominent political advocate of the rights of black people and of people from minority ethnic groups) has written that, while 'different cultures are to be valued', it is nevertheless 'always wrong for them to take precedence over fundamental human rights' (Alibhai-Brown, 2000: 57). She regrets the 'increasing balkanisation of identities', or 'tribal multiculturalism', because, she believes,

> at their worst, [tribal multiculturalisms] take differences as essentialist and never-changing, and seek to divide people into separate and mutually exclusive categories which do not reflect either the complexities of our identities or the ways in which we must all interact deeply with each other in our shared society. (*ibid.*: 45–6)

In short, such general defences from the political left of universal principles are based on a point which Beiner makes in a critique of Iris Marion Young:

> The rejection of moral universalism is clearly a moral and philosophical dead-end, for if there are no moral universals, then one cannot appeal to equality or justice, and if there is no possibility of appealing to these universals, then multiculturalism itself makes no sense. (Beiner, 2006: 32)

There is also a deeper sense in which these ideas do not have to be developed by the left at all, since they have become so embedded in democratic society. That is perhaps the major change since the time of the socialist intellectuals whom we discussed earlier, who were writing when the ideals of equal worth and equal rights were not yet fully accepted, even in principle, and when the left was their main carrier. Now, as Joppke says, they are everywhere, and only the undemocratic far right denies them as a matter of public political philosophy. Multiculturalism is not in doubt as a description of a state of affairs, but since 'the liberal, difference-blind state with its universal citizenship' emerged precisely as a 'peacemaker' in a 'hyper-diverse society' following the religious wars of seventeenth-century Europe which gave rise to it, relegating cultural differences to the private realm and deliberately out of the world of politics, there is 'no convincing explanation... why *this* solution... no longer works' (Joppke, 2004: 239–40; his emphasis). The real sources of discrimination and inequality are socio-economic.

Such general re-assertions of liberal universalism on the left then have specific implications for education, though with scant memory of any of the history we have traced here. Alibhai-Brown develops her argument in connection with the school curriculum. She says that 'traditional multiculturalism... is essentially an education of redress and cultural competition, not an education which teaches children the skills of critical interrogation' (Alibhai-Brown, 2000: 70). Like the socialist thinkers of early in the twentieth century (but not explicitly so), she believes the aim of the curriculum ought to be creating a common culture, embracing all strands certainly, but as firmly including the majority culture as any other: extending 'the appeal of Shakespeare to enable black and Asian children to feel this is part of their heritage' as well as insisting that 'white children need to see Benjamin Zephaniah as their poet too.' Nevertheless, the relativism implicit even in that liberal tolerance remains a contrast with the earlier writers, for whom Zephaniah—for all his merits—would not have been on the same plane as Shakespeare.

There has also been a questioning of the tendencies to see essential differences between men and women. Brotman and Moore (2008), reviewing some recent research on the matter of girls' interest in science, have noted an inclination to reject essentialist claims based on the 'commonly made link between masculinity and traits such as objectivity, rationality, and lack of emotion' (Brotman and Moore, 2008: 987). That new research investigates, rather, the diversity among both males and females, such that 'there are women who are attracted to the very aspects of science typically associated with masculinity and men' (*ibid.*: 992). The research notes that 'masculinity and femininity are cultural constructions that have come to be seen as mutually exclusive—associated exclusively with either males or females—when in fact traits culturally associated with masculinity can be part of females' identities and vice versa.' Brotman and Moore call this new way of looking at the question 'a focus on identity', but it seems to be much the same as a combination of the classical liberal recognition of individual uniqueness with an awareness that uniqueness is influenced by social context; and in that sense this new way of looking at gender and the curriculum seems little different from the universalist views of an old kind of socialism.

Rediscovery of the importance of knowledge

One of the most extensive challenges to radical views about education that date to the 1960s and 1970s was from one of their original exponents, Michael Young. His espousing in 1971 of a view of knowledge as socially constructed and therefore socially relative was doubted by Moore and Muller in their critique of Bourdieu which we discussed in Chapter 5. Young describes his book written in 2008 as in part a response to them which largely agrees with them, and therefore in effect moves fundamentally away from his 1971 view to one in which knowledge is universal and, for that very reason, liberating. The early sociology of knowledge was, Young now says, a form 'of "voice discourse" which reduces knowledge to knowers, their standpoints and interests' (Young, 2008: 3). He goes even further, decrying

> the intellectual dishonesty of the voice discourse theorists... in appearing to be democratic and even populist both in their deference to experience and in their critique of expertise. (*ibid.*: 16)

That position, he says, 'is at best nihilist', denying knowledge altogether (*ibid.*: 16). The emergence of such ideas in the 1960s and 1970s was based on 'a politics that linked constructivist ideas to the privileging of subordinate (as opposed to ruling class or official) knowledge' (*ibid.*: 203). The subordination could be—as we have seen—of the working class, of women, of non-white groups: what all such political discourse had in common, he says, was 'a celebration of the culture of those who were rejected by and failed at school'. The fallacy, even the hypocrisy, he now believes, is that 'by undermining any claims to objective knowledge or truth about anything, social constructivism... denies the possibility of any better understanding, let alone of any better world' despite its radical political claims (*ibid.*: 204). He links this point also to a critique of various kinds of child-centred education, referring to

> today's fashionable language of facilitation, group work and 'teaching is a conversation,'... increasingly linked to the 'promise' of e-learnng, mobile phones and the internet. (*ibid.*: 204)

His new position is that, though there are social processes involved in discovering knowledge—and indeed which are necessary to ensuring that claims to knowledge are valid (through rigorous public discussion, for example)—these do not reduce knowledge to any social position. We might paraphrase this by saying that whereas *claims* to knowledge are socially positioned, knowledge is not.

Young also insists that he is still on the left politically, and distinguishes his position from what he calls 'neo-conservative traditionalism' as well as from the enthusiasts for industrial training (*ibid.*: 19–20). His main disagreement with right-wing thought is its failure (as he sees it) to acknowledge the social character of the production of knowledge. That is an implausible claim in the light of much distinguished conservative writing about tradition—including some which we have discussed in Chapter 2, and maintained by, for instance, Oakeshott (1989) and Scruton (1991). Nevertheless Young says that 'the neo-conservative position may be flawed, but it is not false', reminding us, as it does, of the desirability of seeing education as an end in itself, and that

> tradition, though capable of preserving vested interests, is also crucial in ensuring the maintenance and development of standards of learning in schools, as well as being a condition for innovation and creating new knowledge. (Young, 2008: 23)

Theoretical debates about what counts as left-wing thought have not ever, since the 1960s, been as close to practical politics on the left as they were up to about the 1945 Labour government. Nevertheless, for different reasons there are some stirrings of interest in a common culture of the older kind not only from the recent doubts about multiculturalism but also from an interest in the idea of 'cultural literacy', originally developed by E.D. Hirsch in the USA. Hirsch—a professor of English at the University of Virginia—was astonished at students' lack of knowledge of the ideas that underpin American democracy, when he was working at a community college in Richmond serving a population which was almost entirely African American. He argued that 'democracy depends on shared knowledge' (Hirsch, 2009: 1) and is the necessary egalitarian condition for a shared civic life. These ideas have appealed to British politicians of many ideological persuasions; one Labour instance is Michael Barber, an adviser to Labour on education when it was in power between 1997 and 2010. He accepted the importance of 'cultural inheritance' and 'cultural transmission' (Barber, 1996: 174). He said that the left's abandonment of inherited culture as 'a capitalist culture, an imperialist culture, a patriarchal culture or a Eurocentric culture' in favour of a 'process' view of education has led to a position where cultural transmission is defended only by the political right (*ibid.*: 175). In a sentiment that might appear to fit squarely in the mainstream of thought about liberal education, he said that 'not passing on the tradition... implies raising a generation less able to distinguish goodness, truth and beauty than its predecessors' (*ibid.*: 176). But he took this no further, and certainly not anywhere nearly as far (or as subtly) as the socialist thinkers from every generation up to the 1950s: in supporting a compulsory national curriculum, all that he specified in its content—rather like James Callaghan in his 1976 speech—is basic standards of literacy and numeracy (Barber, 1996: 260 and 277).

Conclusions

Three points may be made in conclusion from the century-long trajectory of ideas on the left about liberal education. The first is that the socialist version of liberal education, though temporarily eclipsed after the 1960s, no more vanishes than—as Rothblatt notes—does liberal education generally. There is always a memory, a sense that part of what democracy brought was not only a welfare state that catered for people's material needs but also a set of new institutions that nurtured their minds. Education was always potentially a means to personal advancement, to securing a better and more secure job, but it was always more than that, and even perhaps—in the views of many early socialists—was other things before that. It created the grounds for civic engagement, and did that by creating a common culture. If there are many ways of interpreting that aspiration to a common culture, it was nevertheless something which the early socialists did not doubt. The problem then was that a common culture had to rest on cultural standards that could be maintained only by a process of cultural selection, which seemed to require the selection of the best minds to take responsibility for that task. Since cultural selection of people inevitably means indirectly selecting by social rank, socialist thought turned away from the difficult task of defining how the best that has been thought and said would be chosen for wide dissemination. That was understandable but has evaded the problem. Unless there is some thought given again to how selection from a common tradition might contribute in an egalitarian manner to a common culture, while also maintaining the cultural standards that are the only grounds on which the tradition is worth maintaining, the left will surrender the task of cultural selection to those with whom it profoundly disagrees.

The challenge for the left is all the greater now than in the past because there barely survive any of the specifically socialist milieu in which such ideas and challenges might be debated. That is the second point in conclusion. No longer would it be likely that a Tawney or a Hoggart could have their whole worldviews shaped by teaching working-class students from close communities who wanted to engage with universal concerns. That is not to say that such adult-education classes no longer exist, but they are not any longer embedded in a self-confident socialist culture. If Laski or Lindsay spent their daily lives in some of the most privileged of academic places—the London School of Economics or Balliol College—that did not prevent their ideas being also shaped by their simultaneous connections to Labour movement politics. Their experience confirmed that liberal education of an inherited kind could be adapted to a new, democratic age while remaining in touch with what Leavis called a humane centre: people like these could inhabit both worlds simultaneously and have their ideas about a cultural tradition tested by those who had been excluded from it but who admired it and sought their aid in tasting its fruits. It may be in fact that the period between, say, the founding of the Workers' Educational Association in 1903 and the end of the Labour government in 1951 was an unrepeatable moment, in which the pressures of democratisation had still not discredited the old hierarchies of knowledge—still not brought them into disrespect—but had gone far enough to inspire people who had been excluded from the traditions to seek entry to them, and also had inspired leading thinkers to seek to extend the benefits of these traditions to all.

It may be then, finally, that if a general idea of liberal education as universal persists it cannot ever again owe much specifically to the left. If liberal education does survive (as Rothblatt's comment gives reason to suppose), it may be simply because universalism is now so pervasive in liberal democratic cultures such as in Britain that there is no longer a need for socialist intellectuals to make the case. That larger question of what the left now is, and whether it has been superseded by history, cannot be addressed as a general matter here, but if the fragmentation of left-wing views about liberal education since the 1960s is any guide then it does seem reasonable to say that it is unlikely that the left will ever again hold a coherent view of a democratic liberal education which also marks it off from curricular thinking based on other political positions, or on none at all: liberal universalism is now just the taken-for-granted common sense of society. Nevertheless, even if left-wing thought about education is no longer particularly relevant to society in general, the ideas which it produced early in the twentieth century remain available for debate. If the left has indeed been superseded, and is no longer as culturally unified as it once was, that is in part because it successfully did achieve something of a common culture through education, persuading the society more generally that liberal education could be conceptually universal only if it was socially, in principle, for all. That is a tradition of thought worth remembering.

Appendix

Biographical Notes

These notes are brief summaries of the public roles of the main thinkers whose ideas and influence are discussed at some length or recurrently in the book, concentrating on the reasons why they are relevant to this work. The main sources of the notes are the *Dictionary of National Biography*, newspaper obituaries and institutional websites.

Yasmin Alibhai-Brown

Alibhai-Brown is a journalist, and was a member of the Commission on the Future of Multi-Ethnic Britain that was chaired by Bhikhu Parekh. She is a founder of British Muslims for Secular Democracy.

Hannah Arendt (1906–1975)

Arendt was active in German socialist politics in the 1920s, fleeing to Paris in 1933 and then imprisoned by the Vichy government. She escaped to New York, and worked at various universities in the USA. Her most influential writing was on the nature of mass democracy, on revolution, and on the totalitarianism of both the left and the right.

Matthew Arnold

Arnold was one of the most influential liberal thinkers in Britain in the nineteenth century, through his writing and his public speaking. His legacy for the twentieth century has mainly been based on his ideas about culture, education and democracy, but in his lifetime he was as well-known as a poet and as a theologian, and indeed his poetry remained in school syllabuses until well into the twentieth century. His understanding of education gained a practical edge from his work as a school inspector in England, and as an advisor to official committees of enquiry into school education.

W.H. Auden (1907–1973)

Auden was the most influential English poet of the 1930s, shaping a whole generation in how they saw the social responsibility of the imaginative writer. He taught for a while in schools, and also in adult education. He was on the left politically, especially after the early 1930s, and spent some time as an ambulance worker in Spain during the Civil War, where he developed a distrust of any kind of totalitarian political programme.

G.H. Bantock (1914–1997)

Bantock was professor of education at Leicester University, writing in the philosophy of education (though resisting that label). He was closely involved with the Leavises in the journal *Scrutiny*, becoming one of its main contributors on educational topics. He was consistently sceptical of what came to be known as progressive educational methods.

Basil Bernstein (1924–2000)

Bernstein was professor of the sociology of education at the Institute of Education in London. He was best-known for his detailed study of language and social class, and of the implications for how children learn.

Pierre Bourdieu (1930–2002)

Bourdieu was probably the most influential sociologist in the world in the second half of the twentieth century, cited in all sociological fields and far beyond. His appeal lies in the attention which he gave in his work to questions of culture, in place of the structural approaches that were thought to have dominated hitherto. He became professor of sociology at the Collège de France, and was regarded highly on the political left in France and elsewhere.

G.D.H. Cole (1889–1959)

Cole became professor of political and social theory at Oxford University. From 1941, while at Nuffield College, he directed the Social Reconstruction Survey, a sociological investigation of Britain with the aim of informing the development of social policy for the post-war world. He taught for the Workers' Educational Association. He was influential on the development of the Labour Party's economic policy in the 1930s.

Anthony Crosland (1918–1977)

Crosland was a Labour MP in the UK Parliament, becoming Secretary of State for Education and Science in the Labour government of the 1960s, where he presided over the shift to non-selective secondary schooling and the initial phases of the expansion of higher education. His writing in the 1950s and after was influential in modernising the ideas of democratic socialism.

John Dewey (1859–1952)

Dewey was professor of education at Chicago University and professor of philosophy at Columbia University (and at the Teachers' College there). He was a philosopher whose work covered a very wide range (including ethics, democracy and aesthetics), but his main relevance here is his educational liberalism. He adapted the ideas of child-centred education for the twentieth century, and became the main intellectual source internationally of these ideas.

T.S. Eliot (1888–1965)

Eliot's relevance to this study is not so much in his poetry—although that mattered in helping to create a widespread sense of tradition under threat (for which, see Chapter 2)—but rather because of his critical writing from the 1930s onwards, in which he formed a conception of an organic culture undermined by modernity that appealed to many thinkers on the left.

Nancy Fraser

Fraser is professor of political and social science at the New School for Social Research in New York, writing influentially about feminist conceptions of justice.

Victor Gollancz (1893–1967)

Gollancz was a publisher and writer, first with his own company at which he employed striking, modernist design and effective commercial advertising, and then in the Left Book Club (as explained in Chapter 3). His influence on left-wing thought in the 1930s was thus very great, though indirect.

T.H. Green (1836–1882)

Green was a leading exponent of idealist philosophy in the middle of the nineteenth century, influencing directly or indirectly several generations of thinkers about the nature of the state as it grew to take on a much greater role in social life than at the high point of Victorian industrialism. He was a tutor at Balliol College, and later a professor of moral philosophy at the University of Oxford.

R.B. Haldane (1856–1928)

Haldane was a Liberal politician who served in the cabinet of the 1906 Liberal government with responsibility for the army, and later as Lord Chancellor, a post which he also held in the first Labour government in 1924. He took a strong interest in education throughout his political life, for example working with Sidney Webb to create the University of London, and with R.H. Tawney, Albert Mansbridge and others to found the British Institute of Adult Education.

L.T. Hobhouse (1864–1929)

Hobhouse was a fellow of two Oxford colleges before becoming a journalist on the *Manchester Guardian* and then (from 1907) the first holder of the chair of sociology at the London School of Economics. He was the best-known exponent of the new liberalism, though, unlike many who shared his views, he remained wary of the Labour Party and of socialism.

Richard Hoggart (1918–2014)

Hoggart was professor of English at Birmingham University (1962–73), and founder there of the Centre for Contemporary Cultural Studies. From 1971 to 1975 he was an assistant director general of U.N.E.S.C.O. He was a member of several public committees, such as the Arts Council and the Pilkington Committee on Broadcasting (in the early 1960s). He taught for the W.E.A., and was a prolific journalist and public lecturer.

T.H. Huxley (1825–1895)

In the second half of the nineteenth century, Huxley was the leading exponent of the ideas of evolution by means of natural selection and random variation, becoming more prominent as a lecturer on these topics than the shy Darwin, his friend. He was a consistent advocate of science education in schools, and ran large classes training school teachers in how to teach science, at the Natural History Museum in London. He taught at, and was principal of, the south London working men's college.

Henry Jones (1852–1922)

Jones was a lecturer in philosophy at the University College of Aberystwyth, and professor of philosophy at University College, Bangor, and at St Andrews and Glasgow Universities. He was an influential exponent of the British idealist philosophy, teaching many of the rising generation who would become the civil servants and politicians of the new welfare state inaugurated by the reforms of the Liberal government of 1906.

Allen Lane (1902–1970)

Lane founded Penguin Books, inaugurating thereby a revolution in book design, distribution, marketing and affordability. During his time at the company, it always had an edge of social radicalism, but it never patronised its customers; it thus caught the changing mood of the mid-twentieth century from deference to an increasingly well-educated democracy.

Harold Laski (1893–1950)

Laski was professor of political science at the London School of Economics, having also held academic posts in several universities in the USA and Canada. In his academic work he wrote on the nature of the state, on democracy, and on capitalism and socialism. He taught classes of the Workers' Educational Association as well as in the L.S.E. He was prominent in the Labour Party, becoming chair of its National Executive Committee in 1945.

F.R. Leavis (1895–1978)

F.R. Leavis was a fellow of Downing College, Cambridge, but his wider influence was through his editorship of the journal *Scrutiny*, which he co-founded with L.C. Knights. His literary criticism shaped several generations of teachers of English, notably in the new meritocratic system of secondary schooling in the years after the Second World War. He took a close interest in education, specifically in the place of English at the heart of a liberal curriculum. He was married to Q.D. Leavis.

Q.D. Leavis (1906–1981)

Q.D. Leavis's most notable influence was through her *Fiction and the Reading Public* (1932), a pioneering study of popular taste in an era of mass democracy, which was a precursor in method, though not in ideological commitment, of the cultural studies which rose in the second half of the century. She was married to F.R. Leavis.

A.D. Lindsay (1879–1952)

Lindsay was professor of philosophy at Oxford University, master of Balliol College, vice-Chancellor of Oxford in the late-1930s, and—in 1950—founder of Keele University. His academic writing, in the idealist tradition, analysed the role of the state and its reciprocal relationship with the ethical basis of society. He taught for the Workers' Educational Association.

Albert Mansbridge (1876–1952)

Mansbridge founded the immediate predecessor of the Workers' Educational Association in 1903, and was the leading influence on the Association's development to the 1920s, paying particular attention to securing its links with the established universities, notably Oxford. He served on several advisory committees to government in the 1920s and 1930s.

Tariq Modood

Modood is professor of sociology at Bristol University, and was an adviser to the Commission on the Future of Multi-Ethnic Britain that was chaired by Bhikhu Parekh.

John Henry Newman (1801–1890)

Newman was an Anglican priest and theologian who led the Tractarian movement (aiming in the 1830s to give a developed doctrine to the Anglican Church as both Reformed and Catholic) and then moved closer to Roman Catholicism to which he converted in 1845. He was invited by the Catholic Church in Ireland to be principal of a new Catholic university in Dublin, and his specific influence on educational debates was due mainly to lectures which he gave in that city in the 1950s on what he later summed up as 'the idea of a university'.

Percy Nunn (1870–1944)

Nunn was professor of education at the University of London, and principal of the London Day Training College, having started his career as a secondary-school teacher of science.

George Orwell (1903–1950)

Orwell wrote surprisingly little explicitly about education, did not like the schooling which he had had in a minor preparatory school and at Eton, and did not attend university. His relevance to debates about the curriculum thus rests on what he taught himself, which in Bernard Crick's words in the *Dictionary of National Biography* came from his having 'read widely for himself in the canon of English literature and books by rationalists, freethinkers, and reformers like Samuel Butler, George Bernard Shaw, and H.G. Wells'. Orwell's thoughts on the content of a core liberal culture have thus come to enter the mainstream of debate about liberal education.

Bhikhu Parekh

Parekh has been a professor of political theory at several universities; his longest association has been with Hull University. He chaired the Commission on the Future of Multi-Ethnic Britain that was set up by the Runnymede Trust in 1997.

Lawrence Stenhouse (1926–1982)

Stenhouse started his career as a teacher in Glasgow and Dunfermline; after periods lecturing at Durham University and at Jordanhill College of Education in Glasgow he became head of the Humanities Curriculum Project, which was funded by the Nuffield Foundation and the Schools Council and which moved with him to the University of East Anglia, where he also became professor of education.

R.H. Tawney (1880–1962)

Tawney was Professor of Economic History at the London School of Economics. In his academic work he was distinguished as an historian of seventeenth-century England. His main influence on socialist thought was through his teaching of economic history and related matters to classes in the Workers' Educational Association, and through his work on developing the Labour Party's policy on education, notably in *Secondary Education for All* (1922).

William Temple (1881–1944)

Temple was Anglican Bishop of Manchester, Archbishop of York and Archbishop of Canterbury (from 1942); early in his career, he had been headmaster of Repton School in Derbyshire. He wrote, spoke and worked to link Christian concerns with the need for social reform, describing himself as a socialist.

E.P. Thompson (1924–1993)

Thompson was a social historian, activist on the new left in the 1950s and 1960s (though ousted in 1962 from the editorial board of *New Left Review* by a younger generation) and – in the 1980s – prominent supporter of the Campaign for Nuclear Disarmament. He started his career in the extra-mural department of Leeds University.

Ellen Wilkinson (1891–1947)

Wilkinson was Minister of Education in the 1945 Labour government until her death in 1947. She was MP for Jarrow in north-east England, and had been active in many causes on the left of the Labour Party and on behalf of women in the 1920s and 1930s.

Raymond Williams (1921–1988)

Williams was professor of drama at Cambridge University, having taught in adult education classes for the W.E.A. and at Oxford University. He was a very frequent contributor to public debates both in writing and as a speaker, and was associated with the New Left of the 1960s.

Iris Marion Young (1949–2006)

Young was professor of political science at the University of Chicago, gaining strong influence on radical debates world-wide with her writing about justice, democratic theory and feminism.

Bibliography

Albrecht, F.M., 'A Reappraisal of Faculty Psychology', *Journal of the History of the Behavioral Sciences*, 6, 1970, 36–40.

Aldrich, R., *A Century of Education*, London, RoutledgeFarmer, 2002.

Alibhai-Brown, Y., *After Multiculturalism*, London, Central Books, 2000.

Anderson, P., 'Components of the National Culture', *New Left Review*, No. 50, 1968, 3–57.

Angell, N., *Why Freedom Matters*, Harmondsworth, Penguin, 1940.

Apple, M., 'Ideology, Reproduction, and Educational Reform', *Comparative Education Review*, 22, 1978, 367–87.

Arendt, H., 'The Crisis in Education', in H. Arendt, *Between Past and Future*, London, Faber and Faber, 1961 [1954], 173–96.

Armytage, W.H.G., 'Matthew Arnold and T.H. Huxley: Some New Letters, 1870–80', *The Review of English Studies*, 4, 1953, 346–53.

Arnold, M., 'General Report for the Year 1852', in F. Sandford (ed.), *Reports on Elementary Schools, 1852–1882*, London, Macmillan, 1889, 1–20.

Arnold, M., *Irish Essays*, London, Smith, Elder, 1891.

Arnold, M., *Letters of Matthew Arnold, Vol. I*, ed. G.W.E. Russell, London, Macmillan, 1895.

Arnold, M., *Culture and Anarchy*, J. Dover Wilson (ed.), Cambridge, Cambridge University Press, 1960 [1869].

Arnold, M., 'Democracy', in Arnold, 1980 [1861], 436–68.

Arnold, M., 'The Function of Criticism at the Present Time', in Arnold, 1980 [1864], 234–66.

Arnold, M., 'Equality', in Arnold, 1980 [1878], 573–608.

Arnold, M., *The Portable Matthew Arnold*, ed. L. Trilling, Harmondsworth, Penguin, 1980.

Arnot, M., David, M. and Weiner, G., *Educational Reforms and Gender Equality in Schools*, Manchester, Equal Opportunities Commission, 1996.

Arnot, M. and Miles, P., 'A Reconstruction of the Gender Agenda: The Contradictory Gender Dimensions in New Labour's Educational and Economic Policy', *Oxford Review of Education*, 31, 2005, 173–89.

Ashby, E., 'Growing Points in Adult Education: Strategy and Tactics', *Scottish Adult Education*, 15, December 1955, 5–12.

Atherton, C., 'Public Intellectuals and the Schoolteacher Audience: the First Ten Years of *The Critical Quarterly*', *English*, 58, 2009, 75–94.

Atkinson, P., *Language, Structure and Reproduction*, London, Methuen, 1985.

Auden, W.H., 'Private Pleasures', in Mendelson (ed.), 1977 [1932], 312–14.

Auden, W.H., 'Review', in Mendelson (ed.), 1977 [1933], 317–18.

Auden, W.H. and Worsley, T.C., *Education Today – and Tomorrow*, London, Hogarth Press, 1939.

Ball, S., *Politics and Policy Making in Education*, London, Routledge, 1990.

Bantock, G.H., 'Matthew Arnold, H.M.I.', *Scrutiny*, XVII, 1951, 32–44.

Bantock, G.H., *T.S. Eliot and Education*, London, Faber and Faber, 1970.

Barber, M., *The Learning Game*, London, Gollancz, 1996.

Barker, E., 'The Conception of Empire', in C. Bailey (ed.), *The Legacy of Rome*, Oxford, Clarendon, 1923, 45–89.

Barker, R., *Education and Politics, 1900–1951*, Oxford, Oxford University Press, 1972.

Barry, B., *Culture and Equality*, Cambridge, Polity, 2001.

Barry, B., 'Second Thoughts – and Some First Thoughts Revived', in P. Kelly, *Multiculturalism Reconsidered*, Cambridge, Polity, 2002, 204–38.

Beiner, R., 'Multiculturalism and Citizenship: A Critical Response to Iris Marion Young', *Educational Philosophy and Theory*, 38, 2006, 25–37.

Bell, D., *The Coming of Post-Industrial Society*, Harmondsworth, Penguin, 1976.

Bentley, D. and Watts, D.M., 'Courting the Positive Virtues: A Case for Feminist Science', *European Journal of Science Education*, 8, 1986, 121–34.

Bentley, T., *Learning Beyond the Classroom*, London, RoutledgeFarmer, 1998.

Bernstein, B., 'Code Theory and Its Positioning: A Case Study in Misrecognition', *British Journal of Sociology of Education*, 16, 1995, 3–19.

Bernstein, B., *Class, Codes and Control, Volume 1*, London, Paladin, 1971.

Bernstein, B., 'Education Cannot Compensate for Society', in Rubinstein and Stoneman (eds.), 1972, 104–16.

Bernstein, B., *Class, Codes and Control, Volume 3*, 2nd edition, London, Routledge and Kegan Paul, 1977.

Bernstein, B., *Class, Codes and Control, Volume 4*, new edition, London, Routledge, 2003.

Blair, T., 'Tony Blair's First Keynote Speech of the Campaign', *Guardian*, 31 May 2001, http://www.theguardian.com/politics/2001/may/13/labour.tonyblair [downloaded 6 April 2014].

Blair, T., Speech to IPPR and Demos at Beveridge Hall, University of London, 11 October 2004, http://news.bbc.co.uk/1/hi/uk_politics/3733380.stm [downloaded 27 February 2014].

Blunkett, D., 'Education into Employability: The Role of the DfEE in the Economy', 2001, London, Institute of Education, Digital Education Resource Archive, http://dera.ioe.ac.uk/id/eprint/3668 [downloaded 27 February 2014].

Blyth, J.A., *English University Adult Education*, Manchester, Manchester University Press, 1983.

Board of Education [the Spens Report], *Secondary Education with Special Reference to Grammar Schools and Technical High Schools*, London, HMSO, 1938, http://www.educationengland.org.uk/documents/spens/spens1938.html#01

Bogdanor, V., 'Oxford and the Mandarin Culture: The Past that is Gone', *Oxford Review of Education*, 32, 2006, 147–65.

Bolgar, R.R., *The Classical Heritage and its Beneficiaries*, Cambridge, Cambridge University Press, 1954.

Boli, J., Ramirez, F.O. and Meyer, J.W., 'Explaining the Origins and Expansion of Mass Education', *Comparative Education Review*, 29, 1985, 145–70.

Bottomore, T., 'Foreword', in Bourdieu and Passeron, 1977, xiv–xvii.

Boucher, D. and Vincent, A., *British Idealism and Political Theory*, Edinburgh, Edinburgh University Press, 2000.

Bourdieu, P., *Distinction*, London, Routledge and Kegan Paul, 1984.

Bourdieu, P., *Language and Symbolic Power*, tr. G. Raymond and M. Adamson, Cambridge, Polity, 1991.

Bourdieu, P., 'The Forms of Capital', in J.E. Richardson (ed.), *Handbook of Theory of Research for the Sociology of Education*, 1986, reprinted in A.H. Halsey, H. Lauder, P. Brown, and A.S. Wells (eds.), *Education: Culture, Economy, Society*, Oxford: Oxford University Press, 1997, 46–58.

Bourdieu, P. and Passeron, J.-C., *Reproduction in Education, Society and Culture*, tr. R. Nice, London, Sage, 1977.

Brooks, J.R., 'The Council for Educational Advance During the Chairmanship of R.H. Tawney, 1942–49', *Journal of Educational Administration and History*, 9, 1977, 42–8.

Brooks, J.R., 'Labour and Educational Reconstruction, 1916–1926: A Case Study in the Evolution of Policy', *History of Education*, 20, 1991, 245–59.

Brotman, J.S. and Moore, F.M., 'Girls and Science: A Review of Four Themes in the Science Education Literature', *Journal of Research in Science Teaching*, 45, 2008, 971–1002.

Brown, G., 'Full Text of the Chancellor's Speech', 9 March 1999, http://news.bbc.co.uk/1/hi/events/budget_99/news/293669.stm [downloaded 27 February 2014].

Brown, G., 'Gordon Brown's Speech to Labour Conference', 2009, http://www.ukpolitics.org.uk/node/3508 [downloaded 7 April 2014].

Buxton, C.S., 'Ruskin College: An Educational Experiment', *Cornhill Magazine*, 25, 1908, 192–200.

Callaghan, J., Speech at Ruskin College, Oxford, 18 October 1976, http://www.ukpolitics.org.uk/node/3508 [downloaded 7 April 2014].

Campbell, F., 'Latin and the Elite Tradition in Education', *British Journal of Sociology*, 19, 1968, 308–25.

Campbell, I., 'Carlyle and Education', in P.E. Kerry and M. Hill (eds.), *Thomas Carlyle Resartus*, Madison, NJ, Fairleigh Dickinson University Press, 2010, 49–61.

Carey, J., *The Intellectuals and the Masses*, London, Faber and Faber, 1992.

Carpenter, H., *The Envy of the World*, London, Weidenfield and Nicolson, 1996.

Carpenter, L.P., *G.D.H. Cole*, Cambridge, Cambridge University Press, 1973.

Centre for Contemporary Cultural Studies, *Unpopular Education*, London, Hutchinson, 1981.

Chitty, C., *Towards a New Education System: The Victory of the New Right?*, London, Falmer, 1989.

Cohen, A., 'The Educational Philosophy of Tolstoy', *Oxford Review of Education*, 7, 1981, 241–51.

Cole, G.D.H., 'The W.E.A. and the future', *The Highway*, 1925, 97–101.

Cole, G.D.H., 'The Tutorial Class in British Working-Class Education', *International Quarterly of Adult Education*, 1932, 127–40.

Cole, G.D.H., 'The Dream and the Business', *Political Quarterly*, 20, 1949, 201–10.

Cole, G.D.H., *Essays in Social Theory*, London, Macmillan, 1950.

Cole, G.D.H., 'Education and Politics: A Socialist View', in J.A. Lauwerys and N. Hans (eds.), *The Yearbook of Education*, London, Institute of Education, 1952, 42–63.

Cole, G.D.H., *A History of Socialist Thought, IV: Communism and Social Democracy, 1914–1931*, London, Macmillan, 1958.

Cole, M., *Growing Up Into Revolution*, London, Longmans, Green and Co., 1949.

Coleman, J.A., 'Why the British Do Not Learn Languages: Myths and Motivation in the United Kingdom', *Language Learning Journal*, 37, 2009, 111–27.

Collini, S., *Matthew Arnold*, Oxford, Oxford University Press, 1988.

Collini, S., *English Pasts*, Oxford, Oxford University Press, 1999.

Collini, S., 'Arnold, Matthew (1822–1888)', *Oxford Dictionary of National Biography*, Oxford, Oxford University Press, 2004; online edn, 2008a.

Collini, S., *Absent Minds: Intellectuals in Britain*, Oxford, Oxford University Press, 2006.

Collini, S., 'Richard Hoggart: Literary Criticism and Cultural Decline in Twentieth-Century Britain', in Owen (ed.), 2008b, 33–56.

Commission on Social Justice, *Social Justice*, London, Vintage, 1994.

Commission on the Future of Multi-Ethnic Britain, *The Future of Multi-Ethnic Britain*, London, Profile, 2002.

Connolly, C., *Enemies of Promise*, Chicago, University of Chicago Press, 1983 [1948].

Cooke, A., *From Popular Enlightenment to Lifelong Learning: A History of Adult Education in Scotland, 1707–2005*, Leicester, National Institute of Adult Continuing Education, 2006.

Creech Jones, A. (ed.), *R.H. Tawney: A Portrait by Several Hands*, privately published, 1960.

Crick, B., 'Blair, Eric Arthur [pseud. George Orwell] (1903–1950)', *Dictionary of National Biography*, 2004.

Crosland, A., *The Future of Socialism*, London, Jonathan Cape, 1956.

Crosland, S., *Tony Crosland*, London, Jonathan Cape, 1982.
Crossman, R.H.S., 'The Public School System', *New Statesman and Nation*, 16 July 1949, 59–60.
Croxford, L. 'Equal Opportunities in the Secondary-School Curriculum in Scotland, 1977–91', *British Educational Research Journal*, 20, 1994, 371–91.
Dalrymple, W., *White Mughals*, London, HarperCollins, 2002.
Darling, J., 'New Life and New Education: The Philosophies of Davidson, Reddie and Hahn', *Scottish Educational Review*, 13, 1981, 12–24.
Darling, J., 'A.S. Neill on Knowledge and Learning', *British Journal of Educational Studies*, 32, 1984, 158–71.
Darling, J., *Child-Centred Education and its Critics*, London, Paul Chapman, 1994.
Darling, J. and Nisbet J., 'Dewey in Britain', *Studies in Philosophy and Education*, 19, 2000, 39–52.
Davies, L., 'Gender and Comprehensive Schooling', in S.J. Ball (ed.), *Comprehensive Schooling: A Reader*, London, Falmer, 1984, 47–65.
Dean, D.W., 'Planning for a Postwar Generation: Ellen Wilkinson and George Tomlinson at the Ministry of Education, 1945–51', *History of Education*, 15, 1986, 95–117.
Department for Education and Employment, *The Learning Age*, London, DfEE, 1998.
Dewey, J. and Dewey, E., *Schools of Tomorrow*, New York, E.P. Dutton, 1915.
Dietz, M.G., 'Citizenship with a Feminist Face: The Problem with Maternal Thinking', *Political Theory*, 13, 1985, 19–37.
DiMaggio, P., 'Cultural Capital and School Success: The Impact of Status Culture Participation on the Grades of U.S. High School Students', *American Sociological Review*, 47, 1982, 89–201.
Donald, J. and Grealy, J., 'The Unpleasant Fact of Inequality: Standards, Literacy and Culture', in A. Wolpe and J. Donald (eds.), *Is There Anyone Here from Education?*, London, Pluto, 1983, 88–101.
Douglas, J.W.B., Ross, J.M., Maxwell, S.M.M. and Walker, D.A., 'Differences in Test Score and in the Gaining of Selective Places for Scottish Children and Those in England and Wales', *British Journal of Educational Psychology*, 36, 1966, 150–7.
Dower, R.S., 'Thomas Carlyle', in Hearnshaw (ed.), 1930, 31–52.

Doyle, B., 'The Invention of English', in R. Colls and P. Dodd (eds.), *Englishness: Politics and Culture, 1880–1920*, London, Croom Helm, 1986, 89–115.

Ecclestone, K. and Hayes, D., *The Dangerous Rise of Therapeutic Education*, London, Routledge, 2009.

Eliot, T.S., *Notes Towards a Definition of Culture*, London, Faber and Faber, 1948.

Elliott, J., 'A Curriculum for the Study of Human Affairs: The Contribution of Lawrence Stenhouse', *Journal of Curriculum Studies*, 15, 1983, 105–23.

Ellis, C., 'Relativism and Reaction: Richard Hoggart and Conservatism', in Owen (ed.), 2008, 198–212.

Emmet, D., 'Lindsay as Philosopher', in Scott, 1971, 389–415.

Entwistle, H., *Child-Centred Education*, London, Methuen, 1970.

Entwistle, H., *Antonio Gramsci*, London, Routledge and Kegan Paul, 1979.

Favretto, I., '"Wilsonism" Reconsidered: Labour Party Revisionism 1952–64', *Contemporary British History*, 14, 2000, 54–80.

Fenwick, I.G.K., *The Comprehensive School, 1944–1970*, London, Methuen, 1976.

Fieldhouse, R., 'The Ideology of English Adult Education', *Studies in Adult Education*, 15, 1983, 11–35.

Fieldhouse, R., 'Conformity and Contradiction in English Responsible Body Adult Education, 1925–1950', *Studies in the Education of Adults*, 17, 1985, 121–34.

Flexner, A., 'The Burden of Humanism', *Taylorian Lecture*, Oxford, Clarendon Press, 1928.

Forster, E.M., 'What I Believe', in *Two Cheers for Democracy*, Harmondsworth, Penguin, 1965, 75–84.

Francis, M., 'A Socialist Policy for Education?: Labour and the Secondary School, 1945–51', *History of Education*, 24, 1995, 319–35.

Fraser, N., 'From Redistribution to Recognition? Dilemmas of Justice in a "Post-Socialist" Age', *New Left Review*, 212, 1995, 68–93.

Fryer, R., *Learning for the Twenty-First Century*, London, National Advisory Group for Continuing Education and Lifelong Learning, 1997.

Gallie, D., 'The Labour Force', in Halsey and Webb (eds.), 2000, 281–323.

Gillborn, D., 'Racism, Identity and Modernity: Pluralism, Moral Antiracism and Plastic Ethnicity', *International Studies in Sociology of Education*, 5, 1995, 3–23.

Gillborn, D., 'Racism and Reform: New Ethnicities/Old Inequalities?', *British Educational Research Journal*, 23, 1997, 345–60.

Giroux, H., 'Theories of Reproduction and Resistance in the New Sociology of Education', *Harvard Educational Review*, 53, 1983, 257–93.

Giroux, H., Shumway, D., Smith, P. and Sosnoski, J., 'The Need for Cultural Studies: Resisting Intellectuals and Oppositional Public Spheres', in Munns and Rajan (eds.), 1995 [1985], 647–58.

Glover, J. and Fielding, J., 'Women and Science in Britain: Getting In?', *Journal of Education and Work*, 12, 1999, 57–73.

Goldman, L., 'Intellectuals and the English Working Class 1870–1945: The Case of Adult Education', *History of Education*, 29, 2000, 281–300.

Goldman, L., 'Tawney, Richard Henry (1880–1962)', *Oxford Dictionary of National Biography*, 2004.

Goldthorpe, J., '"Cultural Capital": Some Critical Observations', *Sociologica*, 2007, 1–23.

Gordon, P., 'Curriculum', in Aldrich (ed.), 2002, 185–205.

Gray, J., *Enlightenment's Wake*, London, Routledge, 1995.

Haldane, R.B., 'A Vision of the Future', in O.F.G. Stanley (ed.), *The Way Out: Essays on the Meaning and Purpose of Adult Education*, Oxford, Oxford University Press, 1923, 7–19.

Hall, S., 'Cultural Studies: Two Paradigms', in Munns and Rajan (eds.), 1995 [1980], 195–205.

Halsey, A.H., 'Further and Higher Education', in Halsey and Webb (eds.), 2000, 221–53.

Halsey, A.H. and Webb, J., *Twentieth-Century British Social Trends*, Houndmills, Macmillan, 2000.

Hargreaves, D., *The Challenge for the Comprehensive School*, London, Routledge and Kegan Paul, 1982.

Harker, R. and May, S., 'Code and Habitus: Comparing the Accounts of Bernstein and Bourdieu', *British Journal of Sociology of Education*, 14, 1993, 169–78.

Harris, J., 'Political Thought and the Welfare State 1870–1940: An Intellectual Framework for British Social Policy', *Past and Present*, 135, 1992, 116–41.

Harrison, J.F.C., *Learning and Living, 1790–1960*, London, Routledge and Kegan Paul, 1961.

Harrop, S., 'Introduction', in S. Harrop (ed.), *Oxford and Working-Class Education: New Edition*, Nottingham, University of Nottingham, 1987, 1–10.

Hartley, D., 'The Convergence of Student-Centred Pedagogy in Primary and Further Education in Scotland: 1965–1985', *British Journal of Educational Studies*, 1987, 115–28.

Hartley, D., 'New Economy, New Pedagogy?", *Oxford Review of Education*, 29, 2003, 81–94.

Hearnshaw, F.J.C. (ed.), *The Social and Political Ideas of Some Representative Thinkers of the Victorian Age*, Westport, CT, Greenwood, 1930.

Hergenhahn, B.R., *An Introduction to the History of Psychology*, Pacific Grove, CA, Brooks-Cole, 1997.

Hewison, R., 'Ruskin, John (1819–1900)', *Oxford Dictionary of National Biography*, Oxford, Oxford University Press, 2004, online edn, Sept 2013.

Heyck, T.W., 'Myths and Meanings of Intellectuals in Twentieth-Century British National Identity', *Journal of British Studies*, 37, 1998, 192–221.

Hillcole Group, *Rethinking Education and Democracy*, London, Tufnell, 1997.

Hilliard, C., *English as a Vocation: the* Scrutiny *Movement*, Oxford, Oxford University Press, 2012.

Hirsch, E.D., 'Creating a Curriculum for the American People', *American Educator*, Winter 2009–10, 6–13 and 38.

Hirst, P.Q., 'Quangos and Democratic Government', *Parliamentary Affairs*, 48, 1995, 341–59.

Hirst, P.H., *Knowledge and the Curriculum*, London, Routledge and Kegan Paul, 1974.

Hobhouse, L.T., 'Oxford and the People', *The Nation*, 6 February 1909, 710–11.

Hobsbawm, E., *Interesting Times*, London, Allen Lane, 2002.

Hoggart, R., *The Uses of Literacy*, Harmondsworth, Penguin, 1957.

Hoggart, R., 'Higher Education and Cultural Change', in Hoggart, 1970 [1965], 84–105.

Hoggart, R., 'Education in the Next Few Decades', in Hoggart, 1970 [1967a], 75–83.

Hoggart, R., 'Professor Bantock and Authority', in Hoggart, 1970 [1967b], 117–21.

Hoggart, R., *About Society*, London, Chatto and Windus, 1970.

Hoggart, R., 'Teaching Literature to Adults', in R. Hoggart, *About Literature*, Harmondsworth, Penguin, 1973 [1959], 205–30.

Hoggart, R., 'The Divisive Society', *Observer*, 21 February 1982, 27.

Hoggart, R., *A Local Habitation*, London, Chatto and Windus, 1988.

Hoggart, R., *A Sort of Clowning*, London, Chatto and Windus, 1990.

Hoggart, R., *The Way We Live Now*, London, Chatto and Windus, 1995.

Holland, J., 'Social Class and Changes in Orientations to Meanings', *Sociology*, 15, 1981, 1–18.

Holmes, O.W. and Laski, H., *Holmes–Laski Letters*, M. deWolfe Howe (ed.), Oxford, Oxford University Press, 1953.

Howson, S. and Winch, D., *The Economic Advisory Council, 1930–1939*, Cambridge, Cambridge University Press, 1977.

Hunt, A., 'The Tyranny of Subjects', in Rubinstein and Stoneman (eds.), 1972, 26–33.

Huxley, T.H., 'Universities: Actual and Ideal', in T.H. Huxley, *Collected Essays Vol. III*, Macmillan, 1874, 189–233.

Huxley, T.H., 'A Liberal Education; and Where to Find it', in C. Bibby (ed.), *T.H. Huxley on Education*, Cambridge, Cambridge University Press, 1971 [1868], 74–98.

Hynes, S., *The Auden Generation*, London, Bodley Head, 1976.

Jackson, B. 'Notes from Two Primary Schools', *New Left Review*, 1, 1961, 4–8.

Jackson, B. and Marsden, D., *Education and the Working Class*, London, Routledge and Kegan Paul, 1962.

Jenkins, R., *Pierre Bourdieu*, London, Routledge, 1992.

Jennings, B., *Knowledge is Power: A Short History of the W.E.A., 1903–78*, Hull, Department of Adult Education, University of Hull, 1979.

Jennings, B., *Albert Mansbridge*, Leeds, University of Leeds, 2002.

Joad, C.E.M., *About Education*, London, Faber and Faber, 1945.

Joicey, N., 'A Paperback Guide to Progress', *Twentieth Century British History*, 4, 1993, 25–56.

Joppke, C., 'The Retreat of Multiculturalism in the Liberal State: Theory and Policy', *British Journal of Sociology*, 55, 2004, 237–57.

Judges, A.V., 'The Educational Influence of the Webbs', *British Journal of Educational Studies*, 10, 1961, 33–48.

Judt, T., *Thinking the Twentieth Century*, London, Heinemann, 2012.

Kelly, T., 'The Extra-Mural Function of the Universities', *The Universities Review*, 25, 1953, 99–103.

Kingston, P., 'The Unfulfilled Promise of Cultural Capital Theory', *Sociology of Education*, 74, 2001, 88–99.

Knights, L.C., 'Will Training Colleges Bear Scrutiny?', *Scrutiny*, I, 1932, 247–63.

Kogan, M., 'Anthony Crosland: Intellectual and Politician', *Oxford Review of Education*, 32, 2006, 71–86.

Kramnick, I. and Sheerman, B., *Harold Laski*, London, Hamish Hamilton, 1993.

Laclau, E., *Emancipation(s)*, London, Verso, 1996.

Lamont, M. and Lareau, A., 'Cultural Capital: Allusions, Gaps and Glissandos in Recent Theoretical Developments', *Sociological Theory*, 6, 1988, 153–68.

Lane, A. (1938), 'Books for the Million', *Left Review*, 1938, 968–70.

Lanvers, U. and Coleman, J.A., 'The UK Language Learning Crisis in the Public Media: A Critical Analysis', *Language Learning Journal*, 2013, DOI: 10.1080/09571736.2013.830639.

Laski, H., 'Knowledge as a Civic Discipline', in H. Laski, *The Way Out: Essays on the Meaning and Purpose of Adult Education*, Oxford, Oxford University Press, 1923, 47–59.

Laski, H., *A Grammar of Politics*, London, George Allen and Unwin, 1925.

Laski, H., *The Dangers of Obedience, and Other Essays*, New York, Harper and Brothers, 1930.

Laski, H., *Where Do We Go From Here?*, Harmondsworth, Penguin, 1940.

Laski, H., *The Dilemma of Our Times*, London, Frank Cass, 1952.

Lawrence, D.H., 'Education of the People', in E.D. McDonald (ed.), *Phoenix: the Posthumous Papers of D.H. Lawrence*, London, Heinemann, 1936, 587–665.

Lawson, J. and Silver, H., *A Social History of Education in England*, London, Methuen, 1973.

Lawton, D., 'Lawrence Stenhouse: His Contribution to Curriculum Development', *British Educational Research Journal*, 9, 1983, 7–9.

Leavis, F.R., 'The Spens Report: A Symposium-Review', *Scrutiny*, VIII, 1939, 242–56.

Leavis, F.R., 'Education and the University', *Scrutiny*, XI, 1943, 162–7.

Leavis, Q.D., *Fiction and the Reading Public*, London, Pimlico, 2000 [1932].

Lewis, Jeremy, *Penguin Special: The Life and Times of Allen Lane*, London, Viking, 2005.

Lewis, John, *The Left Book Club*, London, Gollancz, 1970.

Lindsay, A.D., 'T.H. Green and the Idealists', in Hearnshaw (ed.), 1930, 150–64.

Lindsay, A.D., 'Philosophy as a Criticism of Standards', paper read to The Scots Philosophical Club, September 1950, reprinted in A.D. Lindsay, *Selected Addresses*, privately published, 1957.

Livingstone, R.W., *A Defence of Classical Education*, London, Macmillan, 1916.

Lukes, S., *Power: A Radical View*, London, Palgrave, 2005.

Mack E.C., *Public Schools and British Opinion Since 1860*, Westport, Greenwood, 1941.

Mann K., *Kind Dieser Zeit*, Berlin, Transmare, 1932.

Mannheim, K., *Ideology and Utopia*, London, Routledge and Kegan Paul, 1936.

Martin, K., *Editor*, London, Hutchinson, 1968.

Maxwell, N., *From Knowledge to Wisdom*, Oxford, Blackwell, 1984.

May, S., *Language and Minority Rights*, Harlow, Pearson, second edition, 2012.

McArthur, E., *Scotland, CEMA and the Arts Council, 1919–1967*, Farnham, Ashgate, 2013.

McCulloch, G., 'Secondary Education', in Aldrich (ed.), 2002, 31-53.

Mendelson, E., *The English Auden: Poems, Essays, and Dramatic Writings*, London, Faber and Faber, 1977.

Mill, J.S., 'Inugural Address Delivered to the University of St Andrews', in Mooney and Nowacki, 2011 [1867], 215–62.

Mill, J.S., 'The Idea of a University', in Mooney and Nowacki, 2011 [1873], 165–200.

Miller, K., 'Soap Opera and Kabuki', *Times Literary Supplement*, Issue 5296, 1 October 2004, 24.

Mills, C.W., 'Mass Society and Liberal Education', in J.H. Summers (ed.), *The Politics of Truth: Selected Writings of C. Wright Mills*, Oxford, Oxford University Press, 2008 [1954], 107–24.

Mills, C.W., 'The Decline of the Left', in J.H. Summers (ed.), *The Politics of Truth: Selected Writings of C. Wright Mills*, Oxford, Oxford University Press, 2008 [1959], 213–22.

Modood, T., *Multiculturalism*, Cambridge, Polity, 2007.

Mooney, T.B. and Nowacki, M., *Understanding Teaching and Learning: Classic Texts on Education by Augustine, Aquinas, Newman and Mill*, Exeter, Imprint Academic, 2011.

Moore, R. and Muller, J., 'The Discourse of "Voice" and the Problem of Knowledge and Identity in the Sociology of Education', *British Journal of Sociology of Education*, 20, 1999, 189–206.

Morgan, K., *Labour in Power, 1945–1951*, Oxford, Oxford University Press, 1984.

Morgan, K., *Labour People*, Oxford, Oxford University Press, 1987.

Mulhern, F., *The Moment of 'Scrutiny'*, London, New Left Books, 1979.

Munns, J. and Rajan, G. (eds.), *A Cultural Studies Reader*, London, Longman, 1995.

Nash, R., 'Bourdieu, "Habitus", and Educational Research: Is It All Worth the Candle?', *British Journal of Sociology of Education*, 20, 1999, 175–87.

National Commission on Education, *Learning to Succeed*, London, Heinemann, 1993.

National Institute of Adult Education (NIAE), *Liberal Education in a Technical Age*, London, Max Parrish, 1955.

Neavill, G.B., 'Victor Gollancz and the Left Book Club', *Library Quarterly*, 41, 1971, 197–215.

Newman, M., 'Laski, Harold Joseph (1893–1950)', *Oxford Dictionary of National Biography*, Oxford, Oxford University Press, 2004; online edn, Jan 2011.

Numata, H., 'What Children Have Lost by the Modernisation of Education: A Comparison of Experiences in Western Europe and Eastern Asia', *International Review of Education*, 49, 2003, 241–64.

Nunn, T.P., *Education: Its Data and First Principles*, London, Edward Arnold, 1920.

Nunn, T.P., 'The Education of the People', address to section L of the British Association for the Advancement of Science, in *The Advancement of Science: Addresses Delivered at the Ninety-first Annual Meeting of the British Association for the Advancement of Science*, Liverpool, London, John Murray, 12–19 September 1923.

Oakeshott, M., *Michael Oakeshott on Education*, T. Fuller (ed.), New Haven, CT, Yale University Press, 1989.

Oelkers, J., 'Rousseau and the Image of "Modern Education"', *Journal of Curriculum Studies*, 34, 2002, 679–98.

Orr, P., 'Prudence and Progress: National Policy for Equal Opportunities (Gender) in Schools since 1975', in K. Myers (ed.), *Whatever Happened to Equal Opportunities in Schools?*, Buckingham, Open University Press, 2000, 13–26.

Orwell, G., 'Review of Penguin Books', in S. Orwell and I. Angus (eds.), *The Collected Essays, Journalism and Letters of George Orwell*, Harmondsworth, Penguin, 1970 [1936], 189–92.

Owen, S. (ed.), *Richard Hoggart and Cultural Studies*, London, Palgrave, 2008.

Oxford University, *Oxford and Working-Class Education*, Oxford, Oxford University Press, 1908.

Palmer, H.M., 'Livingstone, Sir Richard Winn (1880-1960)', revised M.C. Curthoys, *Oxford Dictionary of National Biography*, Oxford, Oxford University Press, 2004.

Parekh, B., *Rethinking Multiculturalism*, London, Palgrave, 2006.

Parkinson, M., *The Labour Party and the Organisation of Secondary Education, 1918-65*, London, Routledge and Kegan Paul, 1970.

Paterson, L., *Scottish Education in the Twentieth Century*, Edinburgh, Edinburgh University Press, 2003.

Paterson, L., 'The Modernising of the Democratic Intellect: The Role of English in Scottish Secondary Education, 1900-1939', *Journal of Scottish Historical Studies*, 24, 2004, 45-79.

Paterson, L., 'The Reinvention of Scottish Liberal Education: Secondary Schooling, 1900-1939', *Scottish Historical Review*, 90, 2011, 96-130.

Paterson, L., Pattie, A. and Deary, I.J., 'Social Class, Gender and Secondary Education in Scotland in the 1950s', *Oxford Review of Education*, 37, 2011, 383-401.

Phillips, T., 'After 7/7: Sleepwalking to Segregation', speech given at the Manchester Council for Community Relations, 22 September 2005, http://www.humanities.manchester.ac.uk/socialchange/research/social-change/summer-workshops/documents/sleepwalking.pdf [downloaded 21 January 2014].

Playfair, L., 'The Evolution of University Extension as a Part of Popular Education', *Aspects of Modern Study: University Extension Addresses*, London, Macmillan, 1894, 1-16.

Premat, C., 'L'Engagement des Intellectuels au sein des Universités Populaires', *Tracés. Revue de Sciences Humaines*, 11, 2006, 67-84.

Pring, R., 'Political Education: Relevance of the Humanities', *Oxford Review of Education*, 25, 1999, 71-87.

Pring, R., 'Education as a Moral Practice', *Journal of Moral Education*, 30, 2001, 101-12.

Raffe, D., 'As Others See Us: a Commentary on the O.E.C.D. Review of the Quality and Equity of Schooling in Scotland', *Scottish Educational Review*, 40, 2008, 22-36.

Raybould, S.G., *The English Universities and Adult Education*, London, Workers' Educational Association, 1951.

Read, H., *Education Through Art*, London, Faber and Faber, 1943.

Reardon, B.M.G., 'Maurice, (John) Frederick Denison (1805–1872)', *Oxford Dictionary of National Biography*, Oxford, Oxford University Press, online edn, May 2006.

Rée, J., 'Socialism and the Educated Working Class', in C. Levy (ed.), *Socialism and the Intelligentsia*, London, Routledge and Kegan Paul, 1987, 211–18.

Rose, J., *The Intellectual Life of the British Working Classes*, New Haven, CT, Yale University Press, 2002.

Rosen, H., *Language and Class*, Bristol, Falling Wall Press, 1972.

Rothblatt, S.R., *Tradition and Change in English Liberal Education*, London, Faber and Faber, 1976.

Rothblatt, S.R., *Education's Abiding Moral Dilemma*, Oxford, Symposium, 2007.

Rubinstein, D., 'Ellen Wilkinson Re-Considered', *History Workshop*, 1979, 161–9.

Rubinstein, D. and Simon, B., *The Evolution of the Comprehensive School, 1926–1972*, London, Routledge and Kegan Paul, 1969.

Rubinstein, D. and Stoneman, C. (eds.), *Education for Democracy*, Harmondsworth, Penguin, 1972.

Ruskin, J., 'Ad Valorem', in J.D. Rosenberg (ed.), *The Genius of John Ruskin*, London, Routledge and Kegan Paul, 1979 [1860], 254–72.

Ruskin, J., 'Fors Clavigera', in J.D. Rosenberg (ed.), *The Genius of John Ruskin*, London, Routledge and Kegan Paul, 1979 [1871], 362–433.

Rylance, R., 'Reading with a Mission: the Public Sphere of Penguin Books', *Critical Quarterly*, 47, 2005, 48–66.

Sadler, J.H., 'William Temple—a Classic Definition', *W.E.A. News Supplement*, 28, Spring 1985a.

Sadler, J.H., 'William Temple's Educational Work and Thought', *British Journal of Religious Education*, 8, 1985b, 3–8, 12.

Sanderson, M., 'Vocational and Liberal Education: A Historian's View', *European Journal of Education*, 28, 1993, 189–96.

Sassoon, D., *One Hundred Years of Socialism*, London, I.B. Tauris, 1996.

Scott, D., *A.D. Lindsay*, Oxford, Blackwell, 1971.

Scottish Education Department, *The Structure of the Curriculum in the Third and Fourth Years of the Scottish Secondary School*, Edinburgh: HMSO, 1977.

Scruton, R., 'The Myth of Cultural Relativism', in R. Moore and J. Ozga (eds.), *Curriculum Policy*, Oxford, Pergamon, 1991, 77–84.

Sharp, R. and Green, A., *Education and Social Control*, London, Routledge and Kegan Paul, 1975.

Shaw, G.B., *Misalliance*, London, Constable, 1910.
Simon, B., *The Politics of Educational Reform, 1920–1940*, London, Lawrence and Wishart, 1974.
Simon, B., *Education and the Social Order, 1940–1990*, London, Lawrence and Wishart, 1991.
Smith, D., 'Williams, Raymond Henry (1921–1988)', *Oxford Dictionary of National Biography*, Oxford, Oxford University Press, 2004, online edn, Oct 2009.
Smith, G., 'Schools', in Halsey and Webb (eds.), 2000, 179–220.
Smith, S., 'Loyalty and Interest: Auden, Modernism, and the Politics of Pedagogy', *Textual Practice*, 4, 1990, 54–72.
Spender, S., 'Poetry', *Fact*, July 1937, 18–30.
Spender, S. *The New Realism*, London, Hogarth Press, 1939.
Standish, P., 'Heidegger and the Technology of Further Education', *Journal of Philosophy of Education*, 31, 1997, 439–59.
Stears, M., 'Cole, George Douglas Howard (1889–1959)', *Oxford Dictionary of National Biography*, Oxford, Oxford University Press, 2004.
Steedman, H., 'Defining Institutions: The Endowed Grammar Schools and the Systematisation of English Secondary Schooling', in D.K. Müller, F. Ringer and B. Simon (eds.), *The Rise of the Modern Educational System: Structural Change and Social Reproduction, 1870–1920*, Cambridge, Cambridge University Press, 1987, 111–34.
Steele, T., *Cultural Studies, 1945–65*, London, Lawrence and Wishart, 1997.
Stenhouse, L., *Culture and Education*, London, Nelson, 1967.
Strachey, J., 'The Education of a Communist', *Left Review*, 1, 1934, 63–9.
Strachey, L., *Eminent Victorians*, London, Chatto and Windus, 1918.
Strauss, L., *Liberalism, Ancient and Modern*, London, Basic Books, 1968.
Strike, K.A., 'The Moral Role of Schooling in a Liberal Democratic Society', *Review of Research in Education*, 1991, 413–83.
Strike. K.A., 'Is Liberal Education Illiberal? Political Liberalism and Liberal Education', in C. Higgins (ed.) *Philosophy of Education*, Urbana, IL, Philosophy of Education Society, 2004, 321–9.
Summerfield, P., 'Education and Politics in the British Armed Forces in the Second World War', *International Review of Social History*, 26, 1981, 133–58.

Summerfield, P., 'Mass-Observation: Social Research or Social Movement?', *Journal of Contemporary History*, 20, 1985, 439-52.
Sutherland, J., 'Introduction', in Leavis, Q.D. (2000), v–xxvii.
Swindells, J. and Jardine, L., *What's Left?*, London, Routledge, 1990.
Tawney, R.H. (ed.), *Secondary Education for All*, London, Labour Party, 1922.
Tawney, R.H., *Education: The Socialist Policy*, London, Independent Labour Party, 1924.
Tawney, R.H., 'Educational Policy', *Guardian*, 9 June 1938, unsigned leader (for confirmation of Tawney's authorship, see Terrill, 1973: 299).
Tawney, R.H., *The Attack and Other Papers*, London, George Allen and Unwin, 1953.
Tawney, R.H., *The Acquistitve Society*, London, Fontana, 1961 [1921].
Tawney, R.H., *Equality*, London, George Allen and Unwin, 1964 [1931].
Tawney, R.H., *The Radical Tradition*, Harmondsworth, Penguin, 1964.
Tawney, R.H., 'An Experiment in Democratic Education', in Tawney, 1964 [1914], 74–85.
Tawney, R.H., 'William Lovett', in Tawney, 1964 [1920], 15–32.
Tawney, R.H., 'The Problem of the Public Schools', in Tawney, 1964 [1943], 55–73.
Tawney, R.H., 'Social Democracy in Britain', in Tawney, 1964 [1949a], 144–75.
Tawney, R.H., 'Social History and Literature', in Tawney, 1964 [1949b], 191–219.
Tawney, R.H., 'British Socialism Today', in Tawney, 1964 [1952], 176–88.
Tawney, R.H., 'Robert Owen', in Tawney, 1964 [1953a], 33–41.
Tawney, R.H., 'The Workers' Educational Association and Adult Education', in Tawney, 1964 [1953b], 86–97.
Teese, R. and Lamb, S., 'Social Inequalities: Enlarging the Scope of Public Policy Through Reflection on Context', in R. Teese, S. Lamb and M. Duru-Bellat (eds.), *International Studies in Educational Inequality, Theory and Policy Volume 3: Inequality: Educational Theory and Public Policy*, 2007, 293–307.
Temple, W., 'National Education', *The Pilgrim*, 2, 1922, 334–43.
Temple, W., 'The Perils of a Purely Scientific Education', in *Religious Experience*, 1958 [1932], 166–70.

Terrill, R., *R.H. Tawney and His Times*, London, Andrew Deutsch, 1973.

Thomas, H., *John Strachey*, London, Eyre Methuen, 1973.

Thompson, E.P., 'The Long Revolution', *New Left Review*, 9, 1961a, 24–33.

Thompson, E.P., 'The Long Revolution—II', *New Left Review*, 10, 1961b, 34–39.

Thompson, E.P., *The Poverty of Theory*, London, Merlin, 1978.

Tight, M., 'Education, Education, Education! The Vision of Lifelong Learning in the Kennedy, Dearing and Fryer Reports', *Oxford Review of Education*, 24, 1998, 473–85.

Times Educational Supplement, 'Tate Condemned for "New Racism"', 27 June 1997.

Trilling, L., *Matthew Arnold*, Oxford, Oxford University Press, 1939.

Troyna, B. and Vincent, C., 'The Discourses of Social Justice in Education', *Discourse: Studies in the Cultural Politics of Education*, 16, 1995, 149–66.

Ulam, A.B., *Philosophical Foundations of English Socialism*, Cambridge, MA, Harvard University Press, 1951.

Vernon, B.D., *Ellen Wilkinson*, London, Croom Helm, 1982.

Wacquant, L., 'Pierre Bourdieu', in R. Stones (ed.), *Key Contemporary Thinkers*, London, Macmillan, 2008, 261–77.

Walcott, F.G., *The Origins of Culture and Anarchy*, Toronto, University of Toronto Press, 1970.

Waldron, J., 'Theoretical Foundations of Liberalism', *The Philosophical Quarterly*, 37, 1987, 127–50.

Walkerdine, V., 'Developmental Psychology and the Child-Centred Pedagogy: The Insertion of Piaget into Early Education', in J. Henriques (ed.), *Changing the Subject*, London, Routledge, 1998, 153–202.

Wallis, J. and Allman, P., 'Adult Education, the "Critical Citizen" and Social Change', in J. Wallis (ed.), *Liberal Adult Education: The End of an Era?*, Nottingham, University of Nottingham Continuing Education Press, 1996, 163–79.

Warren, A., 'Sir Robert Baden-Powell, the Scout Movement and Citizen Training in Great Britain, 1900–1920', *English Historical Review*, 101, 1986, 376–98.

Webb, S., *London Education*, London, Longmans, Green and Co., 1904.

Weiner, G., 'Education and the Sex Discrimination Act', *Educational Research*, 20, 1978, 163–73.

West, E.G., *Education and the Industrial Revolution*, London, Batsford, 1975.

Williams, R., *The Long Revolution*, Harmondsworth, Penguin, 1961.
Williams, R., *Culture and Society, 1780–1950*, Harmondsworth, Penguin, 1963.
Williams, R., 'Culture and Revolution', in T. Eagleton and B. Wicker (eds.), *From Culture to Revolution*, London, Sheed and Ward, 1968, 24–34.
Williams, R., 'Fiction and the Writing Public', in R. Williams, 1989 [1957], 15-23.
Williams, R., 'A Kind of Gresham's Law', in R. Williams, 1989 [1958], 93-7.
Williams, R., 'Marx on Culture', in R. Williams, 1989 [1983], 195-225.
Williams, R., 'Seeing a Man Running', in R. Williams, 1989 [1984], 24–9.
Williams, R., 'Writing, Speech and the Classical', in R. Williams, 1989 [1985], 44–56.
Williams, R., *What I Came to Say*, London, Hutchinson radius, 1989.
Williams, R., 'Culture is Ordinary', in B. Highmore (ed.), *The Everyday Life Reader*, London, Routledge, 2002 [1958], 91-100.
Willis, P., *Learning to Labour*, Farnborough, Saxon House, 1977.
Wilson, J.D., 'Matthew Arnold and the Educationists', in Hearnshaw, 1930, 165–93.
Wiltshire, H.C., 'The Great Tradition in University Adult Education', *Adult Education*, 29, 1956, 88–97.
Wolf, A., *Does Education Matter?*, London, Penguin, 2002.
Wood, N., *Communism and British Intellectuals*, London, Victor Gollancz, 1959.
Woodhams, S., 'Forgotten History: A Radical Platform for Workers' Education', *Changing English: Studies in Culture and Education*, 10, 2003, 73–89.
Woolf, L., *After the Deluge*, Harmondsworth, Penguin, 1937.
Woolf, V., 'The Leaning Tower', *Folios of New Writing*, London, Hogarth Press, 1940, 11–33.
Workers' Educational Association, 'Education for a Changing Society: The Role of the WEA', *Adult Education*, 31, 1958, 6-13.
Wright, A., *R.H. Tawney*, Manchester, Manchester University Press, 1987.
Wyse, B., *Factive/Non-Factive Predicate Recognition within Question Generation Systems*, Milton Keynes, Open University, Faculty of Mathematics, Computing and Technology, 2009.

Yeaxlee, B.A., *An Educated Nation*, Oxford, Oxford University Press, 1920.

Young, I.M., 'Polity and Group Difference: A Critique of the Ideal of Universal Citizenship,' *Ethics*, 99, 1989, 250–74.

Young, M., *Bringing Knowledge Back In*, London, Routledge, 2008.

Index

www.ingramcontent.com/pod-product-compliance
Lightning Source LLC
Chambersburg PA
CBHW030639270326
41929CB00007B/138

* 9 7 8 1 8 4 5 4 0 7 5 2 0 *